"This is that rare thing that is a pleasure to discover – a text which manages to present important philosophical ideas in ways which are both challenging and accessible, and which in the process illuminates a significant area of clinical practice.

Chris Mawson has written a remarkably lucid and scholarly book which offers a much-needed bridge between psychoanalytic and existential formulations of anxiety. It will be required reading for anyone interested in contemporary psychoanalytic or existential therapy, not least because of its rigorous account of the common roots of both in the ancient world, and the engaging way in which it traces these influences down the centuries to the present day. This is a finely-crafted book which shines with veracity and knowledge – a joy to read and a valuable resource for all practitioners, regardless of their theoretical orientation, who are concerned to engage as fully as possible with those who consult with them.

Some of the material presented here will be familiar to existential therapists, but the comparisons between the work of, in particular, Heidegger and Bion provide enlightening and compelling new contributions to an understanding of the irreducible fact of anxiety which unifies both the psychoanalytic and existential communities. Mawson's work promises to stimulate and provoke practitioners in equal measure. A ground-breaking book which deserves the widest possible readership."

—**Professor Simon du Plock**, Metanoia Institute & Middlesex University, Editor, Existential Analysis

"Chris Mawson offers us a fascinating set of ideas that clarify and develop some of the fundamental theories of Klein and Bion. For example, he attempts to illuminate the meaning of Bion's otherwise obscure recommendation to suspend memory and desire. He discusses the role of 'intuition' in understanding and responding to the patient, and the value of attending to 'the world of the drama of internal relations'. In each case he brings a thoughtful and refreshing perspective to these areas, thereby enriching our clinical and theoretical perspectives."

—**Dr Michael Feldman**, British Psychoanalytical Society and The Institute of Psychoanalysis

"When Chris Mawson and I met for the first time in 2016, he brought me the book 'Transformations' because of a question Bion asks on page 148 about 'how to pass from "knowing" phenomena to "being" that which is "real"' – a question which was just a puzzle for me at that time. In the meantime, Chris Mawson has written a book which is dedicated to the legacy which is contained in this very question. It is an excellent book because its author is – as the Editor of the collected works of Bion – best suited not only for elucidating the shift of Bion's thinking expressed in this question, but also, what is much more, for exploring and elaborating the consequences of this shift for psychoanalytic practice, especially for a new understanding ⟨ ̄ ̄ ̄ ̄ ̄ 'being with') and a new 'indicative' form of i 'being informed-from-being').

This book is also a model example for the rare capability of a psychoanalyst to feel free to look beyond their own psychoanalytic garden fence (namely towards existential philosophy for one thing and towards the field of drama for the other), but not as an end in itself, but as a necessary means for unfolding and answering Bion's question in its deepness and complexity. What Chris Mawson has won by doing so he defines as 'inspirations'. I am happy that some of my daseinsanalytic ideas were able to work in this way too."

—**Alice Holzhey–Kunz, Ph. D.**, President of the Society for
Hermeneutic Anthropology and Daseinsanalysis, Zürich

PSYCHOANALYSIS AND ANXIETY: FROM KNOWING TO BEING

Psychoanalysis and Anxiety: From Knowing to Being combines psychoanalytic, existential and dramaturgical perspectives on the study of anxiety.

The book explores the implications for psychoanalysis of including a consideration of the being of the patient, and of the analyst. The central principle throughout is that the psychoanalytic and the existential belong together since it is the irreducible fact of anxiety that unifies them. It is in relation to anxiety that we are helped by other human beings to bear what is, and what we are.

Divided into four parts, the book begins with the distinction made in antiquity between anxiety and fear, before discussing its treatment by philosophers such as Heidegger, who regarded anxiety as the mood most disclosive of our being, and Kierkegaard, who distinguished between fear and angst. The book then explores how anxiety has been understood by major psychoanalytic theorists, including Freud, Klein, Winnicott and Bion, before a third part discusses how key principles of drama relate to therapeutic practice and theory, including a re-evaluation of the concept of catharsis, as well as Brecht's concept of making strange the familiar. The pursuit of insightful knowledge in psychoanalysis is reconsidered in the book's concluding section, with a shift of emphasis from psychoanalytic interpretations as statements of *knowing* to interpretive activity as a continuous process of *becoming informed*.

This insightful and wide-ranging volume will fascinate practising psychoanalysts and psychotherapists, anyone working in mental health, as well as scholars of philosophy and theatre.

Chris Mawson is a Training and Supervising Analyst of the British Psychoanalytical Society and works in private practice as a psychoanalyst. He is Editor of *The Complete Works of W. R. Bion* (2014), with Francesca Bion as Consulting Editor.

PSYCHOANALYSIS AND ANXIETY: FROM KNOWING TO BEING

Chris Mawson

Routledge
Taylor & Francis Group

LONDON AND NEW YORK

First published 2019
by Routledge
2 Park Square, Milton Park, Abingdon, Oxon OX14 4RN

and by Routledge
52 Vanderbilt Avenue, New York, NY 10017

Routledge is an imprint of the Taylor & Francis Group, an informa business

British Library Cataloguing-in-Publication Data
A catalogue record for this book is available from the British Library

Library of Congress Cataloging-in-Publication Data
Names: Mawson, Chris, 1953- author.
Title: Psychoanalysis and anxiety / Chris Mawson.
Description: Abingdon, Oxon ; New York, NY : Routledge, 2019. |
    Includes bibliographical references and index. |
Identifiers: LCCN 2018048262 (print) | LCCN 2018050415 (ebook) |
    ISBN 9780429055812 (Master eBook) | ISBN 9780367152246
    (hardback) | ISBN 9780367152277 (pbk.)
Subjects: LCSH: Anxiety. | Psychoanalysis.
Classification: LCC BF575.A6 (ebook) | LCC BF575.A6 M34 2019
    (print) | DDC 152.4/6—dc23
LC record available at https://lccn.loc.gov/2018048262

ISBN: 978-0-367-15224-6 (hbk)
ISBN: 978-0-367-15227-7 (pbk)
ISBN: 978-0-429-05581-2 (ebk)

Typeset in Bembo
by Swales & Willis Ltd, Exeter, Devon, UK

No writer, including Dante, sees more clearly than Shakespeare does the impassable fissure between knowing and being.

R. Allen Shoaf, *Lucretius and Shakespeare on the Nature of Things*

For Eileen and Bob, my mother and father

CONTENTS

ACKNOWLEDGEMENTS

I would like from the outset to thank Oliver Rathbone of Karnac Books, who showed support, and shortly after offered a publication contract, when I shared with him the idea that grew into this book – the suggestion, in a single short passage by Bion, that analysis held the potential to further the capacity of the patient for being real, for becoming themselves, and that the scope of analysis is not limited to the accumulation of insightful knowledge only. Oliver's understanding and enthusiasm for publishing the ideas of Bion led him to consider it a book worth writing, and for this I am very grateful. The work has since passed into the hands of Routledge, and I would like to acknowledge the detailed and thoughtful contributions of their staff in bringing it to print.

I thank the Bion Estate for their kind and continuing help, and their permission for me to reproduce the up-to-date and corrected textual material from *The Complete Works of W. R. Bion*, which has been absolutely essential to my work. I would like to acknowledge appreciation too, even where formal permission is unnecessary, of the *International Journal of Psychoanalysis* as a crucial resource in the writing of the book, in giving me ready access to the scholarship of others who have included the question of being in their psychoanalytic thinking. I thank the editor of the *IJP*, Dana Birksted-Breen. Thanks are due also to the creators of the online resource Psychoanalytic Electronic Publishing (PepWeb).

I also want to acknowledge the inspiration I drew, during my analytic training, from Dr Eric Brenman, who brought into his work and supervision his awareness of the relevance to psychoanalysis of the wisdom of the ancient Greek world, its thinkers and its dramatists. Also to Robin Anderson, Ronald Britton and Betty Joseph for psychoanalytic inspiration, and to Michael Feldman not only for clinical inspiration but also for putting me in touch with the writings of Lucretius, which have been absolutely invaluable for the early part of this book. I also thank warmly the Swiss analyst Alice Holzhey-Kunz, as a friend and a colleague, for making me aware of the significance to psychoanalysis of her particular daseinsanalytic approach – psychoanalysis under a philosophical perspective. Thanks to Jo Hurn, the artist whose painting graces the cover of the book.

Thanks are due also to Hill & Wang (USA) and Bloomsbury (UK) for permission to reproduce passages from Brecht's "Theatre for pleasure or theatre for instruction" and "A short organum for the theatre", from *Brecht on Theatre*, edited and translated by John Willett (tr. © 1964, renewed 1992 by John Willett, and reprinted in the USA by permission of Hill & Wang, a division of Farrar, Straus and Giroux; and in the UK by Methuen Drama, an imprint of Bloomsbury Publishing Plc).

The reproduction of Picasso's painting *Les Demoiselles d'Avignon* is by kind permission © Succession Picasso/DACS, London, 2018.

Finally, my heartfelt thanks to Donna Christina Savery, without whom this book would not have been started. Her inspiration and encouragement, and her understanding of the way I work, are at the heart of this book.

ABOUT THE AUTHOR

Chris Mawson is a Training and Supervising Analyst of the British Psychoanalytical Society. He trained at the Tavistock Clinic in psychoanalytic psychotherapy with children and adolescents, and in psychoanalysis at the British Psychoanalytical Society and Institute. He worked for nine years in St Mary's Hospital Department of Child Psychiatry, Paddington Green, in the days when children at that clinic were offered intensive psychoanalytic treatment within the care of the National Health Service. He now works as a psychoanalyst in private practice.

As well as the clinical practice of psychoanalysis, he is interested in the study of groups from a psychoanalytic perspective. He has a special interest in the work of Wilfred Bion and is the editor of *The Complete Works of W. R. Bion* (2014, Karnac Books).

Other publications include *Three Papers of W. R. Bion* (editor, 2018, Routledge); "Interpretation as Freud's specific action, and Bion's container–contained" (2017, *International Journal of Psychoanalysis*); "Review: *Between Mind and Brain: Models of the Mind and Models in the Mind* by Ronald Britton" (2017, *International Journal of Psychoanalysis*); *Bion Today* (editor, 2010, Routledge); "The use of play technique in understanding disturbed behaviour in school" (1986, *Psychoanalytic Psychotherapy*); and "Containing anxiety in work with damaged children" in Anton Obholzer and Vega Zagier Roberts (eds), *The Unconscious at Work: Individual and Organisational Stress in the Human Services* (1994, Routledge).

FOREWORD BY RONALD BRITTON

O, as a term of Wilfred Bion in the realm of L (loving), H (hating) and K (knowing), stands for being. O for ontological as opposed to K for epistemological: what it is rather than what is known about it. This distinction applies particularly strongly when the object of enlightenment, the 'it' in the sentence, is the self.

The core sense of self has been the subject of investigation in neuro-science and neurology as well as in psychoanalysis and philosophy particularly since the second half of the twentieth century. The complexities of those developing ideas I will not describe here, but two things can be said of relevance to this book. One is that the proto-self, the brain's potential basis of the 'I' (Freud's *das Ich*), comes from its oldest part, in an evolutionary and developmental sense, and once a core self is established it is remarkably resilient. Even when the autobiographical self is lost through damage or dementia, the phrase used is 'I don't know who I am'. The 'I' remains even when stripped of its powers and memories. It is also clear that *das Ich* is as Freud said originally a body ego but the brain's receptive and interactive awareness of the body's activities is much more complex than he knew, and parts of the body can be neurologically disowned by the self. This proto-self needs to be in close conjunction with the perceptual patterns developed in the brain for a core self to exist that can be the recipient and responder to perceived events.

This core self can register the body's changes and the history of its experiences that gives it an autobiographical dimension: a continuous selfhood. All this has been garnered from a rich combination of studies of neurological disorder and experimental brain scanning.

Meanwhile in psychoanalysis, in parallel, but not in concert, with neuro-scientific ideas, Bion was devising his theories of the beginning of a mental self. His notion of a pre-conception that needs to find an experience that fulfils its imageless expectation in order to become a concept parallels the proto-self notion of Damasio. This theory of pre-conception would include one of the self waiting to emerge as a realised entity on the basis of its somatic and perceptual experience. Bion's outstanding further contribution to this emergence is his notion of the container and the contained. In this developmental theory for the processes just described to take place satisfactorily is only accomplished by the infant in interaction with the mother.

Chris Mawson is suggesting, as I understand it, that change in O, the ontological self, requires a repetition of an interaction of a comparable kind between patient and analyst. This implies that first we need to find and meet the O of the patient and not some more diplomatic representative of the person such as that described by Winnicott as a false self or by John Steiner as a pathological organisation. Being a more true self might mean we are more authentic but not necessarily more agreeable or virtuous. It is likely however that becoming more aware objectively of one's authentic, subjective self, 'warts and all', might lead to an improvement in personal relations – as our nearest and dearest may well affirm. That might in itself produce a change in the O of the self.

Ultimately we hope the analysand can observe himself (K) whilst being himself (O). I have suggested elsewhere that this requires triangular space, the development of which depends on tolerating a non-participatory role in observing the relationships between others. This dynamic situation and resistance to it is the daily business of many analyses. But in this book Chris Mawson is addressing ontological development and possible change.

I would say that the self only comes into real existence through interaction and that change in its nature is likely to occur only through interaction. It is perhaps easier to accept the idea nowadays when physicists are saying the same things about the basic particles of the material world, that things only exist when they interact, that there are only events not things; and neuroscientists, similarly, saying that it is only interaction between neurones and neuronic systems that is relevant. It is a long way from the picture of the physical world that existed in 1895 when Freud started out on psychoanalysis.

In this book Chris Mawson is concerned particularly with ontological anxiety. This is what Jean-Paul Sartre would have called existential anxiety and Rilke, who suffered from it greatly, the fear of losing himself, his *Dasein*.

In this context Mawson refers to Bion's clinical descriptions of a psychotic patient who was preoccupied by the insubstantiality of his knitted socks as containers for his feet. He saw them as inadequate threads of wool spread around large, menacing spaces where others would have seen solid woollen woven material. This microscopic view of woollen threads encompassing empty space in contrast to an ordinary macroscopic view that sees a solid, continuous material is a vivid clinical description of an anxious view of the material world: one where the wholesome, everyday, macroscopic illusion of continuity is lost. Similarly the illusion of a seamless continuity of the self made out of particles of experience that the brain knits together and the mind consolidates can be lost. It is not lost by neuroscientists simply because they know that this illusion is provided by an active brain not a mirror of nature; they can carry on pulling on socks without questioning the reality of their perception or themselves. Ontological anxiety like this does not come from knowing better the true fundamental nature of matter or experience of how the perceptual apparatus works, it comes from the loss of what David Hume called our 'natural beliefs' – beliefs that ignore such knowledge and remain our logically indefensible, common-sense shared beliefs.

We are fortunate if we have a natural, assumptive belief in our own continuous existence: if we for example are not like Rilke who felt his sense of self was under threat from interaction with another person. We are fortunate if we have an expectation of meeting an approximately complementary objective view of ourselves to our own subjective version, unlike Jean-Paul Sartre who felt his quintessential subjectivity would be compromised by the objective view of other people. We are fortunate if with our unconscious basic assumptions and common-sense illusions we possess ontological security.

One notable example of a fortunate possessor of ontological security was David Hume who was also the most rigorously searching, questioning mind of his age. As an Enlightenment philosopher of the eighteenth century he examined rigorously what could be known about our existence and the world by the use of reason. He concluded that it was a great deal less than was previously thought; the discards included the concepts of cause and effect which we imposed on what could only be observed as 'constant conjunctions'. Hume however added that he could not live a sane and normal life if he carried such a desert of reason from his study into his living room. There he was happy to resume his 'natural beliefs' that he shared with his friends. Hume had abundant ontological security that survived his intellectual curiosity and enabled him to question the most basic assumptions about himself and reality. His philosophical scepticism, particularly about cause and effect, was much criticised and held to be an obstacle to science. The twentieth century however vindicated him, the findings and theories of modern physics being consonant with his philosophical analysis. He anticipated in many ways the gap between common sense and the mathematical reasoning of quantum mechanics. Heisenberg, the creator of the uncertainty principle, similarly saw the gap between his quantum physics theories and the common-sense view of the macroscopic world and went so far as to say that the moment we use language we have introduced Newtonian classical physics because it is embedded in it. And he suggests this is so because our brains evolved on our planet where macroscopically it seems to be an accurate picture of reality.

But as Hume would have said we don't need to ruminate on the difficulties of quantum counter-logic to use our mobile phones, even though they actually rely on one of its most ingenious applications. We live in a probabilistic world with a sense of certainty and we have somatically based particulate sensations of ourselves which we transform into a sense of continuous existence. Our sense of security depends on this sense of self and the unsubstantiated belief in the continuous well-being of our absent loved ones allows us to leave home without a crisis of anxiety. In this everyday world we constantly transform probability into certainty: it is the basis of psychic reality. Psychoanalysis explored and exposed this as subject to illusion at a mental level, now it looks likely that this is also the case at the brain level. The brain it seems can deceive itself as we previously learnt the mind can do.

But we rely neuronically on the transformation of probability into certainty in order to perceive and we rely at a mental level on our ability to transform belief into assumed fact for our security.

However in our field of clinical psychoanalysis we meet some who lack Hume's natural beliefs, whose beliefs may not include certainty as to their own existence or that 'the sun also rises', that the moon will reappear, that things may continue out of sight. There are those who suffer ontological anxiety, a fear of not being, or of not really being who they are. It is from exploring the psychic reality of those who suffer ontological anxiety that we can learn more about our brain-/mind-based ability to achieve the security of certainty in a probabilistic world. To explore this requires a readiness to question all our common assumptions and to pay serious and minute attention to other minds than our own. Probably it requires a good deal of ontological security that I believe can be enhanced by analysis, yet another justification for a searching, thorough training analysis. Chris Mawson, in his post–Bion mode has bravely embarked on this, and in this book the spirit of inquiry is paramount. It raises questions for all of us, several of which we probably would rather not ask, a sure sign of a good question.

INTRODUCTION

In the mid–1960s there was a decisive shift of emphasis in Bion's psychoanalytic attitude, discernible in his book *Transformations* (1965), and developed further in *Attention and Interpretation* (1970). Traditionally psychoanalysis has emphasised the goal of insight – at root a form of knowing based on the transformation from derivatives of the unconscious as made detectable by the specific method of psychoanalysis. In *Transformations* Bion considered how interpretive work might hold the potential to effect a further transition, from knowing to being and becoming. The book takes further key aspects of Bion's later work, one principle of which is that the activity of interpretation should stem first and foremost from a sojourn with the *being* of the patient and the particular suffering that comes from their being. This is the crucial passage:

> When, as psychoanalysts, we are concerned with the reality of the personality, there is more at stake than an exhortation to 'know thyself, accept thyself, be thyself', because implicit in psychoanalytic procedure is the idea that this exhortation cannot be put into practice without the psychoanalytic experience. The point at issue is how to pass from 'knowing' 'phenomena' to 'being' that which is 'real'. . . . Is it possible through psychoanalytic interpretation to effect a transition from knowing the phenomena of the real self to being the real self?
>
> *(Bion, 1965a, p. 148)*

Bion argued from an implicitly existential perspective that whereas the phenomena that we meet in the consulting room are aspects of knowledge, reached by what he termed 'transformations in K', the reality of the patient and the analyst cannot itself be known, only 'become', that is to say, lived. This is not only a philosophical statement, it concerns – as I detail in the book – the practice of analysis.

The principle means that in order to further psychic growth, interpretation must stem from contact with something real and yet out of reach of the accretion of knowledge. Although Bion understood that many analysts would not consider the patient's being and becoming to be an important part of psychoanalysis, he wanted to explore the potential for interpretive work in this area.

It seems to have been Bion's work on anxiety, its opacity and its non-sensuous aspect in particular, that suggested to him that something of the psychoanalytic attitude had the potential for making that further step – in which the patient in analysis could be helped not only to gain insight *about* themselves, but that they may come to experience something of the reality of their own being, and the potential for becoming. These are terms that tend to be found more in existential accounts of psychotherapy than the psychoanalytic, and this book attempts to redress the balance. In the later chapters of this book, after much preliminary discussion to prepare the ground, I will show how we can make use of some of Bion's later work to investigate obstacles, including those introduced by the personality of the analyst, to a movement from knowing towards being, and back again to a form of knowing to which I give the term 'becoming informed from being'. One way to consider the ideas in this book, therefore, is as an investigation of learning from experience, in the psychoanalytic experience, from a philosophical perspective. In addition to the psychoanalytic and philosophical perspectives, I include a third – the dramaturgical dimension of mental life. Without all three, I maintain, the practice of psychoanalysis is incomplete.

In this book I will attempt to pursue this project, making use of some of Bion's more difficult writing on what he called the domains of 'K' and 'O', and his later emphasis on an analytic attitude in which the suspension of memory, desire and apperception became the central recommendations to the practitioner. I show how these technical concepts and their underlying philosophy have a close affinity with the existential concepts of Heidegger and Sartre, and with the study of drama, from antiquity and in its modern forms in which deconstruction of meaning has both philosophical and psychoanalytic relevance.

It is a book with anxiety at its heart, and it is with anxiety in mind that it explores the implications for psychoanalysis of including a consideration of the *being* of the patient, and of the analyst, as inseparable from the particular kind of anxiety pertaining to this perspective, ontological anxiety.

The inspiration and impulsion for the book came from several sources simultaneously. Having spent ten years editing the *Complete Works of W. R. Bion* in close collaboration with Francesca Bion I had become increasingly drawn, from the entirety of his published and unpublished writings and recorded lectures and his many scattered notes, to one passage in particular. This passage, reproduced in the opening paragraph of this introduction, appears in chapter 11 of his 1965 *Transformations*. Through editing his work I came to feel that it expresses in concise form an essential growing point for Bion in the last fourteen years of his life, at a time when his colleague in the British Psychoanalytical Society, Donald Winnicott, was also interested in the being of the patient. I advance it here as the beginning of a project revealing a fascinating hidden dimension of psychoanalytic work, one worth exploring for its therapeutic possibilities and for the theoretical avenues opened up by its connections to other disciplines.

This book, therefore, pursues and takes further the implications for psychoanalysis of Bion's inclusion of the ontological in considering mental growth, from the perspective of the authenticity of the being and the becoming of the patient in analysis. Attempting to do so involves exploring the application of the philosophical distinction underlying Bion's thinking in this regard, together with one to which it holds a close affinity, to be found in the work of Martin Heidegger in *Being and Time*.[1] This will be explored as the distinction between the spheres of the 'ontic' and the 'ontological', where the latter term takes on a meaning unique to Heidegger. This philosophical distinction permits of a clinical application,[2] or – more accurately, a recognition of its already existing dimension – by which I mean that, as I hope to demonstrate, it helps in our orientation to all that our patients bring to us in the consulting room. In pursuing this latter orientation to psychoanalysis I have been helped by studying the work of the Swiss analyst Alice Holzhey-Kunz, who has developed a particular version of a daseinsanalytic approach to psychoanalysis, that is to say, an approach informed by a philosophical perspective on the being of the patient in analysis. I have found it helpful in pursuing my line of thinking throughout this book to bear in mind, as Holzhey-Kunz (2014, p. 44) has shown, that the patient in analysis has an inherent philosophical interest in their world, as well as a basic orientation towards their object relations. To use a term coined by one of Heidegger's translators, John Macquarrie (2001 [1960]), I regard the two dimensions, those of object relations and attunement to the philosophical, as equiprimordial[3] in the human being. I have also found valuable Holzhey-Kunz's concept of *Hellhörigkeit* – the special sensitivity to the ontological dimension found in certain patients. As I will discuss later, Holzhey-Kunz made central to her studies the way in which Bion described such a patient in 1954, and later, from a new perspective in 1973 – a man whose special sensitivity to the ontological led him, when aware of the gaps in the material of his socks, to a state of being of absolute horror.

A personal communication from the analyst Neville Symington, received in 2011 while I was editing Bion's works, turned out to be of great help to me. For the purpose of reading Bion's writing on the subject of the domains of 'K' and 'O', I recommend to readers the practice of holding back from ascribing a name to the sign 'O', instead allowing its signification to evolve from the experience of reading, but the term suggested by Symington, which he arrived at by virtue of his combined theological and psychoanalytic experience, *ontological*, I believe to be

---

1 I have, throughout the book, been informed mainly by the revised version, by Dennis Schmidt (2010), of the translation of Heidegger's text by Joan Stambaugh, in which *Stimmung*, an important Heideggerian concept, is taken to refer to *disclosive mood* rather than the anglophile term 'state of mind'.

2 For instance in the contributions of the Swiss analyst Alice Holzhey-Kunz (2014).

3 Etym. exist together as equally fundamental *ab initio*. A term coined by John Macquarrie (1960), as a rendering of Heidegger's concept of *gleichursprünglich*.

helpful in the total context of Bion's later work. It orients us to the realm of being and the philosophical thinking suitable for it.

The primacy of anxiety

Anxiety, which informs us of our being with great immediacy, and which is stimulated by contact with primordial truths of our human condition, is what unifies the various strands of this study. It is in relation to anxiety that we are helped by other human beings to bear what *is*, and what we *are*. It is because of this universal condition that I maintain, as a central principle throughout the book, that the psychoanalytic and the existential belong together. My thesis is that it is the irreducible fact of anxiety that unifies them.

More specifically, the central idea of the book concerns evolutions in the psychoanalytical relationship in which insight and mental growth stem from what Bion calls 'being that which is real', rather than 'knowing about' phenomena. It is the thesis of this book that discerning such moments rests upon the analyst's sensibility for working in a mode of being described by Heidegger as *Mitsein* (being-with) in which the dimensions of the ontological and ontic occur together and yet are maintained as distinct. I will be considering the value of fostering, alongside an attitude of evenly suspended attentiveness (Freud) and a freely roused emotional sensibility (Heimann), an openness to the particular mood of anxiety belonging to the ontological. Transitions in that domain, discussed by Bion as 'transformations in O', with which the mutative interpretation discussed by James Strachey (1934)[4] has an affinity, involve the analyst in listening with what Holzhey-Kunz (2014) calls a philosophical ear.

The orientation to the ontological dimension, the being of the patient, does not replace the attention to the patient's unconscious object relations as they are lived out in the transference–countertransference relationship, or to the unconscious phantasy life of the patient, but rather it complements our understanding.

My response to the challenge of Bion's shift of emphasis, from knowing towards the domain of being, is to consider how this shift is expressed in terms of method, particularly to Bion's recommendations on memory and desire and to the insights and findings of Holzhey-Kunz's particular daseinsanalytic method, a psychoanalysis informed by the core philosophical concepts of Heidegger and Sartre, and which sees the patient as a being with philosophical strivings and ontological anxieties. I will show how an awareness of ontological anxiety is fore-shadowed in Freud's first theory of anxiety, though it is not named as such, and in Bion's explorations of what he called the container–contained relationship and its origins in the infant–mother relationship. I will also be suggesting the presence of a deeply intuitive sensitivity to this kind of anxiety in the psychoanalytical attitude of Melanie Klein in her descriptions of her analytic work with children, though

---

4 See later for a fuller discussion of this important contribution to the difficulty of analytic work.

this was not made explicit philosophically by her. What is thrown up for therapeutic practice by drawing these conceptual links and affinities, in the lines that I trace in the various chapters, and by crossing the borders of different disciplines and their languages, is the subject of this book.

Klein wrote of the necessity for a sensibility in the child analyst enabling her to detect impressions of anxiety, indicated by the particular quality of hesitation in the child's 'play-thoughts', for example, but also by fainter and more subtle pressures – something to which she gave the term "point of urgency" (1932, p. 51). What was urgent was not necessarily indicated by the intensity of the anxiety interfering with the flow of the child's play-communications, nor did the intervention have to be in terms of 'depth' of interpretation, in classical terms. What I will be suggesting is that she had a tacit awareness of the necessity for the child's ontological anxiety to be addressed at the very point of its emergence.

In the emotionally intense relationships encountered in the psychoanalytic session I envisage, alongside what we ordinarily describe as learning, a particular type of momentary contact or 'brush', an intersection of sorts, between the ontical aspects (those which can in principle be known and subject to categorical thought) and the ontological, impressions of which can sometimes be intuited by the quality, or mood, of anxiety present. In other words, the analyst can, in crucial moments, intuit the primordial aspects immanent in, and 'touched on', by the specific anxiety-situation being communicated by the patient. Openness to this level of experience can enhance attention to other, more structured intimations of the Unconscious.

This potential for ontological contact in the analytic relationship will, as I said earlier, be explored in relation both to contemporary psychoanalytic theory and to the therapeutic approach of Holzhey-Kunz, informed by Heidegger's early thinking in *Being and Time*, known as the daseinsanalytic perspective. From this viewpoint another kind of openness to be explored is the heightened sensitivity found in some individuals to this particular source of anxiety. In later chapters I will be taking Holzhey-Kunz's concept of a special sensitivity to the ontological (2014, p. 197) as representing not so much a pathological state as a way of access for attunement to the ontological in the psychoanalytical setting.

This daseinsanalytic concept will also be considered in relation to Bion's concept of *maternal reverie*, the openness to receiving the infant's projected distress, and particularly his discussion of the adverse mental consequences of the denial to the infant of this basic openness to anxiety. The relevance of focusing on Heidegger's writings on openness as a kind of *revealment of being*, arises from its affinity with the Freudian task of addressing what is hidden, and uncovering and bringing out the latent in the manifest.

Donald Winnicott shared with Bion a deep interest in the earliest formative interactions of the mother–infant couple, and he too was interested in considering the being of the child and of the adult patient in analysis. His early approach to the being of his patients (1945) will be discussed, as well as his later views in the 1960s. There is also an important contribution from Michael Parsons (2014) that has interesting methodological implications, which can be usefully compared with those suggested by Bion's writings.

Whether we are considering the central ontological distinction used by Bion in *Transformations*, or the one articulated by Heidegger – which is more suited to taking further Bion's project – such a partition is at the heart of this book, which I have indicated using the shorthand terms knowing and being. They imply a rift,[5] an 'impassable fissure' for which there is, *in principle*, no bridge. The application to psychoanalysis of this axiom, one well known to epistemological philosophers, is the mainspring of this book. In relation to it, Shoaf (2014, p. xxi) wrote that "No writer, including Dante, sees more clearly than Shakespeare does the impassable fissure between knowing and being". Introducing his psychoanalytic theory of transformations, Wilfred Bion expressed it thus:

> My theory would seem to imply a gap between phenomena and the thing–in–itself; all that I have said is not incompatible with Plato, Kant, Berkeley, Freud and Klein, to name a few, who show the extent to which they believe that a curtain of illusion separates us from reality. Some consciously believe the curtain of illusion to be a protection against truth which is essential to the survival of humanity; the remainder of us believe it unconsciously, but no less tenaciously for that. Even those who consider such a view mistaken, and truth essential, consider that the gap cannot be bridged because the nature of the human being precludes knowledge of anything beyond phenomena save conjecture.
>
> *(Bion, 1965a, p. 147)*

The implications of making this a principle central to psychoanalytic methodology will be explored, showing why it is, for example, that we cannot with our interpretive work simply move between what we and our patients come to *know* of themselves and the implications of this insight for their *being and becoming*.

In the book I argue that Bion's distinction between these realms, which he symbolised using the signs 'K' and 'O', requires that we recognise explicitly the importance of contact with ontological anxiety as well as listening to our patients' more tangible fears. These ideas, and the conceptual equipment required for their understanding, will form the early chapters.

In placing the experience of *anxiety* at the centre of my enquiry, I explain how Freud considered the question of the management of mental pain in the personality. In the first psychoanalytic chapter of the book I clarify Freud's first theory of anxiety, which appeared in his pre-psychoanalytic works of 1894 and 1895. Freud's ideas on anxiety were developed further by Melanie Klein, who in 1946 introduced an original concept concerning fundamental projective processes, and her ideas were subsequently expanded by Wilfred Bion. These formulations have been of great importance to the development of psychoanalysis in the UK and beyond, and in later chapters their

---

5 Etym. *c.*725, *ryft*: a cloak, a veil.

relevance to the main themes of the book will be made clear. In relation to the existential aspects of the book, the conceptual distinction which will be linked to Bion's later psychoanalytical writing is to be found in the writings of Søren Kierkegaard in *Fear and Trembling* (1843) and *The Concept of Anxiety* (1844), and developed further by Heidegger in *Being and Time* (1927). This, as I said earlier, is the distinction marked by the terms ontic and ontological. I will make use of clinical vignettes taken from analytic sessions and supervisions to illuminate these ideas where possible.

There has tended to be an unhelpful set of splits or divisions, rationalised in terms of sharply defined intellectual cultures, 'subject areas', or 'schools of thought', in which psychoanalysis has been concerned predominantly with the gaining of insightful self-knowledge, or else inclined principally towards the alleviation of symptoms and the individual's better adaptation to the surrounding societal culture, and the various existential approaches have tended to orient themselves more towards the anxieties of the human condition and the various modes of being associated with them.

In the book I argue that psychoanalytic work is best served by resolutely *not* following the conventional divisions, and, instead, take the psychoanalytic and the existential aspects of human life together. I will describe how Bion's later formulations suggest the importance of developing a psychoanalytic methodology that is suited to becoming aware of, and where possible reducing, obstacles standing between analysts and their contact with the reality that is the patient, however fleeting such contact may be. Bion's work alerts us to the chief hindrances in this contact, which are those brought about through premature knowing, and the smoothing-over or filling-up of lacunae and contradictions. This inevitable tendency is due to the anxiety in the analyst whilst awaiting, "without any irritable reaching after fact and reason",[6] a closer contact with the undisclosed and unknown reality of the patient and of themselves as they involve themselves in the fluid interaction of the analytic hour. The thrust of Bion's argument here is of a relationship between knowing and being in which the equilibrium of the encounter in the consulting room threatens constantly to evolve into an unstable and 'unhomely' dis-equilibrium, through the sudden impingement into the domain of K by unruly elements of the reality of the patient and of the analyst (O). This will be discussed in the book as my idea of an ontological version of countertransference.

In terms of the analytic situation, knowing and being can be considered as superordinate 'vertices' (a 'geometric' term that Bion used instead of 'perspective' in order to discuss the idea of intersection of domains of experience), existing in conjunction with those concepts more familiar to the practising analyst, albeit that they exist on a 'meta-level'. To speak of such 'intersections' in the psychoanalytic situation risks introducing mysteries through the use of allusive language, but in the course of the book I hope to make the ideas understandable through linking them with clinical practice.

6 John Keats (1817).

As well as including the ontological in psychoanalysis, I will also be making a case for the explicit recognition of its *dramaturgical* extension, one which in fact exists already in psychoanalysis as the drama of the figures of the inner world, and which helps span the relations between the intrapsychic and interpersonal realms of our work and thinking. Transference and countertransference are terms which, in their origins and meaning, belong to the representational field of drama. As such, principles derived from the intensive study of drama in its own right will be described, and brought into the discussion of the psychoanalytic and ontological domains which form the central spine of this book. I will be suggesting that core elements of existential and epistemological philosophy, together with a dramaturgical sensibility, form a potentially fertile, creative conjugation for psychoanalysis.

This third perspective in the book takes as its starting point the definitive studies of tragic drama made by Aristotle in his *Poetics*, the earliest surviving work of dramatic theory. I will be revisiting the concept of *katharsis*, which has tended to be marginalised in modern psychoanalysis, by returning to the original text of Aristotle to show its renewed relevance for a psychoanalytic methodology that includes the perspectives of drama and a study of being.

Brecht's experimental theatre, based on the making strange (*Verfremdungseffekt*) of familiar narrative conventions, will be considered in relation to the specific methodology of psychoanalysis in terms of Freud's original recommendations.

A sensibility to the dramaturgical foundations of dreaming and transference was present in Freud's thinking, as we will see from the terms in which he first couched his descriptions of the workings of transference.

The dramaturgical dimension was introduced by Bion too in his early work on group processes in the late 1940s and early 1950s, where he related it to an understanding of the transference–countertransference relationship and projective processes. Leon Grinberg, in South America, pursued these ideas, and in the UK Anne-Marie and Joseph Sandler wrote of role-responsiveness.

The foundation of psychoanalysis as an interpretive phenomenology carried out with openness to the dynamic unconscious will be used as a unifying principle amongst the ideas used in this enquiry, beginning with the most central concept of psychoanalysis, *anxiety*, and moving towards its conjunction with ontological concepts of being and becoming on the one hand, and the dramaturgical production of the complex dynamics of transference and countertransference on the other. A tripartite structure is thus envisaged to study the life of the mind using concepts traditionally associated with the separate domains of psychoanalysis, existential philosophy and the study of drama. My reason for doing so is that my clinical experience convinces me that psychoanalysis requires, together with its intrapsychic focus, a recognition of the basics of its underlying ontological and epistemic philosophy, and an awareness that its specific method precipitates and relies upon, implicitly, an underlying dramaturgical structure. Basic concepts pertaining to each of the principal perspectives explored in this book will be set out in the terms of those fields themselves, but where appropriate their particular affinities and correspondences, their 'family resemblances', to ideas from the other perspectives will be brought in, hopefully with the minimum of 'jarring' due to the differing kinds of discourse.

The principal axiom of the book is that from the beginning of life it is in relation to *anxiety* that we are helped to bear what *is*. Because of this fact I begin this exploration of the domains of knowing and being, the epistemic and the ontological, in psychoanalysis by examining the nature of anxiety itself. Anxiety is the most universal experience which, like pain, is "the most imperative of all processes", and from which there is the most decided tendency to flee (Freud, 1895, p. 307). In the book I will explain how and why it is that the developing human mind becomes populated by representations of its experiences in the animate form of 'objects', functioning as characters in the theatre of an inner world, a private world, largely unconscious, every bit as real as the outer world which we have become more accustomed to sharing. This is a description of the mind's essentially dramaturgical dimension. In my view, theatre exists because this dimension is an essential component of how the mind works.

Additionally, I will argue, psychoanalysis also requires the existential dimension, on the basis that at the inception of mental life the formation of objects in the inner world proceeds from the need to manage overwhelming and boundless anxiety in relation to being and non-being. It is for this reason that I assert throughout this book the importance of including the ontological, the study of being, in psychoanalysis. As I say, this is discussed firstly and principally in relation to *anxiety*, which lies at the foundation of our being in the world, and in relation to all that grows from the original orientation of the mother towards that anxiety – in terms of communication, thinking and the growth of the mind. The purpose of doing so is to provide the necessary groundwork for the recommendations I put forward in later chapters for expanding the function of interpretation to include all forms of anxiety, including that of the ontological.

I will begin with some of the first descriptions ever written concerning the nature of anxiety.

PART I

Anxiety

From the ancient world to ontological philosophy

1

ANXIETY

Antiquity towards modernity

In a letter to Richard Bentley in 1753, Horace Walpole described a small pew hung with green damask as "a *modernity* which beats all antiquities for curiosity" (Wright, 1842, p. 184). An apt epigraph for this chapter would be its transposition: "But here is an antiquity which beats all modernities for curiosity", because in specific Epicurean texts to which I will draw attention there appear some of the earliest systematic writings on the mind, and in those passages it is emotion rather than cognition that is recognised as being at the heart of the mind. In this chapter I will begin with these writings to show how some of the observations concerning anxiety, and of the human being's relations towards it, are startling both in their acuity and contemporary relevance.

In the first century BCE, in his epic philosophical texts, *De rerum natura*[1] (*The Nature of Things*), the Roman philosopher Lucretius,[2] distinguished *anxiety* from *fear* almost two thousand years before Søren Kierkegaard did so. Following the principles of his teacher Epicurus, Lucretius stated that, although in terms of material comforts men may amply (or even richly) be satisfied, "they yet, O yet, within the home, / Still had the anxious heart [*anxia corda*]".

> For when saw he that well-nigh everything
> Which needs of man most urgently require
> Was ready to hand for mortals, and that life,
> As far as might be, was established safe,
> That men were lords in riches, honour, praise,
> And eminent in goodly fame of sons,

---

1 Manuscript rediscovered in 1417 in a monastery in Germany by Poggio Bracciolini (Greenblatt, 2012).
2 Titus Lucretius Carus (*c.*99 BCE–*c.*55 BCE), inspired by the writings of Epicurus (341 BCE–270 BCE).

> And that they yet, O yet, within the home,
> Still had the anxious heart which vexed life
> Unpausingly with torments of the mind.[3]
>> *(Lucretius, 50 BCE, De rerum natura,*
>> *Book VI, 13)*

Lucretius distinguished between anxiety and the more palpable fears and desires, for which he used the term *timor*, upsurges of which prevented the stoical imperturbability that some had considered within their grasp through the operation of reason. In these verses Lucretius can be read as signifying 'home' not only to indicate the literal dwelling place, but the innermost one, the mind itself.[4] The meaning becomes clearer when I return to the verses of Lucretius later in this chapter, when I discuss his historically early depiction of the mind as a *vessel*, a container with its own autonomous potential for creating inner sources of anxiety, independently of external circumstances.

But first, here are two short vignettes from Greek medical texts belonging to the compilation known as the Hippocratic Corpus,[5] in which there appears the description of a man suffering intense anxiety brought on during the night by the eerie sound of flutes. His name was Nicanor of Athens.

> Nicanor's affection,[6] when he went to a drinking party, was fear[7] of the flute girl. Whenever he heard the voice of the flute begin to play at a symposium, *masses of terrors rose up.* He said that *he could hardly bear it* when it was night, but if he heard it in the daytime he was not affected. Such symptoms persisted over a long period of time [my emphasis].
>> *(Hippocrates, 1994)*

The ancient texts describe another sufferer, whose name was Democles.

> Democles, who was with him,[8] *seemed blind and powerless of body*, and *could not go along a cliff, nor on to a bridge to cross a ditch of the least depth*, but he could go through the ditch itself. This affected him for some time.
>> *(Müri, 1986, p. 230)*

True to the nature of *pathos* (πάθος) this phenomenological description of anxiety in the two men – the vignette given did not involve 'diagnosis' or 'treatment' of the condition – has the quality of evoking our pity and fear, reminding us that we are, actually or potentially, fellow-sufferers. We can feel ourselves involved with and alongside Nicanor and Democles in their anxieties – terrors welling up at the

---

3 *anxius angor*, torment of anxiety.
4 Compare Heidegger's use of *Unheimlichkeit* (Ger.), 'unhomeliness' not as an affect, but as an aspect of being.
5 Various authors, dating approximately fifth century to the first half of the fourth century (BCE).
6 πάθος, pathos and pity.
7 φόβοσ, *fovos*, fear, terror, alarm, fright, panic, with the connotation of flight from something.
8 *ho met' ekeinou.*

haunting sounds of the night and the cripplingly vertiginous anxiety felt by a man feeling suspended helplessly over what is, or is felt to be, an abyss. The specific, tangible fears evoke also an awareness of something of the deeply ontological, the human-condition elements immanent in the specifics of the situations depicted. From what unknown place does an eerie, ominous sound emanate? What does it portend? Is the ground, or anything at all, really solid beneath my feet? Will I fall for ever? On what can I truly depend?

The reference here to pity and fear is a specific reference to the writings of Aristotle (*c.*335 BCE) in his *Poetics* (Περὶ ποιητικῆς). It is the earliest known writing on the theory of the structure and dynamics of tragic drama, and the concepts will be considered in detail later in the book, in Chapter 7. Concerning this important concept of Aristotle's, Gotthold Lessing (1767) wrote:

> It is certainly not Aristotle who has made the division so justly censured of tragic passions into terror and compassion. He has been falsely interpreted, falsely translated. He speaks of pity and *fear*, not of pity and *terror*; and his fear is by no means the fear excited in us by misfortune threatening another person. *It is the fear which arises for ourselves from the similarity of our position with that of the sufferer; it is the fear that the calamities impending over the sufferers might also befall ourselves; it is the fear that we ourselves might thus become objects of pity. In a word, this fear is compassion referred back to ourselves.*
>
> (Lessing, 1767, "On Aristotle's pity and fear" [my emphasis])

I have emphasised the latter part of this description by Lessing because it brings out so clearly the striking correspondence of Aristotle's conception to the confluence of two later psychoanalytic concepts which will feature in this book. These are Freud's (1895) concept of the *Nebenmensch*, the fact that the first object internalised into the ego is a fellow human being, and that of introjective *identification* in the work of Melanie Klein. Later I will show how her concept of projective identification, and Wilfred Bion's model of the container–contained, hold affinities with Aristotle's work on the transformations made possible by the functions of purging and catharsis in the dramatic form of tragedy. The contemporary theories of projective identification can be seen in prototypic form in elements of Aristotle's *Poetics* and in passages of Lucretius' epic philosophical poem. This I will describe in a separate chapter, Chapter 7.

Returning now to Lucretius, here are the lines from Book VI of his philosophical work in which, having first stated that anxiety can strike us from within in spite of externally derived sources of security, he goes on to write of the autonomy of the mind, making use of the analogy of a container capable of generating, from within itself, poisonous contents having harmful effects upon whatever comes into it. He pictures the heart/mind, the *anxia corda*, as a containing vessel affecting its contents:

> Then he, the master, did perceive that 'twas
> The vessel itself which worked the bane, and all,
> However wholesome, which from here or there

Was gathered into it, was by that bane
Spoilt from within, – in part, because he saw
The vessel so cracked and leaky that nowise
'T could ever be filled to brim; in part because
He marked how it polluted with foul taste
Whate'er it got within itself. So he,
The master, then by his truth-speaking words,
Purged the breasts of men, and set the bounds
Of lust and terror.[9]

(Lucretius, 50 BCE, De rerum
natura, Book VI)

Lucretius writes that goodness which has been experienced as internalised does not remain so for long, because the mind – as a container for its experience – can never be entirely satisfied, nor can its feelings of frustration and anxiety be wholly relieved for more than a short while. The observation of this universal experience will prove important when we return to the subject of satisfaction and pain in the next chapter, by considering Freud's earliest theory of anxiety.

Lucretius' allusion to the leaky vessel as a symbolic form for dissatisfaction and ingratitude is a reference to the Greek myth of the fifty discontented daughters of Danaus (Δαναΐδες), water-nymphs who were called the *Danaids*, or, in Ovid's account,[10] the *Belides*, forty-nine of whom murdered their new husbands on their wedding nights and were punished by the gods to a fate that calls to mind the curse of Sisyphus. They were made interminably to carry water in vessels with holes in them, and so could never achieve the purpose of washing away their crimes.

It is the second part of the text that holds a greater significance for later theories of mind. Lucretius suggests with poetic imagery that the mind is analogous to a vessel "polluted with foul taste / Whate'er it got within itself". This is the insight that the mind itself is by virtue of its own inner workings a producer of noxious events. It is the workings of the vessel itself, states Lucretius, that can generate destructiveness and the concomitant anxiety stemming from it, *not only* because the container cannot ever be filled to the brim – full and complete satisfaction cannot be attained – but because *the mind itself is capable, by its own processes, of contaminating its contents.*

This is a striking insight into the nature of one of the most important aspects of mental functioning, the existence and the autonomy of an inner world, anticipating by more than two thousand years Freud's conception of a mental apparatus, the concept of psychical reality, and – in particular, as we will consider later, Bion's model of the mind as a container in which contents can be destructive to their container and a container can exercise damaging effects upon those elements contained within it.

9 *timor.*
10 *Metamorphoses*, Book 10, lines 10–63.

Shakespeare, who had read Lucretius' poem, expressed, in the following lines from *As You Like It*, the insight that even good and creative properties could wreak poisonous harm within the mind of the one possessing them:

> Know you not, master, to some kind of men
> Their graces serve them but as enemies?
> No more do yours. Your virtues, gentle master,
> Are sanctified and holy traitors to you.
> O, what a world is this, when what is comely
> Envenoms him that bears it!
> *(Shakespeare, c.1901,* As You Like It,
> *Act II, Scene iii)*

In the final lines of the passage that I reproduced earlier, having depicted the mental vessel as generating its own anxieties from within, Lucretius writes of the necessity for a helpful intervention from outside. I will show in the next chapter how Freud traced a similar arc in relation to the origins of anxiety in the infant. When Lucretius describes the role of the external helper in limiting the dread arising from within the mind of the sufferer, he uses the term 'master' to represent this more experienced one:

> So he,
> The master, then by his truth-speaking words,
> Purged the breasts of men, and set the bounds
> Of lust and terror.

These lines trace a relation between several elements of experience:

(1) the need to purge ourselves of the worst anxieties initially by means of *discharge*;
(2) the need for simple truthful words bearing on reality to meet the pain of such experiences that have been thus discharged;
(3) and that facing overwhelming desire and dread with honest words permits some bounds to be set to them.

On these central principles of anxiety and truthful words, Shakespeare, in *Love's Labour's Lost* (*c*.1901, Act V, Scene ii), wrote the lines: "Honest plain words best pierce the ear of grief", and "A heavy heart bears not a nimble tongue".

Traumatic degrees of anxiety

It is clear from certain of his verses that Lucretius understood another crucial fact about the nature of anxiety. Once the *degree* of unattended anxiety, quantitatively speaking, exceeds a certain threshold limit of tolerability by the individual containing it, a *qualitative* shift can be understood to occur. The individual is subject to trauma that encompasses totally the psyche and the whole person, making impossible the distinction we normally like to make between the psychical and the physical. Lucretius certainly understood this fundamental fact about unbound anxiety. Later we will see how Freud formed a model of anxiety which took account of the phenomenon of traumatisation in two early pre-psychoanalytic works.[11]

Lucretius had foreshadowed the ideas of Freud on anxiety that traumatises us in the following vivid and striking description:

> And as, when head or eye in us is smit
> By assailing pain, we are not tortured then
> Through all the body, so the mind alone
> Is sometimes smitten, or livens with a joy,
> Whilst yet the soul's remainder through the limbs
> And through the frame is stirred by nothing new.
> But when the mind is moved by shock more fierce,
> We mark the whole soul suffering all at once
> Along man's members: sweats and pallors spread
> Over the body, and the tongue is broken,
> And fails the voice away, and ring the ears,
> Mists blind the eyeballs, and the joints collapse, –
> Aye, men drop dead from terror of the mind.
> Hence, whoso will can readily remark
> That soul conjoined is with mind, and, when
> 'Tis strook by influence of the mind, forthwith
> In turn it hits and drives the body too.
> *(Lucretius, 50 BCE, De rerum natura,*
> *Book III, Part 2)*

The description is beautiful, capturing as it does forcefully and concisely the involvement of the whole body as the anguish breaks its mental confines. It is the efficacy of care and attention offered by a helper drawn to such traumatic suffering that Lucretius describes as "purging the breasts of men", enabling bounds to be set to both lust and terror. The conjunction marked by the terms *purging, truth* and *setting bounds* will prove to be one of the central themes of the book, implicated in all three component realms of mental life running through the book, the psychoanalytic, the ontological and the dramaturgical.

Lucretius, in Book IV of his epic verse, wrote of dread by describing vividly that evoked in human beings by the instability of the ground under their feet, the earthquakes of Sidon in Syria and Aegium in Peloponnese:

> And besides many walled towns have fallen through great movements on land, and many cities have sunk down deep into the sea, inhabitants and all. And even if it does not burst forth, yet the very impulse of the air and

11 Freud, 1894, "Draft E: How anxiety originates"; Freud, 1895, "Project for a scientific psychology".

the fierce force of the wind are spread, like a fit of shivering, throughout the riddling passages of the earth, and thereby induce a trembling: even as cold, when it comes deep into our members, shakes them against their will and constrains them to tremble and to move. So men quiver with anxious terror throughout the cities, they fear the houses above, they dread the hollow places beneath, lest the nature of the earth should break them open all at once, and lest torn asunder she should open wide her maw, and, tumbled all together, desire to fill it with her own falling ruins. Let them then believe as they will that heaven and earth will be indestructible, entrusted to some everlasting protection; and yet from time to time the very present force of danger applies on some side or other this goad of fear, lest the earth, snatched away suddenly from beneath their feet be carried into the abyss, and the sum of things, left utterly without foundation, follow on, and there be a tumbling wreck of the whole world.

(Lucretius, 50 BCE, De rerum natura, Book IV, Part 2)

Writing with imagery evocative both of the practical and the ontological instability of the dread brought to human beings by the turmoil of the earth in its foundations, Lucretius summons up the mental and physical sense of dread which Søren Kierkegaard, writing as Johannes de Silentio, apprehended as the fear and trembling in the core of our psyche, the *anxia corda* as Lucretius had called it. In fact "fear and trembling" is not such a good translation of Kierkegaard's title, bearing in mind the distinction he makes between fear and anxiety. The Danish *Frygt og Bæven* is more accurately rendered in English as *Trembling in Apprehension*, or in *Angst*. His title may have been inspired by the following lines from Book II (67) of Lucretius' epic verse:

For even as children tremble and fear everything in blinding darkness, so we sometimes dread in the light things that are no whit more to be feared than what children shudder at in the dark, and imagine will come to pass. This terror then, this darkness of the mind, must needs be scattered not by the rays of the sun and the gleaming shafts of day, but by the outer view and the inner law of nature.

(Lucretius, 50 BCE, De rerum natura, Book II)

Partly drawing on the verses of Lucretius, Kierkegaard, this time writing under the pseudonym Vigilius Haufniensis, described in *The Concept of Anxiety*[12] (1844), the importance to our understanding of ourselves of being willing and able to suffer anxiety: "Whoever has learned to be anxious in the right way", wrote Kierkegaard,

---

12 *The Concept of Anxiety* (*Begrebet Angest*) was translated into English with the title *The Concept of Dread* in 1944 by Walter Lowrie.

has learned the ultimate. . . . Anxiety is freedom's possibility, and only such anxiety is through faith absolutely educative, because it consumes all finite ends and discovers all their deceptiveness. And no Grand Inquisitor such dreadful torments in readiness as anxiety has, and no secret agent knows as cunningly as anxiety to attack his suspect in his weakest moment or to make alluring the trap in which he will be caught, and no discerning judge understands how to interrogate and examine the accused as does anxiety, which never lets the accused escape, neither through amusement, nor by noise, nor during work, neither by day nor by night.

(1844, p. 188)

Compare this insight with the final line from the following passage of a letter that the psychoanalyst Wilfred Bion wrote to one of his children at boarding school. Speaking of homesickness he wrote that all his memories of it were of:

the most ghastly feeling I ever knew – a sort of horrible sense of impending disaster without any idea what it was or even any words in which to express it. Not much better is what I think of as the 2 a.m. feeling when some horrible worry comes on you with such force that it makes your blood run cold. One might write an anthology but it would require skill, almost amounting to genius, to begin to recall the absolute dread that comes on these occasions. But I believe it is from one's ability to stand having such feelings and ideas that mental growth eventually comes.

(Bion, 1985, p. 173; 2014, vol. 2, p. 195)

'Freeing from the encumbrances of the senses': the early contemplative thinkers

The spiritual exercises created by early Christian thinkers known as Contemplatives were practices which led to the 'falling away' of the normal everyday functioning of the senses, of their products, and ideas, as preparation for unencumbered spiritual contemplation of mysteries. The theological-philosophical contemplatives – sometimes referred to as mystics – practised an austere and exacting mental discipline, which they applied in seeking to overcome the obstacles posed by their own knowledge, and inclinations, to their meditative task, which they considered as an approach to a kind of union with their conception of ultimate being.

The general term for enquiry proceeding by way of negation, considering what is *not*, is *apophatic* methodology. The more unknown a situation is, the more suited is this way of inquiring into it. It involves a suspension of the habit of relating new perceptions to a "mass of ideas already possessed".[13] It is, therefore, more suited to philosophical investigation of the unknown, and contrasts with the more familiar

13 The faculty of *Apperception*, as described by William James (see later).

attitude, the *cataphatic*, which means proceeding by defining though positive statements, producing knowledge of what is taken to be cumulative, factual knowledge.

Some writings of the early theo–philosophical thinkers are relevant to the subject of this book. Their spiritual-mental discipline brought them into painful contact with fundamental anxiety, stemming from their attempts to suspend the normal, everyday sensory, perceptual and cognitive functions insofar as they felt these to act as barriers to their contemplation of the unknown. To complete this chapter I describe how two particular early contemplative thinkers described, in their philosophical and theological writings, a kind of severe existential anxiety arising from the suspension of their normal use of the faculties for knowing and perceiving. Of particular interest, in relation to the anxiety of not-knowing, are the writings of the German Dominican theologian and philosopher Eckhart von Hochheim, also known as Meister Eckhart (1260–1328), and the Spanish Carmelite friar, Juan de Yepes y Álvarez, (1542–91), better known as St John of the Cross. He expanded on his poem *Dark Night of the Soul* (*La noche oscura del alma*) with two commentaries, *The Ascent of Mount Carmel* (*Subida del Monte Carmelo*) and *The Dark Night* (*Noche Oscura*).[14] In these he wrote of what he called the "afflictive suffering"[15] brought about by a kind of mental and spiritual emptiness resulting from, as he wrote, "the suspension of these natural supports and perceptions". The 'natural supports of the soul', or as we would say psychoanalytically, the ego, are, in the writings of St John of the Cross, the senses and the faculties served by them. He wrote that for "this dark contemplation" to be possible, which is not contemplation *of* something, but contemplation itself [16] without reference to a particular object at hand:

> All these sensory means and exercises of the faculties must be left behind and in silence. . . . As a result one has to follow this method of disencumbering, emptying, and depriving the faculties of their natural rights and operations to make room for the inflow.
>
> *(St John of the Cross,* The Dark Night of the Soul,
> *Book 2, Chapter II, Section 2)*

What was supposed to take the place of that which the mind dwells upon in its normal everyday condition? And then, subsequently, an 'inflow' of what? What did St John of the Cross hold as the beneficial consequence of tolerating the experiences which were as a long dark night to our being? For now these questions will be left unanswered.

The suspension of the natural habits of mind, those most "deeply rooted in the substance of the soul", lead us, he wrote, to:

---

14 See K. Kavanaugh & O. Rodriguez (tr.) (1964), *The Collected Works of St John of the Cross*.

15 "dark contemplation; wherein the soul not only suffers this emptiness and the suspension of these natural supports and perceptions, which is a most afflictive suffering (as if a man were suspended or held in air so that he could not breathe)".

16 Later this statement will be compared with Freud's fundamental recommendation concerning psychoanalytic listening.

suffer deep undoings and inward torment, besides the said poverty and emptiness, natural and spiritual.

(Book 2, Chapter VI, Section 5)

In other words, in the states of mind being described as resulting from an austere spiritual discipline, there are intense persecutory anxieties, 'deep undoings', which go beyond an experience of the pains of lack and loss. St John of the Cross writes of the dread of annihilation, death of the soul. He suggested that such states could only be endured for moments:

> there are only occasional periods when it is conscious of their greatest intensity. At times, however, they are so keen that the soul seems to be seeing hell and perdition opened.
>
> *(p. 22)*

Just as Lucretius had referred to the mind both as a home and a vessel, one which holds its contents within itself, Meister Eckhart (1260–1328) wrote of what, in today's terms, we would consider as external objects being internalised, their images subsequently 'taking lodging' within us:

> Within, the soul sees clearly the image whereby the creature has been drawn in and taken lodging. For whenever the powers of the soul make contact with a creature, they set to work and make an image and likeness of the creature, which they absorb. That is how they know the creature.[17]
>
> *(Meister Eckhart, 2009, p. 31)*

It is, on this model, an affinity with our 'lodged' images that forms the means by which we 'know' the objects of our perception. Eckhart suggested that all relations of knowledge take place though the setting-up inside us of what he called "presented images". He believed that it was the function of the soul to make internal images of externally presented objects and to make an attempt to unite itself with these images in the service of feeling familiar with them, and thereby to feel united with the objects of its world. These descriptions correspond closely to modern ideas of memory, apperception,[18] and the psychoanalytic concepts of identification and internal objects.

Of the formation of images, Eckhart wrote:

> an image being something that the soul makes of (external) objects with her own powers. Whether it is a stone, a horse, a man, or anything else that she

---

17 Possibly the earliest description of what we would now, following Klein, call *introjective* identification.
18 A term for all mental processes in which a presentation is brought into connection with an already existing and systematised mental structure and can thereby be classified, explained and understood. See later in this chapter.

wants to know, she gets out the image of it that she has already taken in, and is thus enabled to unite herself with it.

(2009, p. 31)

It is clear that these contemplatives were describing hazardous meditative processes for which skilled and experienced assistance was required. Earlier I left open the question of what it was that the mind might be opened *towards*, as a result of being disencumbered of its everyday operations. What might 'inflow', in place of the ordinary input from sensory sources and their many combinations and correlations in the formation of their images and objects? In the second part of his first sermon, Meister Eckhart distinguishes, in the passage following, an inner reality of being, separate from all the objects of knowing, pointing to the fact that what has been made by the self can be known by the self, *but that the being of the self cannot itself be known*:

> But for a man to receive an image in this way, it must of necessity enter from without through the senses. In consequence, there is nothing so unknown to the soul as herself. Accordingly, one master says that the soul can neither create nor obtain an image of herself. Therefore she has no way of knowing herself, for images all enter through the senses, and hence she can have no image of herself. And so she knows all other things, but not herself. Of nothing does she know so little as of herself, for want of mediation.

(2009, p. 31)

In "The Ascent of Mount Carmel" (1, 1–2), by St John of the Cross, there is the following description:

> The first [night of the soul] has to do with the point from which the soul goes forth, for it has gradually to deprive itself of desire for all the worldly things which it possessed, by denying them to itself; the which denial and deprivation are, as it were, night to all the senses of man. The second reason has to do with the mean, or the road along which the soul must travel to this union – that is, faith, which is likewise as dark as night to the understanding.

Earlier in the chapter I asked what might compensate the soul for having been deprived of 'food' by way of its senses, and what is it that could replace the 'inflow' of sensuous information. The following passage by Meister Eckhart is of interest. He distinguished the mind's use of sensory images from that which may be *intuited* through the *suspension* of sensuously based knowledge. Referring to the soul as 'her', he wrote in his first sermon that the faculties which receive only in images

> have to know and lay hold of each thing in its appropriate image . . . and since all things enter from without, that knowledge is hidden from my

soul – which is to her great advantage. This not-knowing makes her wonder[19] and leads her to eager pursuit, for she perceives clearly *that* it is, but does not know *how* or *what* it is. Whenever a man knows the causes of things, then he at once tires of them and seeks to know something different.

(2009, p. 34)

Further to this, Meister Eckhart was aware that the mental discipline preparatory to what he considered a fully *interior act* meant tolerating the anxiety stemming from depriving oneself of the ontological security of knowing. He wrote, in his second sermon:

> Accordingly a master says, "To achieve an interior act, a man must collect all his powers as if into a corner of his soul where, hiding away from all images and forms, he can get to work". Here, he must come to a forgetting and an unknowing. There must be a stillness and a silence for this Word to make itself heard. We cannot serve this Word better than in stillness and in silence: there we can hear it, and there too we will understand it aright – in the unknowing. To him who knows nothing it appears and reveals itself.

(2009, p. 43)

To set against this potential compensation, Eckhart puts into words the refutation of a 'Devil's advocate', one who prizes accumulated knowledge above all else, saying that ignorance is simply a deficit, that is all there is to it, suggesting that "in ignorance there is a lack, something is missing, a man is brutish, an ape, a fool, and remains so long as he is ignorant" (2009, p. 43). Eckhart is aware that this version of knowledge is purely quantitative, and something taken as capable of being possessed. Its ownership is equated with riches, its lack is identified with mental poverty.

There is another mode of knowledge, referred to by Meister Eckhart as *transformed knowledge*, and this, he states, has to evolve from unknowing. He writes that in such a transformation, which comes after a rigorous struggle, we *become* our knowing. Although Eckhart was writing in a theistic context, the underlying principle has, as I will show later, close correspondences with the later work of Bion in psychoanalysis, and the work of Holzhey-Kunz in daseinsanalysis, which is the psychoanalytic approach carried out under a phenomenological-existential perspective.

Holzhey-Kunz (2016, p. 21) has introduced the concept of a special sensitivity to the ontological in relation to traumatisation arising from anxieties of the human condition. She gives to this special sensitivity the term *Hellhörigkeit*, a term with an etymology drawing on the faculty of *hearing* rather than

---

19 A word with an ancient etymology (*c.*700) predating those of *awe* and dread (OE: ondrǽdan), which it also connotes.

seeing – 'clair-*audition*' as contrasted with 'clair-*voyance*'. Concerning this distinction Meister Eckhart's wrote:

> the sense of hearing is nobler than that of sight, for we learn more wisdom by hearing than by seeing, and in it live the more wisely. Hearing draws in more, but seeing rather leads outward – the very act of seeing does this. Therefore in eternal life we shall rejoice far more in our power of hearing than in that of sight. For the act of hearing the eternal Word is within me, but the act of seeing goes forth from me: in hearing, I am passive, but in seeing I am active. In this way your unknowing is not a lack but your chief perfection, and your suffering your highest activity. And so in this way you must cast aside all your deeds and silence your faculties, if you really wish to experience this birth in you.
>
> *(2009, p. 43)*

Eckhart's reference here to what is required for allowing an experience of the genesis of something new is what for Socrates[20] is the *maieutic attitude* – literally that promoting mental midwifery. Eckhart therefore is promoting what today would be termed mental space, encouraging us not to saturate that space with ready to hand knowledge. He wrote that the intellect, when left to its own tendencies, seeks to concretise experience into pictorial images, to make use of memory, cognition and the purposeful activity of the Will to "fasten on something and [to] act on it" (2009, p. 50).

Eckhart sought a method of thinking that would postpone the closure instigated by the mind's normal tendencies, so that the intellect (which I am considering as the operation of 'K') is enabled to await what he calls a "finding of true being", a finding that "penetrates to the ground of being". He writes that such a finding enables an investigator to say, "This is this; it is such and not otherwise". Until this situation evolves, Eckhart writes that the intellect

> has nothing to go by and makes no pronouncement at all, as long as it has not penetrated to the ground of truth with full realization. . . . Meantime the intellect, finding no real object to support it, waits as matter awaits form. Just as matter will never rest until it is filled with all forms, so the intellect cannot rest except in the essential truth that embraces all things.
>
> *(2009, p. 50)*

It is this final term, *realisation*, which later will provide the conceptual link between the ideas discussed in the latter part of this chapter, and the psychoanalytic ideas of Bion in Chapter 5. I have discussed the central principle of Eckhart's treatise because

---

20 OED: the Socratic process of assisting a person to bring out into clear consciousness conceptions previously latent in his mind.

its treatment of the relationship between getting-to-know and allowing sufficient time and depth of experience is expressed so beautifully, and in such a way as to prepare the ground for a later chapter in which I consider Bion's recommendations for the analyst in tolerating anxiety and doubt, whilst awaiting the evolution of a moment for a mature interpretation to the patient in the analytic encounter. Before that, in the next chapter I consider how Heidegger, in *Being and Time* (1927), investigated anxiety as the principal mood in which our Being is disclosed.

2
HEIDEGGER
Care and the anxiety of being

Heidegger placed the question of being, with anxiety as its basic mood of disclosure, on a new philosophical footing by making it the investigation of the being of the human being, whose existence in the world was taken as indivisible and not as fallen into the subject/object division established by the dominant narrative of dualistic thinking:

> the phenomenon of anxiety will be made basic for our analysis. In working out this basic state-of-mind and characterizing ontologically what is disclosed in it as such, we shall take the phenomenon of falling[1] as our point of departure, and distinguish anxiety from the kindred phenomenon of fear, which we have analysed earlier.
>
> *(Heidegger, 2001 [1927], p. 227)*

His project in *Being and Time* was to open up to detailed philosophical investigation the question of the human being's being. For this he used the term *Dasein*, which he used to indicate the human being's being-in-the-world, his existence as such. In a later chapter I will relate some of Heidegger's central ideas to Wilfred Bion's investigation of the capacity of human beings to understand their understanding as an aspect of their being and not only in relation to their cognition. In fact, Heidegger and Bion each in their own ways, in their own fields, were able to make inroads to a study of being, in spite of the great difficulties of working within a language suited, in the main, to articulate the world of sense-based phenomena. Both thinkers coined new expressions for their studies, and both made use of existing terms in new and startling ways.

---

1 Here the translation of Stambaugh is helpful in rendering this as "falling prey to".

By using the term *Dasein*, Heidegger meant to emphasise the fact that human beings are born into, and are from the beginning immersed in an already existing world of other beings and their ways, and that it is in relation to this condition that he makes use of the term 'existence'. Thus, in reading Heidegger, it is important not to take the term being as *objective presence*, which summons up the polarity[2] of objective/subjective, but rather it should be taken as the 'such–so–ness',[3] or 'that–ness' of that which we encounter, insofar as we can, as human beings, have a brush with existence which is not solely interpretive and categorical. From a Heideggerian perspective, the being of the human being, its *Dasein* finds its grounding, or 'declension', in its *being-in-the-world*, in which context it can be examined integrally and phenomenologically, and not by piecemeal analysis.

What is the relationship between anxiety and the existential concept of being-in-the-world

> Our greatest reality lies in the anxiety that reminds us that we are not basically at home, safe or substantial and that calls us to attention, to action and to awareness of Being.
>
> *(van Deurzen, 2010, p. 238)*

In Heidegger's writing, which, like that of Bion, requires forbearance and patience, anxiety is the principal primordial mood[4] capable of disclosing what he called our *Dasein*, the being of our *being-in-the world*. It is in our anxiety that we are found, just as we are. The German word *Befindlichkeit* captures this meaning: 'the mood in which we are to be found'. How did Heidegger arrive at giving such a central place to anxiety? He wrote that anxiety "makes manifest 'how one is'". In this ontological sense, in the 'how we are', and 'the being-found-so' – the literal meaning of *Befindlichkeit* – we are, in our anxiety, *unheimlich*. Freud's translator rendered this word into English as 'uncanny', but Heidegger used it to refer to *the experience of not being at-home*.[5] The English terms 'unnatural' or 'unfamiliar' are closer to the experience, though Strachey wished to give emphasis to the feeling of strangeness.

---

2 As discussed by Holzhey-Kunz, 2014, p. 32.

3 The correspondences of such a formulation to those of Taoism and Zen are not accidental. Heidegger seems to have been influenced in his ideas of *Dasein* by his contact with the Japanese philosopher Tomonobu Imamichi (1922–2012).

4 Heidegger considered moods (*Stimmungen*) to be conditions close to our being. In this book the term *state of mind*, the form of which is exclusive to the English idiom, will generally be used in its psychoanalytic sense, namely as descriptive but ontic, and from an external, non-subjectivised viewpoint.

5 *das Nicht-zuhause-sein.*

From an existential vertex, Heidegger wrote:

> In anxiety one feels '*uncanny*'[6] [*unheimlich*]. Here the particular indefiniteness of that which Dasein finds itself alongside in anxiety, comes proximally to the expression: the 'nothing and nowhere'. But here 'uncanniness' also means 'not-being-at-home'.
>
> *(Heidegger, 2001 [1927], p. 233)*

This understanding of Heidegger had been foreshadowed by Lucretius, who had stated in the following passage that our true being is revealed in anxiety:

> it is more fitting to watch a man in doubt and danger, and to learn of what manner he is in adversity; for then at last a real cry is wrung from the bottom of his heart: the mask is torn off, and the truth remains behind.
>
> *(Lucretius, 50 BCE, De rerum natura, Book III, 55–8)*

In the world of theatre, the revolutionary theorist Antonin Artaud also wrote in a remarkably similar vein of the disclosive power of severe existential anxiety:

> And finally from a human viewpoint we can see that the effect of the theatre is as beneficial as the plague, impelling us to see ourselves as we are, making the masks fall and divulging our world's lies, aimlessness, meanness and even two-facedness. It shakes off stifling material dullness which even overcomes the senses' clearest testimony, and collectively reveals their dark powers and hidden strength to men.
>
> *(Artaud, "Theatre and the plague" [1938], in Artaud, 2010)*

The concept of being-in-the-world

From a conjoined psychoanalytic and daseinsanalytic position, the Swiss analyst Alice Holzhey-Kunz, initially a student of Medard Boss, who had himself studied with Binswanger and with Heidegger, explained the significance to analysis of the concept of being-in-the world as residing firstly in taking a quite different approach to the human being:

> He is not a pure subject separated from the world but is always and never anything other than 'being-in-the-world'. This means that he has to deal with things practically and theoretically without first stepping out from his inner world into the external world. Furthermore, the factical subject does not exist in isolation; the human being is only there as 'being-with', which means among other human beings, approached by them and related to them. This even circumvents the opposition between subjectivity and intersubjectivity.

6 'unhomelike' (or 'unhomed').

> *Second*, the expression 'being-in-the-world' repudiates the widespread notion that the human being relates only to objects or to other subjects in his life, and asserts another more fundamental relationship, namely the *relationship to the world as world* that is the human being's preserve.
>
> *(Holzhey-Kunz, 2014, p. 36)*

As we will see later, the relationship to the world-as-world is an important consideration for psychoanalysis as well as the existential phenomenology of Heidegger. Melanie Klein's pioneering work with children introduced to psychoanalysis the central concept of the *inner world*,[7] as a world in its own right with its own 'objects' and relationships between them, colouring and being coloured in turn by the mutually affecting exchanges between psychical reality and that taken as 'outer' by virtue of the senses. The familiarity with the idea of the inner world can lead us to pay attention so much to the figures of that world and their inter-relationships that we forget the basic context, which is that it *is* a world. In other words, in our eagerness to get to grips with what may be revealed in getting to know its inhabitants, the dramatis personae of that world, we neglect its world-as-world quality. In that 'objective' attitude we find ourselves asking what is going on in that world, and miss the sense of what kind of world it *is*, and what is it to be in that world, to exist within it, and how does that existence feel to the one who lives it. These are ideas relating to *being*.

As Holzhey-Kunz has emphasised, the *world-as-world* is not the same as this interpreted and constructed familiarity. Our senses, perceptions, our language and our knowing cannot even in principle make contact with the *world-as-world*, that which Heidegger called 'objective presence'. This was what Bion meant at first by his use of the sign 'O', as in, for example, the following passage. "What the absolute facts are cannot ever be known, and these I denote by the sign O" (1965a, p. 17). It is in this respect that Bion's initial use of the sign 'O' is, because of its reference to Kant's realm of the *noumenal*, not to be taken as identical with Heidegger's phenomenological term *Dasein*.[8] Later Bion used 'O' to indicate more the being of the patient and that of the analyst.

Being-in-the-world implies both the inevitable human attempt to live with the sense of familiarity, and hence security, coherence, continuity and consistency, *and* the inescapable intimations showing us that it is our habitual practices and ways of interpreting the world that *provide* the familiarity, and not reality itself. It is ontological anxiety that reminds us of the fracture.

Holzhey-Kunz clearly understands the articulation of this apprehension of the difference between the human being's *being-in-the-world* and the *world-as-world* as a crucial discovery. She wrote:

---

7 See Klein, 1940, p. 127.

8 *Dasein*, it will be remembered, points to the potentially unconcealed being of the human being's being-in-the-world. The 'O' of Bion's writing, by contrast, is not available to disclosure, although we may gain an impression of it, or a 'brush' with it.

With his discovery, Heidegger moves on to that ultimate ground from which the human being exists – admittedly one that now proves to be an *abyss*. For how can the human being dwell in the 'nullity of the world'?

(2014, p. 38)

Here she brings Heidegger's descriptions of the existential problem together with that of Sartre, and his formulation of the 'nothing' of existence. Heidegger's version of this is to point to the dread caused by awareness of this abyss, as it renders ineffective the seamlessness of the experience called *being-at-home*. The translator of Holzhey-Kunz's (2014) account drew attention in a footnote to how the German word for *ground*, as in the 'ground of our being', has – etymologically – the contrastive term *Abgrund*, meaning *abyss*. In other words, in that etymology, 'abyss' is implied by 'ground', the vertiginous contained in the substantial.

In being exposed to the particular anxiety of 'the nothing', it is not simply a matter of feeling a 'stranger in a strange land',[9] but a situation in which, as Holzhey-Kunz states, "even the 'alien–familiar' opposition has become obsolete" (2014, p. 38). Meaning is, in itself, on shaky ground – even the basic construct 'insideness' and 'outsideness'. Holzhey-Kunz notes that under such a condition we feel not so much, in our basic predicament, a concrete *fear*, but rather a deeply unhomely feeling.

It is important at this point to emphasise that this loss of meaning with its intense ontological anxiety as discussed by both Heidegger and more recently by Holzhey-Kunz, is not a sign of a deviation from the normal. To regard it thus would be to privilege the existence of meaning and to take it for granted as normative and 'natural' to human beings. Holzhey-Kunz (2014, p. 39) spells out very clearly the opposite view:

Heidegger rejects the dominant notion that human existing is fundamentally held secure in meaning-contexts. He thereby turns the tables: someone who suffers from a sense of meaninglessness or complains of a loss of meaning does not simply yet have to find the meaning and has not temporarily lost it, but is being confronted with the truth that we indeed mostly dwell in meaning-contexts without really being secure in meaning because all meaning is fragile, and 'behind' all meaning 'bare being' always lurks in its facticity that is devoid of all meaning.

(2014, p. 39)

She acknowledges that in this situation we have to orient ourselves to conventional meanings, but that even as we do so we are inescapably driven towards the existential anxiety involved in our being, and our being-with-others, for which the agreed stabilising meanings are inadequate, arbitrary and conventional. It is as

---

9 Exodus, 2:22: "For he said, I have been a stranger in a strange land".

though human beings carried with them, outside consciousness, some premonitory awareness of the fact that their structures for making sense of themselves and their world *are* just that, structures. Holzhey-Kunz believes that although relatively rare, the authentic anxiety pertaining to this can "in principle intrude at any time, without any special cause being required" (2014, p. 39).

Ontological anxiety and mood

What is it that discloses to us the immediacy of our ontological state, in relation to our being-in-the-world, in the sense of the foregoing discussion? In what do 'we find ourselves', in our being? Heidegger's response to this question is that disclosure to our being is by way of our *mood* – 'the state in which one may be found', in contradistinction to what is more commonly called a 'state of mind'. In everyday English the term mood tends not to carry much gravity, often being used to refer to a passing momentary emotional 'state'. It is important to keep this in mind, because the phrase *state of mind*, common to psychiatry and psychoanalysis, is an ontical[10] term, suited to the categorical and diagnostic mode of thought in contradistinction to the meaning of *mood* as indicated by Heidegger, that refers to a state of being. In relation to a mood, suggests Heidegger, it is a question of how one finds oneself to be (*befindung*; OE: 'befind' – to be discovered) – literally to be found in one's being.

To reiterate: phenomenologically, anxiety can be regarded primordially as a mood[11] in the sense intended by Heidegger, rather than in its conventional sense as a 'state of mind'. From this vertex it is by *being-with* the other in their anxiety, a condition in which our being is encompassed, that we meet their *Befindlichkeit*, literally 'the state in which they may be found'. In fact the German root *befinden* is found in the same form in Old English, where its etymology contains the dual meanings of *to find, to discover* and *to invent, to contrive*.[12]

"There but for the grace of God go I" – usually regarded as a statement of recognition of our shared human vulnerability to the condition of being alive, has been attributed to the Christian reformer John Bradford (1510–55). On observing a group of prisoners being led to their execution it is said that he uttered the words, "There but for the grace of God . . .", recognising that the misfortunes of others could as easily be our own.

Bradford's observation expresses the same sense of 'tragic pensiveness'[13] found in the classical form of tragic drama, with elements in it that Aristotle, in the second book of his *Rhetoric*, called *eleos* and *phobos*. These terms are

---

10 Etym. (OED): of or pertaining to knowledge of the existence or structure of being in a given entity.
11 A sense observed by Joan Stambaugh in her translation of *Being and Time*.
12 Later, when I discuss *apperception* and *intuition* as distinct forms of understanding, we will note in the German language a corresponding distinction in the two main words for 'understanding' – *Verstehen* and *Erklären*, the former bearing an ontological connotation, the latter a categorical, ontic meaning.
13 See Gadamer, 1989, p. 131, and a discussion of this in Chapter 7.

translated in our times as the reciprocal pity and fear induced by care for the characters whose predicament we witness with apprehension that their fate is felt inwardly as though it could be our own or belong to our loved ones. From the perspective of Bradford's awareness, as he spoke these words, that he himself could find himself 'in the dock' and subject to a similar specific fate as the prisoners, his experience in identifying himself with the specific situation of the condemned is said to be *ontic*. This ontical link is entirely possible since after having been suspected of treason against the monarch, Mary Tudor, he too became a prisoner in the Tower of London and was burned at the stake in 1555. On the other hand, from his perspective of drawing from this observation that none of us can really know that the day is not our last, he was expressing a painful ontological truth.

Shieldedness against the anxiety of the ontological

Our routine psychic defences and constructs not only protect us by deflecting[14] more tangible fears, they shield us at the same time from the anxieties of the human condition immanent within them, their 'ontological inclusions' (Holzhey-Kunz, 2014, p. 53).

On this model, since we are oriented predominantly towards experiences in which we can locate or construct tangible perceptual objects, categories and causal relationships – the realm of the 'ontic' – the elements stemming from the opaque dimension of the ontological remain for the most part concealed. Ordinary adaptation to the exigencies of life under what Proust called *l'habitude*, the generic 'everyday' (*das Man*[15]) of Heidegger, is from a basic attitude in which the awareness and particular anxieties pertaining to the ontological realm – for which we find special words: dread, awe, wonder, the guilt of existing – are, so to speak, 'unconscioused'[16] (*unbewusst*).

Proust's *l'habitude* and Heidegger's *das Man*: the world of the everyday

Marcel Proust, in his *À la recherche du temps perdu* (1913–27), explores, with his notion of *l'habitude,* similar territory to that of Heidegger's 'everydayness' and the 'they-self':

> Custom [*L'habitude*]! that skilful but unhurrying manager who begins by torturing the mind for weeks on end with her provisional arrangements; whom

---

14 Deflection (*Ablenkung*) refers back to Freud's (1894, p. 108) early description of the defensive use of projection away from the psychical sphere.

15 In the English language a similar meaning is conveyed by the use of 'one does this', or 'one feels this'.

16 See Bion, 1992, p. 353.

the mind, for all that, is fortunate in discovering, for without the help of custom [*sans l'habitude*] it would never contrive, by its own efforts, to make any room seem habitable.

(I, p. 8)

To make a room seem habitable, to feel at home in it, this is the analogy that Proust uses as a picture of how we use the mentality of the *everyday*, a fundamentally averaging attitude to 'tame' the world, to 'civilise' it, to usurp what otherwise would produce the angst belonging to our *not-being-at-home-ness*.

It is necessary for us to make our daily life bearable by the everyday attitude of what Proust calls *l'habitude*, and which Heidegger refers to by *das Man*, and the 'they-self'. In a similar vein, Britton (2015, p. 35) describes how the philosopher David Hume drew a comparable distinction between his mode of functioning whilst being a philosopher in his study, and the practical epistemology of his everyday life. Individuals who are especially sensitive to ontological anxiety, and are thus according to the Swiss analyst Holzhey-Kunz in the position of being 'reluctant philosophers', are unable to do what Britton described Hume as being able to sustain. They bear the brunt of an unshielded and hard to bear exposure to the vertiginous perspective of the view of humanity and knowledge that Hume and other philosophers only had to endure professionally, as it were.

Apart from in those with a special, undefended sensibility to the ontological, and which Holzhey-Kunz terms *Hellhörigkeit*, our normal mode of comprehension in the ordinary use of perception and language supports living in the everyday, in the philosophical use of that term. Everyday ontic structures, with their psychological-linguistic models, are founded upon a model of how 'objects' of the perceived world are taken, conventionally, to interact with one another. Britton (2015, p. 50) has noted that this model has a 'grammar' which is much closer to 'old physics' than the stranger but more penetrative insights of quantum thinking and structural linguistics. The latter show our being-in-the-world as being strange in a way that is very hard to live with, *unheimlich* in the extreme. That state belongs to what Britton (2015) calls *unnatural*, and to Heidegger's mode of *Dasein* called 'not-being-at-home' (*das Nichtzuhause-sein*) (*Being and Time* [BT], I.6). As I will consider later, this not-being-at-home quality, a concept in the existential perspective, has important affinity with two psychoanalytic principles – Freud's use of evenly suspended attentiveness, and Bion's suspension of memory, desire and apperception – and a concept from the study of drama, that of the 'making strange the familiar', the *Verfremdungseffekt* of Brecht.

Gabriel Josipovici (1994), in referring to Proust's description of how we 'tame' our perceptions of a room which we inhabit, clarifies that such a capacity does not come without a cost:

> But here we begin to discern a curious quality of habit: it makes the room habitable by effectively sealing us off from it, by reducing it from this unique room

to a room I know and therefore take for granted, cease to see. Habit allows us to go about our business in the world, but only by reducing everything we encounter to the most general terms, so that it is no longer reality but a cliché of the mind which we take for reality. Thus it is only when Marcel hears his grandmother's voice over the telephone, divorced from the rest of her person, which he has always taken for granted, that he feels that he is hearing it for the first time for what it really is: the voice of an old lady close to death.

(1994, p. 3)

Note here that one important reality occluded by *l'habitude* strikes us at the very end of this passage of text. Being forced to abandon the taken-for-grantedness produced by what Proust calls "the generalised cliché of the mind which we take for reality", and which Heidegger refers to as our *dwelling in tranquillized familiarity* (BT, I.6), brings us into contact with the reality of death. The voice of the old lady, when experienced as *real*, is of a real woman close to her death. I will return later to this point, in considering what Heidegger means by the mode of being-in-the-world that he terms *being-towards-death*.

Proust, brings out clearly how what we ordinarily regard as 'perception' and 'attention' are 'forward-reading' and reconstructive phenomena implicated in *l'habitude*.

Even the simple act which we describe as 'seeing someone we know' is, to some extent, an intellectual process. We pack the physical outline of the creature we see with all the ideas we already formed about him, and in the complete picture of him which we compose in our minds those ideas have certainly the principal place. In the end . . . each time we see the face or hear the voice it is our own ideas of him which we recognize and to which we listen.

(Proust, 1913–27, I, p. 20)

As well as shielding us from ontological anxiety of a more profound order, the attitudes that allow us to remain oblivious, described so well by Proust and by Heidegger, shelter us from even a basic recognition of the strangeness and immediacy of our world in every moment, achieving an imitation of reality that forms the basis of our at-homeness in, and familiarity with, the everyday world. Something of this counterfeit but necessary 'at-homeness' is discussed by Britton (1998, p. 160) in his exploration of how the poet Rilke expressed the idea that the dying might perhaps be exposed to what Britton describes as the 'sham of our everyday comfortable but unreal selves':

If no–one else, the dying must notice how unreal, how full of pretence
is all that we accomplish here, where nothing
is allowed to be itself.

(Rilke, 1989, p. 171)

Apperception: knowing and the everyday

The intellectual process indicated by Proust in these passages is, essentially, that designated by Johann Friedrich Herbart (1776–1841), as *apperception*, a process in which the possibility of the immediacy of a unique perception – say of the face of a friend one already knows, but being open to seeing him as though for the first time – is passed over for the sake of an efficient piece of visual processing and of categorical, calculative thought. We feel 'anchored' to reality by such means. In fact, it has been found that the recognition of a face that we have seen before is one of the most rapid mental calculations made on a daily basis. Apperception is a term for all mental processes in which a presentation is brought into connection with an already existing and systematised mental structure and can thereby be classified, explained, and understood.[17] It is an efficient system of mind utilising memory to make possible the predictive, 'reading-ahead' and 'reading-into' mode of perception.

A formulation of the apperceptive mode by William James (1842–1910) is: "To unite and assimilate a new perception to a mass of ideas already possessed, and thereby to comprehend and interpret it". Apperception is central to what Heidegger, in his *Discourse on Thinking*, called "calculative thinking" (Heidegger, 1969). In therapeutic work, apperception has its place, but an implication of Heidegger's thinking is that while the apperceptive mode is operating in a relationship, its use obstructs an approach to the *being* of the other. This, to be discussed in later chapters, is fundamental to Bion's thinking in his 1965 *Memory and Desire* and his 1967 "Negative capability". In the existential perspective, the principle is expressed in terms such as epoché (suspension of judgement), or 'horizontalization'[18] (Spinelli, 2007).

In order to approach being, by a route that does not rely on categories of knowing, what might open up a way for something of the being of our patients "to be encountered unconcealedly in themselves", as Heidegger put it?

What was required, he wrote, was a "way of disclosure", a means by which we might find access to something integral to ourselves in our being, such that it becomes accessible as "simplified in a certain manner", and can "come to light in an elemental way" (BT, I.6, p. 226). In addition, he specified that it should be found in an experience sufficiently "far-reaching and primordial".

This, as I introduced earlier, is where the central role of anxiety can be found. Anxiety itself, suggests Heidegger, provides the requisite way of disclosure for an approach to being. He used the term *angst* with a connotation close to

---

17 In the sense of *Erklären* as contrasted with *Verstehen*, as discussed earlier.

18 Spinelli (2007, p. 116) refers to *horizontalization*, the practice of paying attention to all aspects without prejudice or the prioritizing of any particular element over another based upon expectancy, prior assumption or preference. In this respect it has great affinity with Freud's concept of *evenly suspended attention* (1912a, p. 111) and with Bion's recommendations on memory and desire (1965b), and his use of the concept of *negative capability* (1970, p. 125; 2014, vol. 6, p. 327).

existential dread as it appears in the writings of Søren Kierkegaard (1843) in *Fear and Trembling* (*Frygt og Bæven*). In the application of Heidegger's principles to understanding others, how can we approach anxiety to become open to something beyond knowing *about* the other? And how can we orient ourselves so that when, eventually, we 'return' from an intersection or contact with their being, our knowledge, and the memorialising and communication of it, is applied to that unique experience without excessive degradation of the real? To begin to address these questions requires us to understand the special meaning given by Heidegger to the concept of *care* as a primordial aspect of being.

Heidegger's concept of care

The concept of care (*Sorge*) is a 'term of art' in Heidegger's analysis – his 'daseinsanalytic'. In other words it is a term with a precise, specialised meaning within the context of his writing, and its meaning for Heidegger is not to be approached by applying what we understand by the term from other contexts, for instance the everyday meaning of 'offering love'. A closer approach to his meaning is to consider *Sorge* as the 'mattering'[19] of the existence of human beings *as* human beings, and, as such, is independent of desire. Before explaining the embodiments of care as they are expressed in human relationships, as forms of *solicitude*, the following passage by Holzhey-Kunz gives us a good sense of Heidegger's intention in taking care as a foundational term in his work in *Being and Time*:

> What is radically innovative about the daseinsanalytic ontology is that it does not merely ascribe a specific being to the human subject but makes this 'being' the concern of every single human being. Heidegger in fact sees it as the crucial point about human being that the human subject does not simply (like all other beings) possess a specific constitution of being but *that he conducts himself towards it*. Therefore he can provocatively state: "The ontic distinction of Dasein lies in the fact that it *is* ontological" (BT, p. 10). With this, every human being is recognised as an ontologist, that means – implicitly knowing about his own being and adopting a position towards it. The widespread notion that only the philosopher freely decides to turn his attention at leisure to the question of being is thus repudiated in favour of the thesis that every human being exists philosophically in an elemental way and that it would not even be possible explicitly to posit the philosophical basic question as to the being of beings if every single human being did not always already have an implicit, *pre*-ontological knowledge of being.
>
> (*Holzhey-Kunz, 2014, p. 43*)

---

19 Compare etym. (OED): mattering, vbl. n. Obs. Caring, minding: 1693 Evelyn De la Quint. [Compl. Gard. I. 35].

Ontologically, as Cohn (2002, p. 37) states, "we cannot but 'be with' others. But how we do this is another matter". He identifies the use of Heidegger's terms *solicitude* (*Fürsorge*) and *care* (*Sorge*), and he emphasises that Heidegger was referring to the concern of one person in their condition of being-in-the-world for that of a fellow human being.

It is important to note at the outset that care, in this context, is not synonymous with love. For Heidegger it is immanent in what we could refer to as the human being's 'being-in-the-world-ness' that its existence as such matters; that it is a central, ever-present concern. Since being-in-the-world involves being with others (*Mitsein*), it necessarily includes being-with-others who also share this central concern with their own being. Being-with others, or 'with-being' (*Mitsein*) is also considered ontological, that is to say, 'of being'.

By quoting a passage from *Being and Time* on two forms of solicitude, Cohn brings out a particular aspect of Heidegger's ontological concept of *Sorge* which will prove important in a later discussion of a therapeutic application of these ideas. After remarking on failures of care in its ontological form – for instance in passing another by, taking the other as not mattering, taking against the other – he offers some text[20] describing two forms of solicitude, both of which can be recognised in the therapeutic encounter. I will use the translation of this passage made by Stambaugh:

> With regard to its positive modes, concern has two extreme possibilities. It can, so to speak, take the other's 'care' away from him and put itself in his place in taking care, it can *leap in* for him. Concern takes over what is to be taken care of for the other.
>
> *(2010, p. 118)*

This kind of concern can be appreciated as being sometimes necessary for human beings when there is no alternative present other than dependency on the care of another. Heidegger does not intend us to regard it as wrongful care, though he does say that it can become "determinative for being-with-one another". The second potential for concern is the:

> concern which does not so much leap in for the other as leap ahead of him in his existentiell[21] potentiality-of-being, not in order to take 'care' away from him, but rather to authentically give it back as such.
>
> *(2010, p. 119)*

Heidegger means that this mode of care concerns itself with the existence of the other, their being, and not narrowly with that to which the provision is made.

---

20 From the Macquarrie and Robinson translation of *Being and Time*.
21 In this translation the term *existentiell* corresponds to the ontic, and *existential* to the ontological.

Because of this, Heidegger writes: "[It] helps the other to become transparent to himself in his care and free for it".

Finally in this section, I will mention an associated concept introduced by Heidegger, that of circumspection. It expresses the principle of care in the relation between vigilant attending and the simultaneous carrying out of requisite actions, and its etymology in English bears this out. Heidegger used the German *Umsicht*, which connotes circumspection as prudence and judiciousness. Of this attitude, Heidegger wrote:

> Just as circumspection . . . belongs to taking care of things as a way of discovering things at hand, concern is guided by considerateness [*Rücksicht*] and tolerance [*Nachsicht*].

Heidegger can be read as 'sketching out' conditions for human beings to relate to one another not as objects but as fellow-beings. This allows "things at hand to be encountered as things discovered in their relevance".

Heidegger follows this statement with one of importance for what I have to say later about the therapeutic possibilities opened up by these philosophical ideas. It concerns the principal field of meaning in a human encounter.

> The referential context of significance is anchored in the being [*Sein*] of Dasein toward its ownmost being – therefore it cannot have relevance, it is rather being [*Sein*] for the sake of which [*worumwillen*] Dasein itself is as it is.

At first sight, this may seem a little obscure, even with the foregoing explanations. One way of reading it is to begin with the three terms: 'significance', 'referential context' and 'anchored', and then to think of the more familiar ways we have of establishing a sense of significance. The earlier discussion of apperception is relevant to this. Heidegger is suggesting another way, that of dwelling with a situation in its immediacy, with its unique features as they strike us, rather than thinking from the outset of that which is not present but that which it reminds us of. Read from this perspective it is an urge to suspend apperception and the sense of epistemic security gained by anchorage to that process. The connection to the earlier chapter on the contemplative thinkers is helpful here. The factor of eschewing the security gained by mental 'anchorage' to existing knowledge will be important in the later chapter on Wilfred Bion and the role he gives to the suspension of memory and desire in psychoanalytic observation and intuition. Partly to provide an eventual 'bridge' to those questions I will now introduce a passage from Heidegger, to serve as a 'place of return' when discussing the ideas of Bion which I think have the most striking affinity with Heidegger in *Being and Time*.

Being-with and getting to know

According to Heidegger's formulations in *Being and Time*, what is already present as a nascent form of understanding of others pre-exists what we normally consider as getting-to-know 'about' others. This understanding, like all understanding, is not a knowledge derived from cognition, but a primordially existential kind of being which first makes knowledge and cognition possible.

(Heidegger, 2010, p. 120)

Heidegger is suggesting that an understanding from being, in which a quality of being–with is primordial, is foundational to the human being in the function of cognition, and is a precondition for it, and not the other way around. Later I will be applying this principle to the practice of psychoanalysis by suggesting that the requisite attitude towards knowing is that it involves a willingness to be impacted and surprised by intimate contact with the being of the patient, and that this necessarily involves exposure to the shared ontological inclusions present in the relationship, as well as the specific ontical fears for which the patient is seeking help. An important corollary of this is that the analyst needs to be prepared for a degree of personal psychic change through the turbulence and turmoil of meeting the patient truthfully, through a relation of being informed from being with them. It is in this sense that I will, towards the close of the book, be reformulating the term 'knowing', in the analytic relationship itself, to *being informed*.

This formulation does not have an accidental relation to the earliest etymology of the term 'informed'. The use of the word 'knowledge' tends to mobilise a word-picture of a possession, and 'knowing' suggests a 'taking hold', similar to that invoked by the term 'apprehend'. To become informed raises a different set of impressions, one of which is incompleteness and openness to further indications of phenomena, whilst in the process of experiencing. It thus spans the functions of comprehending and faith, as expressed in its earliest recorded use in the English language:[22] "Fayth informed, although it be imperfyte yet . . . it is faith. . . . But then fayth is an informed fayth, or a derke fayth". The connection here (in this early etymology) to the foregoing discussion of negative capability, as well as Freud's reference to the analogy of dark-adapted vision in psychoanalysis, should be clear. I will expand upon it in a later chapter, but now I will return to Heidegger's point – from which I diverged – which was concerned with a mode of understanding in which the ontological precedes the ontical.

Heidegger continues his discussion of understanding by stating his view of the relation between self-knowing and being:

> Knowing oneself is grounded in being-with which primordially understands. It operates in accordance with the nearest kind of being of being-together-in-the-world [*mitseienden In-der-Welt-seins*] in the understanding knowledge of what Dasein circumspectly finds and takes care of with others.
>
> *(2010, p. 120)*

---

22 OED: *The Pilgrimage of Perfection* (1531: 190) Wynkyn de Worde.

Such concern cannot however be taken for granted in human relationships and, as Heidegger suggests, more commonly our caring has a relatively indifferent or deficient quality. We more often pass one another by, and in so doing are content to 'know about' them, rather than to derive an understanding through being with them, and they with us. In other words our understanding stops at the ontic without passing to the ontological dimension.

Heidegger continues,

> And when even knowing oneself loses itself in aloofness, concealing oneself and misrepresenting oneself, being-with-one-another requires special ways in order to get close to others or to 'see through them'.
>
> *(2010, p. 120)*

He writes of 'primary being-with' as the ground condition for what he calls the 'disclosure' to us of the other, and in doing so he specifies that the dimension of openness and closedness to contact with the ontological is the determining feature of this mode of being.

> To be sure, being-toward-others is ontologically different from being toward objectively present *things*. The 'other' being itself has the kind of being of Dasein [my emphasis].

Later I will set out those formulations of Bion which seek to clarify why it is, and how it is, that we can fall prey to our anxieties in such a way as to take other human beings not as fellow-sufferers but as inanimate objects – 'objective presences' in Heidegger's terms, and 'beings-in-themselves' in Sartre's:

> [others] are not encountered as objectively-present thing-persons, rather we meet them 'at work', that is, primarily in their being-in-the-world. Even when we see the other 'just standing around', he is never understood as a human-thing objectively present. 'Standing around' is an existential mode of being, the lingering with everything and nothing which lacks heedfulness and circumspection.
>
> *(BT, p. 120)*

For Heidegger, in taking the other as a 'thing-person', such a radical turning away in the central ontological relation of being-with engenders indifference towards them as specifically human beings, which is an inevitable part of what he calls the 'everyday' (*das Man*), or the 'they-self'; it can arise unwittingly from the tendency to rely primarily on generalised models of human situations, described earlier in terms of Proust's *l'habitude*. His description of 'meeting a friend one already knows' is beautifully illustrative of this effect (see p. 132).

In the chapter that follows I examine how the fundamentals of anxiety were first considered by Sigmund Freud in his pre-psychoanalytic writings. It will involve us in considering the centrality given by Heidegger to care, solicitude and openness, from the perspective of processes having their origin in the experiences of the mother–infant couple. Although reading the chapter involves a change of language, it is written to bring out some of the underlying affinities with the foregoing chapters.

PART II

Anxiety and psychoanalysis

Freud, Klein, Bion and Winnicott

3
ANXIETY, COMMUNICATION AND THE MIND

Freud's work of the specific action

> Why is an external person necessary? Why can't the human being be like lumbricus?[1] Why have a partner at all? . . . Why can't one have a relationship with oneself directly without the intervention of a sort of mental or physical midwife? It seems as if we need to be able to 'bounce off' another person, to have something which could reflect back what we say before it becomes comprehensible.
>
> *(Bion, 1978, Discussion three)*

Before he discovered the psychoanalytic method as a way of access to the unconscious, Freud was concerned to place the concept of anxiety at the centre of a theory of the development of mind. With Breuer in 1893 he spoke of mental pain causing traumatic suffering, and he distinguished between different forms of such tribulation – fear, anxiety, shame and mental pain (*Schrecken, Angst, Scham, psychischer Schmerz*). He considered the experience of psychic pain to be "the most imperative of all processes", and on this basis he developed an early theory of anxiety six years before he founded psychoanalysis.

In his first theory of anxiety Freud began with the fact that the young infant cannot by itself manage the anxiety arising within its barely differentiated physical and psychical 'mental apparatus'. Accordingly, the earliest experiences are made bearable for the baby only by the repeated timely intervention of her mother, orienting herself not only in the realm of the satisfaction of basic needs but, crucially, in the domain of anxiety. The earliest anxiety, and the prototypical one for which this work of the mother is necessary concerns the anxiety of the continuation of existence itself.

---

1 An earthworm.

The mother as the essential irreplaceable helper for her infant in distress is at the centre of these ideas, outlined in 1894[2] and in much more detail in his 1895 "Project for a scientific psychology", which he wrote five years before *The Interpretation of Dreams*, considered by Freud to mark the beginning of psychoanalysis. This early model goes some way to account for the beginnings of the functions of communication and thinking, rooted in anxiety and its vicissitudes, stemming from the mother's orientation to, and management of, her infant's painful mounting inner tension.

In seeking a model with which to understand the fundamental basis of anxiety, Freud used the language and ideas drawn from neurology as it existed at that time, and so it was framed, by analogy, on what was known in those days of neuronal-energic systems. In reading this early work it is useful to remember that the terms he used, which today may feel anachronistic and thus be skated over, are less important than are the relationships between the terms. It is their inter-relationship that turns out to be so well suited to understanding the fundamentals of anxiety as a phenomenon, one requiring specific action from another human being. Therefore, although the language belongs to another scientific era, what Freud wrote of anxiety in his "Project" is surprisingly well suited to some key modern ideas on the subject.

To begin, it is important to note that Freud's first theory of anxiety presupposed the existence of a nursing couple, and that the formation of a mind from what he called a 'physico-psychical' system depended on the work of the mother in intervening psychologically in her infant's signals of distress. In his 1894 "Draft E: How anxiety originates", Freud began his first attempt to provide a model for how anxiety might arise from the urgency of cumulative inner tension. In contrast to the experience of pain originating from the outside, he sought to account for the existence of anxiety by considering endogenously arising tension, that which wells up from the interior, and from which the infant cannot pull back or flee. His first question was why should there be a transformation from mounting sensations of inner tension into the experience of anxiety? Why not simply a system for the discharge of the accumulation? Freud supposed that the problem lay in the fact that innermost tension differs from that arising principally from sources outside the body, in that it cannot be evaded like an external painful stimulus and continues to be fed at source without diminution.

> What we are concerned with here is the second case – the case of endogenous excitation. Things are simpler in the case of exogenous excitation. The source of excitation is outside and sends into the psyche an accretion of excitation which is dealt with according to its quantity. . . . But it is otherwise with endogenous tension, the source of which lies in one's own body. . . . In this case only specific reactions are of use – reactions which prevent the further occurrence of the excitation in the end-organs concerned, whether those reactions are attainable with

2 Freud, 1894, "Draft E: How anxiety originates".

a large or small expenditure [of energy]. Here we may picture the endogenous tension as growing either continuously or discontinuously, but in any case as only being noticed when it has reached a certain threshold. It is only above this threshold that it is turned to account psychically. . . . If the specific reaction fails to ensue, the physicopsychical tension . . . increases immeasurably . . . reaches the threshold value at which it can arouse psychical affect; but for some reasons the psychical linkage offered to it remains insufficient. . . . Accordingly, the physical tension, not being psychically bound, is transformed into – anxiety.

(Freud, 1894, p. 192)

There existed, believed Freud, barely any differentiation in what he was later to call the psychical apparatus[3] between physically and psychically experienced tension. Freud described the roots of anxiety burgeoning in the helpless infant from endogenously arising, barely differentiated somatopsychic tension.

Freud supposed that this basic tension, which he discussed using terms borrowed from ideas of the distribution of energy in a bounded system, sought discharge away from the newly forming and unshielded psychical organism. On this first model, it was the failure of unbearably accumulating tension, building from within, to discharge along what he termed psychical pathways, that produced basic anxiety.

Initially Freud used sexual tension as the driving force of his model. He continued his studies on what he termed the 'psychical mechanisms' of anxiety in his "Project". It is important to note that Freud's use of the notion of a 'mechanism' is best understood by reference to a passage that appears in *The Interpretation of Dreams*:

The mechanics of these processes are quite unknown to me; anyone who wished to take these ideas seriously would have to look for physical analogies to them and find a means of picturing the movements that accompany excitation of neurones.

(Freud, 1900, p. 599)

Freud understood early on in his studies of mental life that anxiety of the mind, like pain, is a fundamental principle and a core component of what it is to be human. He began from the proposition that pain is the most imperative and urgent process occurring in the individual human being:

The nervous system has the most decided inclination to a *flight from pain*. We see in this a manifestation of the primary trend against a raising of . . . tension. . . . Pain sets the ϕ as well as the ψ system in motion,[4] there is no obstacle to its conduction, it is the most imperative of all processes.

(Freud, 1895, p. 307)

---

3 *der seelische Apparat* (Freud, 1900, *The Interpretation of Dreams*, p. 6).
4 These symbols refer to the somatic and the psychical systems respectively.

His second axiom in regard to pain was that the nervous system has the most decided propensity to flee from it (p. 307); and thirdly that endogenously arising tension and distress cannot be evaded through means of action because it wells up from within; fourthly he posited that it accumulates and rapidly becomes unbearable to the infant,[5] who is helpless in the face of it; fifthly that however much this is ineffective, the helpless infant seeks to use muscularity to discharge the accretions; and, finally, that an intervention is required from outside.

It will be seen how, on this model, it follows from (4) and (5) above that the attempts of the infant to discharge its accumulating tension are visible and audible, and therefore they possess the potential to function as signals for the external witness of the whole situation, and the human caretaker is thereby in a position to attribute psychological elements to the signals of endogenously arising somatic tension and distress. Freud wrote of the infant's resort to muscular movement in the earliest discharge and expression of the emotions, together with screaming and what he called 'vascular innervation', in the face of the resulting urgency to discharge the painful state:

> an *urgency* which is released along the motor pathway. Experience shows that here the first path to be taken is that leading to *internal change* (expression of the emotions, screaming, vascular innervation). But, as was explained at the beginning, no such discharge can produce an unburdening result, since the endogenous stimulus continues to be received and the ψ tension is restored.
>
> *(Freud, 1895, p. 317)*

Anxiety and the work of the specific action

Having described the infant's urgent predicament in relation to its helplessness in experiencing its own tensions, Freud indicates the only means by which these can be alleviated is for them to be addressed effectively by another:

> At first, the human organism is incapable of bringing about the specific action. It takes place by *extraneous help*, when the attention of an experienced person is drawn to the child's state by discharge along the path of internal change. In this way this path of discharge acquires a secondary function of the highest importance, that of *communication*.
>
> *(Freud, 1895, p. 318)*

Because this concept links, at the earliest stage of human development, the intrapsychic and transactional realms, the effective work of the specific action is important for the later development of what is known in psychoanalysis as object relations theory,[6] since it states that the management of pain for the infant depends on the intervention of an

---

5 "If the specific reaction fails to ensue, the physicopsychical tension . . . increases immeasurably; it becomes disturbing, but there is still no ground for its transformation" (Freud, 1894, p. 80).

6 And see Freud, 1930, *Civilization and its Discontents*, p. 67. in relation to a sense of inner and outer.

outside helper, and that the adequacy of timely and relevant intervention is decisive for mental growth. It should readily be understood that the implication of this is that the basic human unit is the couple[7], a fact emphasised in the work of Wilfred Bion, and the significance of which I will expand on later.

Freud suggests, in the following terms, an internalisation of the process stemming from the psychical work that the mother does for her infant:

> When the helpful person has performed the work of the specific action in the external world for the helpless one, the latter is in a position, by means of reflex contrivances, immediately to carry out in the interior of his body the activity necessary for removing the endogenous stimulus. The total event then constitutes an *experience of satisfaction*, which has the most radical results on the development of the individual's functions.
>
> *(Freud, 1895, p. 318)*

Regarding the sources of inner suffering described by Freud, hunger, or a feeling of dying, are prototypic examples, but it should be noted that dreams and phantasies are, in themselves, capable of constituting innermost sources of intense anxiety[8] leading to efforts of the psyche to expel them – to disburden the psyche, as Freud (1911, p. 221) was to describe it – by screaming and associated bodily reactions. The nervous system, as we saw, has what Freud called "the most decided tendency to flee pain", but it cannot flee what wells up from inside.[9]

When Freud writes that "the attention of an experienced person is drawn to the child's state by discharge along the path of internal change", he seems to be suggesting a directing and matching function emerging in the mother–infant couple, a connection amounting to a *channel* between them in which the mother's *attention* produces a new, emergent function encompassing the two of them, that of communication.

Giovanna Di Ceglie (2013) has written about the importance of a process which she terms *orientation*, as a key component – the initial phase – of Bion's model of container–contained, which I will be discussing later. As I see it, this is the factor which corresponds, in Freud's account, to the importance of the attention of the helper being adequately drawn to the child's real state along the channel which itself indicates the nature of the specific pain by virtue of how the infant is *attempting* to discharge it.

In relation to Bion's theory of the container, which later in the book will occupy a chapter of its own, Di Ceglie refers to the function as *orientation*. It is the

---

7 Compare Bion, 1974; 2014, vol. 7, p. 150.

8 See early reference, in Chapter 1, by Lucretius to the mind as an anxious *vessel* that can, by its own pollutants, affect its contents from within.

9 Freud, 1911, p. 221: "A new function was now allotted to motor discharge, which, under the dominance of the pleasure principle, had served as a means of unburdening the mental apparatus of accretions of stimuli, and which had carried out this task by sending innervations into the interior of the body (leading to expressive movements and the play of features and to manifestations of affect). Motor discharge was now employed in the appropriate alteration of reality; it was converted into *action*".

need for the mother to *place herself* adequately, in order to be able to be with her infant and to attune herself to be open to the infant's projections of parts of themself in distress. In the next section of this chapter I draw attention to the importance of the fact that these early and formative emotional exchanges between the mother and her baby clearly do not only, or even primarily, concern material provisions, but are given in such a way, and with such a capacity for suffering in the mother as a fellow human being, that they possess the potential to impart human qualities to the developing mind of the infant in all of its newly growing mental functions.

Returning to Freud's ideas, it will be recalled from the foregoing discussion that he had emphasised that the requisite intervention needs to come from a person with *experience*. A little later he writes:

> Let us suppose that the object which furnishes the perception resembles the subject – a *fellow human-being*.[10] If so, the theoretical interest [taken in it] is also explained by the fact that an object *like this* was simultaneously the [subject's] first satisfying object and further his first hostile object, as well as his sole helping power. For this reason it is in relation to a fellow human-being that a human-being learns to cognize.
>
> *(Freud, 1895, p. 331)*

Freud seems to be emphasising something close to what I have, in the preceding chapter, been describing under the ontological-philosophical concept of *being-with*. His particular use of the term *Nebenmensch* in the context of this passage suggests that this experienced other can be perceived, however dimly, as sharing a common basic humanity, and not solely on the basis of identifiably similar *physical* characteristics. Secondly, the term *Nebenmensch* is not being used to connote another person merely 'being around' – in the vicinity – it is altogether more intimate. In other words, the indispensable helpful object, the person who understands and reduces suffering – and who, simultaneously, is the infant's first satisfying object, his first enemy, and yet his sole helping power – attracts interest *as a similar kind of being*. I believe that implicit in this is the fact that as the child suffers, *she* also suffers, albeit not in an identical way, and I consider this to be the central and indispensable factor in the humanisation of all mental functioning.

On this model, therefore, I take the *Nebenmensch* of Freud's "Project" as the mother in her position as her infant's first and foundational fellow human being, who – like Shylock in Shakespeare's *Merchant of Venice* – also has "eyes . . . hands, organs, dimensions, senses, affections, passions"; is "fed with the same food, hurt with the same weapons, subject to the same diseases, heal'd by the same means, warmed and cool'd by the same winter and summer" (*c.*1901, Act III, Scene i). The mother also, when pricked (or bitten by the infant during feeding) is similarly hurt, feels

---

10 *Ein Nebenmensch.* Freud, 1895, p. 331. I am indebted to Prof. Rosine Perelberg for first drawing my attention to this important term, translated by Strachey as 'a fellow human being'.

pain and bleeds. The total context suggests that the term *experienced*, used by Freud in the "Project", is not necessarily restricted to knowledge of child-rearing, but to the fact that the mother brings her experience of being a fellow human being into her engagement with her baby, and makes use of what we would now recognise, following Klein, as a capacity for full *introjective* recognition. We will see later that in Bion's model of the processes this involves both love and openness in offering herself as a container for the infant's earliest and most forceful projections; in Freud's terms it is this requirement that marks the difference in the mother's intervention between mothering as a set of *procedures* and mothering as Freud's work of the specific action.

So, to reiterate, the performance of the specific action, according to Freud, consists of extraneous help from an experienced person whose attention is drawn to the urgency of the infant's painful physical and emotional state, and whose intervention is made specific and relevant by virtue of her being a fellow human being, capable and willing to experience inside herself something of the suffering of her infant. Freud understood that the worsening internal anxiety situation could only be alleviated by help from an outside source, referring to this as an *intervention*, one which *for the time being* is effective in halting the mounting distress arising from internal sources.

The action that can bring this about for the infant has to be relevant to the actual, real source of the pain, and it has to be delivered specifically in relation to the causes. It has to be an action, otherwise it would not intervene effectively. This was why Freud called it the *specific* or *adequate* action. The special combination of the mother's attention and psychic work permitted what Freud termed a 'pathway' to the endogenous suffering, in a way that we would now recognise as a communicative link to an object, or a conduit.

Some mental consequences of the performance of the work of Freud's specific action

Through the maternal work that Freud, in his earliest theorising called the specific, relevant action, *a longer-lasting reduction of anxiety is effected* than could be achieved by the infant's muscular attempts at disburdening themself, and so the painful urgency which had produced the suffering is, at least for a while, brought to an end.

Secondly, a *correlation*, what Bion (following David Hume) terms a constant conjunction, is formed as a result of reliable repetitions of the experience, resulting in the perception of a real object and the formation through introjection of an inner *object* which becomes established in the psyche of the infant. Thirdly, a *link* is formed, and with repeated cycles further facilitated, between the availability of the object and the indications which are oriented to and responded to, in the outer world; *these indications become signals*. Nowadays we would say that these images of the objects are, in psychic reality, what we call internal objects. The experience of unmoderated and unmediated pain, and the non-realisation of sought-for help with it, leads (in Freud's view) on the other hand to a repulsion

(Freud, 1895, p. 322), a disinclination to maintain a link with and an investment in a hostile stored image, which constitutes a hostile object. The favourable situation, with its diminution of anxiety and the attention of the needed, experienced external helper, is a primary instance of what Freud (1895, p. 319) called a *wishful activation*. In other words, I am suggesting that the work of the specific action may be implicated in the formation of what in psychoanalysis is known by the term object relations.

Through repeated cycles, a mind develops that orients the individual towards a care-giving and containing mother through mutual understanding – referred to by Freud as *Übereinstimmung*. A better translation of this term is *concordance*,[11] or better still, *in accord*, which means, literally, heart to heart – a term which reminds us of the *anxia corda*, Lucretius' term for the mind as the vessel called the anguished heart. Repeated failures of the specific action would be expected, on this model, to reinforce a negative pattern of relating internally and externally, as well as leaving the major portion of anxiety in an unprocessed and 'unbound', state. I will be returning to this later when I consider the binding function provided by a mental container, as described by Wilfred Bion, in work that builds, over ninety years later, on Freud's first model of anxiety.

In the next chapter I describe two major contributions of the pioneering child analyst Melanie Klein to the psychoanalytical study of anxiety.

---

11 An early use of this word (1481) brings out its affinity with music and with the auditory: 1481 Caxton Myrr. i. v. 27: "They fonde the science of musyque for to sette alle thinges in concordaunce".

4

MELANIE KLEIN

The primary projective process and two forms of anxiety

> [T]here is in the unconscious a fear of annihilation of life. . . . Thus in my view the danger arising from the inner working of the death instinct is the first cause of anxiety . . . this source of anxiety is never eliminated and enters as a perpetual factor into all anxiety-situations.
>
> *(Klein, 1975 [1948], p. 29)*

Melanie Klein's accumulated experience of seeing young children in analysis led her to the conclusion that anxiety originates in the fear of annihilation from within. In its original form this anxiety reminds us of that described in the writings of Lucretius, and that of Kierkegaard – a nameless and boundless anguish without an identifiable name or object within which to locate and to isolate it. I will consider in this chapter two forms of anxiety described by Melanie Klein, together with the mind's principal means of protection against them. This I will follow by discussing a technical principle that she called the *point of urgency*, a concept helpful in considering moments of anxiety where timely interpretation is necessary to further the analytic process.

Melanie Klein had a particular gift for understanding the anxieties and the unconscious mental life of small children. She placed the understanding of the anxiety of the infant and the child at the heart of her method. Her first analysis, begun in Budapest in 1914, with Sándor Ferenczi, encouraged her to develop an authentically Freudian psychoanalytic method suitable for working intensively with small children. About Ferenczi, Ernest Jones had written:[1]

---

1 As discussed by Hernandez-Halton (2015) in connection with what Klein learned from Ferenczi.

> I have never known anyone better able to conjure up, in speech and in gesture, the point of view of a young child. These were invaluable qualities for psycho-analytic work, but he possessed others equally so. He had a very keen and direct intuitive perception, one that went well with the highest possible measure of native honesty. He instantly saw into people, but with a very sympathetic and tolerant gaze.
>
> *(Jones, 1958, p. 189)*

These qualities were evidently shared by Klein, and Ferenczi encouraged her to work analytically with children, in spite of Freud's belief, later shown to have been mistaken, that in the case of children, and of adults in psychotic states, the analytic process was incapable of being carried forward by the process of transference.

Klein suggested that the infant from the beginning of life is prone to suffer severe anxiety about its continuing existence, a dread that only the mother is able to alleviate. She also considered that the new-born baby is predisposed to relate to the earliest objects of her perception, namely the salient parts of the mother and her body, and later the father. From these transactions with the external objects, the actual mother and her feeding-comforting breasts, her holding-caressing hands, her skin, eyes, face, voice, the developing infant builds an internal world of figures formed on these first experiences, but highly influenced by early and intense feelings of frustration, hostility and love in relation to them, and much elaborated by various phantasies. The word *phantasy* in her work refers to unconscious events, inferred in the playing out by the child with her analyst, concerning the internal relationships between these figures, which occur with a significant degree of *autonomy*, outside conscious awareness. Child analysis, with its language of play, discloses a dynamic inner world with its own distinctive forms and forces, and, once experienced, we cannot *not* see these phenomena as evidence of the dramaturgical nature of the inner world. That is to say, it is a world in which its various moods and forces are cast as animated characters, that we call (for convenience) 'objects'. These objects are felt to interact with one another, and in relation to the self, and, accordingly, throughout this book, I take the concept of phantasy as indicating the inherently dramaturgical dimension of mental life.

Something of the autonomous nature of the mind had, as we saw earlier, been grasped as early as the first century BCE by Titus Lucretius Carus, in his epic philosophical poem *De rerum natura*. In 1667 John Milton, who had read Lucretius' verses, wrote at the beginning of *Paradise Lost*:

> The mind is its own place, and in it self
> Can make a Heav'n of Hell, a Hell of Heav'n.

Of this world, Freud, in *The Interpretation of Dreams*, had written:

> The unconscious is the true psychical reality; *in its innermost nature it is as much unknown to us as the reality of the external world, and it is as incompletely*

presented by the data of consciousness as is the external world by the communications of our sense organs.

(1900, p. 612)

For Melanie Klein, projective identification and the phantasies engendered by it affect the relationship between this psychical reality and the perception of external reality. The inner world possesses therefore undeniable psychic reality despite its subjectivity, and despite the fact that it may contain and engender distorted views of external situations. As Joan Riviere pointed out, everything in the inner world is perceived as happening or referring to the self, to our urges and desires towards others, and reactions to others as objects of our desires. She describes with great clarity in the following passage the absence of a one-to-one correspondence between the external and internal worlds:

> Although in psycho-analysis we speak of the inner world, it must be remarked that this phrase does not denote anything like a replica of the external world contained within us. The inner world is exclusively one of personal relations, in which nothing is external, in the sense that everything happening in it refers to the self, to the individual in whom it is a part. It is formed solely on the basis of the individual's own urges and desires towards other persons and of his reactions to them as the objects of his desires. This inner life originates at least at birth and our relation to our inner world has its own development from birth onwards, just as that to the external world has. Our relation to both worlds is at first of an extremely primitive character, based on bodily needs such as sucking at the breast; this relation comprises also the emotional elements, the love and hate, springing from our two main instincts – desire and aggression – at first felt only in relation to such limited objects as the nipple or breast. (But to the baby this one and only object is to begin with the be-all and end-all of existence.) The bodily sensations of taking in and containing are accompanied by the emotional corollary of pleasure, or of pain when frustration occurs, in varying degrees. These early experiences of taking in, with their accompaniment of emotional pleasure, constitute the foundation and prototype of the phantasy-process of internalization, which persists throughout life in more developed forms as a main feature of our mental functioning. The inner world of our instinctual objects in its primitive form is thus first peopled with our mother and father or the parts of them internalized at this time.
>
> *(Riviere, 1952, p. 162)*

The child's play within an analytic setting can be observed in detail for manifestations of such inner relationships as they are externalised and dramatised in the relationship to the analyst. Attempts to formulate and convey to the child some recognition of the potential meaning of these communications are called interpretations, and where appropriate an attempt is made to interpret the evolving transference situation, insofar as the analyst has managed to perceive it, and this means seeing in what way the child is experiencing the total situation with the child analyst in the here and now of the session. It is useful to be able to convey to the child the main anxiety felt in relation to the analyst in the situation, together with the child's attempts to evade or modify the experience by use of various defensive measures. This is particularly helpful at moments in which upsurges of the child's anxiety have inhibited the free flow of play and communication.

The following account, by Klein's colleague Susan Isaacs, of the relationship in child analysis between phantasy and the evolving transference relation in the room, is illuminating at this point. It helps us to understand the nature of Klein's analytic attitude[2] to her young patients in terms of their fears and anxieties aroused moment by moment in the total context of the relationship to her:

> The personality, the attitudes and intentions, even the external characteristics and the sex of the analyst, *as seen and felt in the patient's mind*, change from day to day (even from moment to moment) according to changes in the inner life of the patient (whether these are brought about by the analyst's comments or by outside happenings). That is to say, *the patient's relation to his analyst is almost entirely one of unconscious phantasy*. Not only is the phenomenon of 'transference' as a whole evidence of the existence and activity of phantasy in every patient, whether child or adult, ill or healthy; its detailed changes also enable us to decipher the particular character of the phantasies at work in particular situations, and their influence upon other mental processes.
>
> *(Isaacs, 1948, p. 79)*

Isaacs writes clearly and with great confidence of the way the concept of unconscious phantasy was being developed by Klein and her colleagues and students, and, in the following passage, she clarified also how the phantasies played out in the transference relation were thought to possess some invariant representational features corresponding to the early preverbal history of the infant – called the 'genetic' dimension of mental life:

> Repetition of early situations and 'acting out' in the transference carry us back far beyond the earliest conscious memories; the patient (whether child or adult) often shows us, with the most vivid and dramatic detail, feelings, impulses and attitudes appropriate not only to the situations of childhood but also to those of the earliest months of infancy. In his phantasies towards the analyst, the patient *is* back in his earliest days, and to follow these phantasies in their context and understand them in detail is to gain solid knowledge of what actually went on in his mind as an infant.
>
> *(p. 80)*

---

2 The *analytic attitude* is a phrase introduced by Klein at the outset of the first of her 1936 lectures on technique. These previously unpublished lectures, and notes concerning them, have been published by John Steiner (2017).

Before describing two major contributions to psychoanalysis, both of which relate to the nature of anxiety in infancy and childhood, I will outline one of Klein's important recommendations, relating to the question of how to intuit the moment and the level for intervention in the analytic relationship. This is preceded by her description of the attitude of the analyst to her work.

Melanie Klein: the analytic attitude

Klein introduced, at the outset of the first of six lectures given to students at the British Psychoanalytical Society in 1936,[3] her conviction that the mental attitude with which we approach our patients is of crucial importance.

> Since we come to look at the other person's mind through the medium of our own mind, it is evident that very much, if not everything, depends on the frame of mind in which we set out to work.
>
> *(Steiner, 2017, p. 29)*

After cautioning us about the difficulty in using words to define a dynamic, living process separated from its clinical context, she described some of the key features of what she termed the analytic attitude, beginning with its first and most important aspect:

> our whole interest is focused on one aim, namely, on the exploration of the mind of this one person who for the time being has become the centre of our attention. Correspondingly everything else, including our own personal feelings, has temporarily lost importance.
>
> *(p. 29)*

The attitude Klein is describing will, in the light of earlier chapters, be recognised not only as a technical recommendation of observation, but as a mode of being, in the sense indicated by Heidegger. Specifically, I mean by this that Klein's analytic attitude is a specific form of being-with, with its connections to Heidegger's descriptions of care (*Sorge*) as solicitude. What Klein cared for more than anything else in this attitude was truthful curiosity, coupled with a deep respect for the ways in which the mind works. She wrote that,

> if the urge to explore is coupled with an unfailing desire to ascertain the truth, no matter what this may be, and anxiety does not interfere too much with it, we should be able to note undisturbed what the patient's mind presents to us.
>
> *(p. 30)*

3 Published in 2017 and edited with a critical review by John Steiner.

Klein was aware that this analytic attitude could easily be disturbed by categorical and calculative thinking and she went on in the lecture to warn against labelling and diagnosing and thinking too much about where the analysis might lead and what the outcome might be. To retain the exploratory benefits of the attitude she was outlining there should, she said, be no preconceived plan, no attempt to provoke desired reactions from the patient. She also recommended to the students that they be prepared to "rediscover or revise whatever analysis has taught us before" (p. 30). Clearly Klein was suggesting that having established a reliable and consistent setting for the work, it was best to learn from the unfolding process itself, much as Freud had taught (1912a, p. 112). She taught that nothing should be taken for granted and that we should be especially curious about whatever appeared to present itself as familiar.

Melanie Klein was not concerned with interpretation and its accuracy alone. She reminded her students that interpretation of unconscious events took place within the wider context of exploration, and that this meant a great deal of listening, listening with interest and respect for the unique expressions of individual patients, their ways of experiencing the setting, including the analyst herself, and the intricate intimate details of how they experience their relationships in the world. This "rather curious state of mind" she described in language revealing a complete acceptance of the paradoxes involved in expressing the attitude. It is, she said, "eager and at the same time patient, detached from its subject and at the same time fully absorbed in it" (Steiner, 2017, p. 30). She suggested that such a way of being with the patient must arise from a good cooperation between different parts of the analyst's mind, between conscious and unconscious areas and between intellectual and emotional aspects.

On this subject of the analyst's contact with her own emotions whilst with her patient, Klein wrote very positively:

> For if I have so far given you the impression that the analytic attitude is devoid of feelings and somehow mechanical then I should hasten to correct this impression. The analyst is only capable of approaching and understanding his patient as a human being if his own emotions and human feelings are fully active, though they are well kept under control. If the analyst sets out to explore the mind of his patient as if it were an interesting and complicated piece of machinery he will not, however strong and sincere his desire to find out the truth, do fruitful analytic work. This fundamental desire will only be effective if it is coupled with a really good attitude towards the patient as a person. By this I do not mean merely friendly human feelings and a benevolent attitude towards people, but in addition to this, something of the nature of a deep and true respect for the workings of the human mind and the human personality in general.
>
> *(p. 30)*

Paula Heimann introduced into this approach a further element – the analyst's contact with her own emotional responsiveness as a means of access to her countertransference to her patient, and thereby to become capable of being informed through another route of the workings of the unconscious in the relationship. Her thesis was that the analyst's emotional response to his patient within the analytic situation

> represents one of the most important tools for his work. The analyst's counter-transference is an instrument of research into the patient's unconscious.
>
> *(Heimann, 1950, p. 81)*

This strand has become central to modern analytic method in spite of Klein's doubts about its validity. To develop her idea, Heimann first took issue with how the presence of the analyst's emotions could be misunderstood during the training of analysts:

> If an analyst tries to work without consulting his feelings, his interpretations are poor. I have often seen this in the work of beginners, who, out of fear, ignored or stifled their feelings. We know that the analyst needs an evenly hovering attention in order to follow the patient's free associations, and that this enables him to listen simultaneously on many levels. . . . I would suggest that the analyst along with this freely working attention needs a freely roused emotional sensibility so as to follow the patient's emotional movements and unconscious phantasies.
>
> *(p. 82)*

Writing of the enhanced emotional contact between analyst and patient made possible when the analyst is encouraged to consult their feelings in the work, to value them as information, and no longer to persist in confusing analytic abstinence with emotional blankness, Heimann continued:

> This rapport on the deep level comes to the surface in the form of feelings which the analyst notices in response to his patient, in his 'counter-transference'. This is the most dynamic way in which his patient's voice reaches him. In the comparison of feelings roused in himself with his patient's associations and behaviour, the analyst possesses a most valuable means of checking whether he has understood or failed to understand his patient.
>
> *(p. 82)*

In her introductory lectures Klein made the point that the analyst should be open to whatever is *new* in what the patient communicates, in whatever form this takes. In being receptive to the unknown she reassured her students that prior knowl-edge based on experience is "by no means put out of action", but that the critical faculties are allowed to reside in the background, 'suspended' as Bion was later to express it, in order to allow a free response from the whole mind of the analyst to the unique and fresh experience of the patient in the moment. I go on later to expand on the importance of the analyst's willingness, as well as their capability, for being impacted and affected by their patients in the service of coming to understand them. Existentially this willingness is a part of what I have been describing as the 'being-with' relationship.

Klein made another important contribution on the subject of analytic listening which links with the thesis of this book, again in terms of the quality of the being-with relationship. Because the particular quality or mood of anxiety present is so important in coming to an understanding of the patient, Klein realised in her work with small children that there were specific moments in their play, often but not exclusively when the child had *included the analyst* in the sequence of play, at which anxiety obtruded to the point where the play could no longer continue freely along the same path. Some sense of the underlying anxiety – and not only its intensity, and I emphasise this point – could be intuited by the analyst if she happened to be suitably open to it. She called such a moment a 'point of urgency'.

The point of urgency

Klein introduced her idea in the following passage:

> One of the greatest, if not the greatest psychological task which the child has to achieve, and which takes up the larger part of its mental energy, is the mastering of anxiety. . . . We must never lose sight of the presence of this apprehension in small children and also, to some degree, in older ones. . . . [The analyst] should ensure the continuance of analytic work and establish the analytic situation by relating it to himself, at the same time referring it back, by means of interpretation, to its original objects and situations, and in this way resolve a certain quantity of anxiety. His interpretation should intervene at some *point of urgency* in the unconscious material and so open a way to the child's unconscious mind.
>
> . . . If the analyst overlooks urgent material of this kind, the child will usually break off its game and exhibit strong resistance or even open anxiety and not infrequently show a desire to run away.
>
> *(Klein, 1932, p. 51)*

Although Klein suggested that the presence of such a point of urgency might be detectable by attention to the timing of frequent repetitions of 'play ideas', and by what she called "the intensity of feeling attached to such representations", my own view is that it is very hard to be certain that the intuition of such moments stems from such sensuously apprehensible sources. Writing as she did in the early days of child analysis, in which she was striving to get her methods accepted by the analytic community, Klein would have not been very likely to have left this concept as an undefined intuitive capacity. Widening the role of receptiveness to anxiety as encompassing *ontological* anxiety, as part of the analyst's analytic attitude, as I have done in this book, raises the very real possibility that the sensibility indicated by Klein's point of urgency concept is, essentially, an intuitive openness to the ontological (O). If this is correct we would expect it to be more difficult to gain a satisfyingly clear definition of the point of urgency concept. To put it briefly, this is because it is always easier to define concepts that rely on sense-based evidence (observation), than those based primarily on relationships between relationships. The latter description is an attempt to indicate a qualitatively different kind of 'event', a 'meta-order' of phenomena.[4] I am suggesting that Klein's 'point of urgency' is discerned purely intuitively[5] rather than it being an observational skill, and that the intuition requires the analyst to be very present to their own ontological anxiety whilst with the patient.

The word *apprehension* that Klein uses in relation to small children seems particularly well chosen. Its etymology from the late fourteenth and early fifteenth century brings together the two ideas (a) the mind's capacity, or lack of it, to grasp its contents, and (b) anxiety concerning the future. Shakespeare is credited in the OED with the first recorded instance of the term in the English language, to mean "representation to oneself of what is still future; anticipation; chiefly of things adverse":

> The sence of death is most in apprehension.
> *(Shakespeare, 1603,* Measure for Measure, *Act III, Scene i, line 78)*

Most notably, apprehension is also associated with the anxiety of loss,[6] and also to dread,[7] and to the anxiety of that which is unfamiliar.[8] Its usage suggests that the mind, in its capacity to lay hold on what it comprehends, suffers inevitably as a consequence the present and future anxiety of the implications of its knowledge.

Melanie Klein was concerned to reach and to respond to such anxieties in the children she analysed. It is clear that early on in her work Klein emphasised that the child analyst has to be receptive to the point of urgency of such apprehension, and to give an interpretation that addresses the small child's experience of it in a specific and relevant way. It will be seen that this requirement, as well as the statement of the imperative nature of mental pain, follows naturally from the account of the role of the external helper in Freud's "Project".

To interpret effectively with small children, and with adults too, Klein felt it necessary to alleviate what she termed "a certain quantity" of the anxiety that has been stirred up, not through reassurance but through understanding. The primary aim

4 Sometimes this manifests as the capacity to intuit the *difference that makes a difference*, in the communications of the experience of the patient, and in one's own.
5 See Bion, 1970, pp. 7 and 27.
6 1693: "Sorrow had filled their Hearts upon the Apprehension of his Departure" (Owen, Holy Spirit 12).
7 1648: "The bare fears of such things and apprehensions of their approach" (Sanderson, 21 Serm. Ad Aul. xvi. [1673] 227).
8 1709: "I looked about with some Apprehension . . . for Fear any Foreigner should be present" (Tatler No. 108 para 1).

of intervening verbally at the point of urgency was not *amelioration*, but to address excessive and petrifying anxiety in order to prepare the way for analytic work by deepening the relationship, and by opening a way for the unconscious elements to surface and to be conveyed through the medium of the transference relationship. There is a close resemblance between this important aspect of Klein's analytic attitude in relation to anxiety, and the words of Lucretius that I quoted in Chapter 1:

> So he,
> The master, then by his truth-speaking words,
> Purged the breasts of men, and set the bounds
> Of lust and terror.[9]
> > *(Lucretius, 50 BCE,* De rerum natura,
> > Book VI)

The easing of the tight noose exerted by anxiety on what otherwise would be the freely moving play of the child in the child analytic setting discussed by Klein, and of the movement of free-associative speech and thought by the adult patient in analysis, is done through appropriately pitched and timed spoken attempts at understanding, expressed by interpretive activity. It can only ever be a loosening and not a cessation of anxiety. The following lines from Kierkegaard offer a touching picture of the kind of provision that can be offered in this regard. The text lays emphasis on the human presence which takes on the distress and loosens its hold:

> He visits the man whose soul is beset with sorrow, whose breast for stifled sobs cannot draw breath, whose thoughts pregnant with tears weigh heavily upon him, to him he makes his appearance, dissolves the sorcery of sorrow, loosens his corslet,[10] coaxes forth his tears.
> > *(Kierkegaard, 1843, p. 119)*

Kierkegaard in this short passage puts us in mind of a state of human suffering requiring a human being to meet it, to lower the defences, and to take it on – as Klein did in her analytic work with children and adults.

Melanie Klein cautioned against intervening at a level which may be 'correct' in regard to knowledge, but which neglected being with the most urgent anxiety of the child:

> if we model ourselves on the principles of adult analysis and proceed first of all to get into contact with the superficial strata of the mind – those which are nearest to the ego and to reality – we shall fail in our object of establishing the analytical situation and reducing anxiety in the child.
> > *(Klein, 1932, p. 25)*

---

9 *timor.*
10 Etym. OED: a piece of defensive armour covering the body (1563).

Klein warned also against being over-attracted by readily available *symbolic* content, and our habit of choosing interpretations based on metaphor over addressing anxiety and phantasy more directly. Although she did not, in her brief comments about the point of urgency, refer to explicitly existential anxiety as such, her clinical work and her early formulations in *The Psycho-Analysis of Children* (1932) make it clear that she understood that the small child can feel an unconscious awareness of the imminent danger of losing his life, and that this can break through at moments and reveal something of itself in their play or the inhibition of it. She wrote, of her child patient Ruth,

> she had suffered very severely at the age of two. . . . Saying good-night before she went to sleep meant saying goodbye for ever. For, as a result of her desires to rob and kill her mother, she was afraid of being abandoned by her for ever or of never seeing her alive again, or of finding, in place of the kind and tender mother who was saying good-night to her, a 'bad' mother who would attack her in the night. These were the reasons, too, why she was afraid of being left by herself. Being left alone with me meant being abandoned by her 'good' mother; and her whole terror of the 'punishing' mother was now transferred to me. By analysing this situation and bringing it to light I succeeded, as we have seen, in dispelling her anxiety-attacks and in making it possible for normal analytic work to be begun.
>
> *(1932, p. 29)*

In a footnote to this passage, Klein wrote that her colleague Helene Deutsch had, in 1928,[11] written that the commonly experienced anxiety of the child concerning the total loss of the mother through her death is often closely associated not only with the anxiety of being separated from her personally, but also with what she refers to as 'homesickness'. Klein had felt it important to include this element of anxiety. It relates not only to the fears of what hostility may bring in relation to the child's inner and outer objects, but also to an awareness of the kind of loss of 'homeliness' that I described in the existential chapter. As such, this element is an ontological one, alongside but not identical with the specific fear of losing a particular person.

I will now introduce two important contributions of Klein to show their affinity with what I developed earlier in terms of Freud's earliest theory of anxiety. Historically these two sets of ideas paved the way for Wilfred Bion's container–contained theory of the growth of meaning and thinking throughout life, which, in turn, will be central to the line of thinking to be pursued later in this book. I begin with Klein's description of something she referred to initially simply as a projective process, followed by her description of two configurations occurring in the mental life of all human infants, continuing to operate throughout life.

---

11 Deutsch, 1929.

For Melanie Klein, anxiety, and how it was managed by the early ego, was at the core of psychoanalysis. In this she was following Freud, who, as we saw in Chapter 3, had described the imperative nature of inner tensions and the need for an experienced mother to intervene in order to prevent it escalating beyond bearable bounds. Melanie Klein considered brief, truthful and timely interpretation of the anxiety-situation as fulfilling this function for the child in analysis. The equivalent, for her, of the purging function I identified in the writings of Aristotle and of Lucretius, was a specific type of projective process which I discuss in this chapter. As I now explain, Klein was to describe how an early projective process propelled the distress into the mother, who – she wrote – came to contain it.

Anxiety and the central projective process

In her work with children and adults, Klein identified a particular form of projection, a response to the fear of being overwhelmed by persecutory experience, which at first she simply called a projective process (1946, p. 102). Even before the mother can be conceived of as a whole person, wrote Klein, there arises an early form of projection and introjection in which the first object of satisfaction, hostility and protection – the breast – is attacked in phantasy by the infant in distress, in experiences which suggest that the psychic reality is one in which the infant, in unconscious phantasy, (a) has pushed, with violence, parts of itself together with associated bodily products, right into the body of the mother, and (b) has sucked and scooped out of the mother her beneficial contents. The former is an early form of what Freud called deflection, that is to say, projection. The latter is the prototype of introjection. Klein wrote that the mother is, as a consequence of these operations, felt to contain[12] the unwanted 'bad' parts of the self (1946, p. 102), and also, crucially, to be the vessel for relocated good parts of the self (p. 104). By this mechanism the mother may also be experienced both as having been depleted, by the infant's forcible introjective process, of good parts of herself, and as having deposited her own unwanted contents into the infant. These complex processes, even in their earliest raw forms, were felt to lead to a particular early kind of identification, and this is because the mother containing these projections was believed, concretely, to *become* those split-off parts of the infant.

Under these conditions, according to Klein, the nascent identity, the being, that is, of the infant, is also affected by the associated introjection of the altered mother. According to this model, primitive hatred and consequent rejection of parts of the self are directed by the infant against the mother and take residence inside her, a set of events which affect the actual relationship between mother and infant, and although they take place in phantasy, the effects and consequences are real.

---

12 The element of something felt to be contained by another, developed by Bion, is present in Klein's description. It underlies the difference in terminology in discussions of the central projective process, the terminology of projection *into* and projection *onto* the objects of perception.

Klein theorised that the structure of the infant's self, or ego, was altered by these processes. In the original 1946 paper in which Klein described this theory, she mentioned this kind of identification as a prototype of an object relation (p. 102), and, in passing, and alongside the term excessive splitting, she used the term *projective identification*.

In the 1952 version of the paper she introduced some footnotes to show how the idea had already been applied in clinical situations, and also a paragraph making the new term for the concept more definite. In the expanded form, the concept was used to show how much of the hatred felt initially against parts of the self is now directed towards the mother, which Klein believed reflected the first aggressivity in the object relationship. Klein wrote that good parts of the self can also be separated off and projected in this way – into an object. This too affects the normal development of object relations, permanently if the processes are carried out with excessive violence and excessive splintering of parts of the self. In Klein's formulations, it is the moment-by-moment impact of these processes on the unconsciously perceived integrity of the self around its principal object of inner security and love, originally the breast, that is crucial for psychic growth and the management of anxiety. Two qualitatively distinct types of anxiety concerning these processes can be identified in work with children and adults.

The two positions: configurations of mental pain and defences against them

As well as introducing a theory of projective identification, Klein had also described what she called two 'positions' – emotional patterns of phantasies, anxieties, and defences against them – both detectable in the early mental life of infants, present in all of us throughout life and never transcended, in constant oscillation throughout life. She favoured this formulation over 'stages' of development. The term 'position' indicates a more mobile and fluid pattern than a 'stage' – a combination of attitude and readiness to receive and to respond with a particular 'set', or cast of mind.

Klein had described an early persecutory experience in the mental life of infants, sometimes called a 'paranoid position'.[13] Klein agreed with Fairbairn's use of the term 'schizoid position', which she felt was appropriate if it included both persecutory anxiety and schizoid (splitting) processes, because the leading anxiety is a fear of imminent extinction of the self, and the principal defence against the dread of annihilation is held to be psychic splitting, an earlier defence than repression. She combined these two aspects, the principal anxiety and its characteristic defence, with the term 'paranoid–schizoid' position.

In addition, Klein introduced the idea of a second position, a shift in the whole disposition of the human infant from relating only towards isolated parts of her mother (and parts of parts) towards a more integrated position of relating to the

13 See, for example, 1950, "International Journal of Psycho-Analysis", *Psychoanalytic Review*, 37(1): 88.

mother as a whole person. It was only when the mother is loved as a whole, she wrote, that her loss – real or imagined – could be experienced as a whole. Whereas the earlier feelings of dread had been bound up with the potential for the ego to be annihilated, associated with objects experienced as the mind's persecutors, a new quality of terror and mental pain was felt by the infant in relation to the uncertainty of preserving the life of its now-incorporated mother as a 'whole object' of the inner world. The infant's world became not only more structured as a result of its greater integration, but it was able to be felt *as* a world, containing a whole maternal object known to be both essential to continued survival and also loved in its own right. This she called the depressive position.

For Klein, anxiety in the depressive position centres on the lost good object, whose welfare is felt to be essential. The fear is that the infant's own uncontrollable destructive impulses and phantasies have damaged or destroyed the loved and needed mother.

In 1946 Klein developed her ideas about the infantile depressive position further. The urge towards reparation of damage done in psychic reality became an important creative urge as well as constituting a defence. She wrote, in a section called "The depressive position in relation to the schizoid position":

> With the introjection of the complete object in about the second quarter of the first year marked steps in integration are made. This implies important changes in the relation to objects. The loved and hated aspects of the mother are no longer felt to be so widely separated, and the result is an increased fear of loss, a strong feeling of guilt and states akin to mourning, because the aggressive impulses are felt to be directed against the loved object. The depressive position has come to the fore. The very experience of depressive feelings in turn has the effect of further integrating the ego, because it makes for an increased understanding of psychic reality and better perception of the external world, as well as for a greater synthesis between inner and external situations.
>
> *(Klein, 1946, p. 105)*

Care for the continued existence and wholeness of the mother, as the principal object of all basic impulses, becomes focussed on the urge to repair damage felt to have been done to her in the realm of unconscious phantasy. No longer are all impulses and events felt to happen exclusively to the self, as long as this orientation is sustained, and the welfare of the self alone is no longer felt to be of such paramount importance. A degree of painful instability comes from feelings of guilt and uncertainty concerning the true state of the loved one, since all impulses and phantasies are felt in the new position to connect to her. To the extent that these painful feelings can be stayed with, without recourse to renewed violent defences such as splitting, the consequent integration promotes not only concern, but also psychic growth and repair.

In the depressive position described by Klein, the growing self has its relationship to the mother as the central part of its being. The developments made possible in this position include growth of the capacity to live and to *symbolise* experience and not just to suffer it passively and concretely. What would otherwise remain as raw, primordial and sensory experience becomes symbolised into animated "characters of and in the mind" (Savery, 2018), dramaturgically perceived mental objects that engage in relationships with one another and with the ego that they both constitute and contain. For Klein and her colleagues, particularly Segal (1957), who made original contributions to the psychoanalytic study of symbol formation, growth made possible through the shift towards the anxieties of the depressive position is the foundation of thinking and creative sublimation. Both positions, the paranoid–schizoid and the depressive, entail inevitable suffering with the concomitant tendency in both towards fragmentation and the associated pain of confusion.

I will return now to Wilfred Bion's extension of Melanie Klein's theory of projective identification, and those ideas stemming from it, which, as you will recall, he had said (1961a; 2014, vol. 15, p. 16) "explain more than what their propounder intended".

5

W. R. BION

The theory of a container to transform anxiety

> [T]he infant, feeling overwhelmed by emotions, resorts to a mental activity that Klein describes as splitting off the feelings and putting them into the mother. The mother apparently is thus made into a container for the feelings that the infant feels unable to contain. After a sojourn in the mother, during which the feelings undergo modification, the infant takes the feelings back into its personality, which can now tolerate and therefore contain them by virtue of the modification that has been effected by the mother.
>
> *(Bion, "The conception of man", 1961a; 2014, vol. 15, p. 16)*

Freud, as I wrote earlier, understood that the mother is "simultaneously the [subject's] first satisfying object and further his first hostile object, as well as his sole helping power" (1895, p. 331). She is thus a true 'Three-in-One' for her helpless infant from the beginning of life. Wilfred Bion took Freud's insight further when he recognised that the mother *exercises* her helping power not solely, or even at times primarily, through her material provisions, but by offering another *function*, one fore-shadowed by Freud in his early writings but not articulated by him. Bion recognised that in the beginning our mothers offer themselves to us as the sole *container* for our anxiety. As we shall see later in this chapter, the insight that this is the vital function that women perform for us, and that it is what makes learning possible, had been anticipated by Shakespeare in *Love's Labour's Lost* (1593).

Making use of the model of a container allows us to consider a mental function all the more clearly because of how it allows us to begin thinking in terms we can depict, which, as Heisenberg stated, is actually the only way that our understanding of complex phenomena can proceed. The static picture of a container is in itself insufficient for this purpose, and one of Bion's most important and lasting contributions to psychoanalytic understanding was to outline a set of theoretical concepts which showed how the primary containing function of the mind might be thought to operate as a dynamic living system. I shall describe it here because of its relevance to the capacity of the human being to bear and to modify anxiety and, in a fundamental way, to make communication and thinking possible.

Before Bion's elaboration of the concept, various writers had indicated the significance of containers in the study of the mind. First, from antiquity I will mention Aristotle (350 BCE), and then Lucretius from the first century BCE.

Shakespeare wrote in several places of a containing relationship. Later I give an example which also shows how indispensable he felt women to be, not only as the nourishers but as the containers of men. I mention an important contribution by Carl Jung from a 1925 paper in which he expressed the idea that in a marriage one mind can be experienced as containing another. In 1936 there are two interesting instances by Joan Riviere, and in 1946 there is a reference to the idea by Melanie Klein – who included explicitly the idea of a container in her first published definition of the splitting and projective process to which she gave the name 'projective identification'. Following these references to mental containers I will concentrate on Bion's dynamic theory of the container–contained and its implications for the ideas developed in this book.

A brief history of the idea of the mind as a container

Aristotle (384–322 BCE) held that our nature is not unitary but that we are beings that contain elements inherently in conflict with one another. In 350 BCE he wrote that even those who appear relatively 'self-restrained' need, in the psyche, to contain elements that do not conform with the rational:

> But there also appears to be another element in the soul, which, though irrational, yet in a manner participates in rational principle. In people we approve their principle, or the rational part of their souls, because it urges them in the right way and exhorts them to the best course; but their nature seems also to contain another element beside that of rational principle, which combats and resists that principle.
>
> *(Aristotle, 1944,* Nicomachean Ethics, *Book I, Ch. 13)*

Lucretius[1] showed in his epic philosophical verses an appreciation of the mind as a vessel for its anxiety. He took the mind to be the *anxious heart*, a vessel whose own properties affected the nature of its contents, and he wrote that the goodness felt to exist within this living receptacle was vulnerable both to attacks from frustration and loss through leakage. As Freud stated nearly two thousand years later in his pre-psychoanalytic "Project", in which the mind as a container of tension is implicit

---

1 See Chapter 1.

because of the distinction between external and endogenous sources of anxiety, the tensions arising within us cannot be wholly relieved for more than a short while, which is why the intervention of an experienced external helper is essential.

In *Love's Labour's Lost*, Shakespeare wrote the following lines describing women as the containers and nourishers of the learning of men. The work as a whole is a hymn to love and gratitude and the passages in Scene iii of Act IV reveal his enormous feeling of gratitude to women:

> From women's eyes this doctrine I derive:
> They sparkle still the right Promethean fire;
> They are the books, the arts, the academes,
> That show, contain, and nourish, all the world,
> Else none at all in aught proves excellent.
> *(Shakespeare, c.1901,* Love's Labour's
> Lost, *Act IV, Scene iii)*

Jung wrote in a paper of 1925[2] that in a marriage a person may act as a container for their partner. Bion may have read the paper, given his interest in Jung's ideas in the mid-1930s, and been struck by Jung's phrase, so similar to the one he was to develop, the 'contained' and the 'container'. Here is Jung's description:

> It is an almost regular occurrence for a woman to be wholly contained, spiritually, in her husband, and for a husband to be wholly contained, emotionally, in his wife. One could describe this as the problem of the 'contained' and the 'container'. The one who is contained feels himself to be living entirely within the confines of his marriage; his attitude to the marriage partner is undivided; outside the marriage there exist no essential obligations and no binding interests. The unpleasant side of this otherwise ideal partnership is the disquieting dependence upon a personality that can never be seen in its entirety, and is therefore not altogether credible or dependable. The great advantage lies in his own undividedness, and this is a factor not to be underrated in the psychic economy.
>
> *(1925, p. 195)*

In 1936 the psychoanalyst Joan Riviere spelled out what she believed to be the prototypical anxiety, *the worst danger-situation possible*, and which all later structures of the mind are required to contain. She believed that the earliest perception of the death instinct within promoted a violent attempt to discharge it through any and all means possible, a massive discharge which, unchecked, "reduces the child for the time being to the same condition of helpless exhaustion and lifelessness as results from a constant deprivation such as starving":

2 C. G. Jung, "Marriage as a psychological relationship: Anima and animus", 1925.

the closest proximity to death. So that, in my view, from the very beginning the internal forces of the death–instinct and of aggression are felt to be the cardinal danger threatening the organism. In spite of all later complications and even reversals, I believe anxiety of helplessness in the face of destructive forces within (a severe depletion of Eros within the organism) constitutes the fundamental pattern of all subsequent anxieties.

(Riviere, 1936, p. 402)

In 1952 she wrote of containing in the context of Melanie Klein's vision of the personality as comprising an inner world of unconscious figures, what I develop in the book as its dramaturgical dimension:

At first sight there appears to be no connection between the proposition that we imagine ourselves to contain within us other persons and the sharp differentiation in feeling just described between good or bad states of mind or body which colour all our emotional experiences. But in fact the connection is simple: the people we unconsciously feel to be within us, parts of ourselves or alien to ourselves, are not neutral, they also are felt as either good or bad. They are essential parts of ourselves and as such we require them to be 'good' – perfect, in fact; all our vanity and self-esteem is disturbed if they are not.

(Riviere, 1952, p. 162)

What Riviere refers to here as a disturbed sense of vanity and self-esteem, based on a sharp division between ideal and bad parts of the self, may, under certain conditions, be experienced as something far worse. This happens when the integrity of the self is felt, as a matter of its survival, to depend absolutely on the structure of its narcissistic organisation. The self in this situation uses all means available to keep to itself its delusionally faultless attributes whilst rejecting and repudiating all else. It will be understood from this that the tendency we call 'splitting', that has existed already as a normal process in producing the scene in which the ideal self and object are entirely separated from the bad and persecuting versions, is carried further in narcissism. That is to say it may be carried out as a violent defence against any awareness that the self is *not* ideal, and against the experience the object sorely needed for help in the situation is good. In other words, measures that may have begun as a need to preserve 'vanity and self-esteem' may be mobilised against the perception of goodness – chiefly potency and creativity – in others. Riviere's clear and beautiful writing captures the essence of what Klein was to go on to formulate as projective identification. This, as I now go on to describe, is a concept that combines these ideas of splitting in the mind, and splitting *of* the mind, with the concept of basic identity, since what is felt to happen in omnipotent phantasy to an object is also felt to affect the part of the self related to that object – the object relation. In Klein's description of the concept it is the sense of *concreteness* with which the phantasy of splitting is mobilised that so strongly affects the whole sense of being, both of the infant and the mother:

> In so far as the mother comes to contain the bad parts of the self, she is not
> felt to be a separate individual but is felt to be the bad self.
>
> *(Klein, 1946, p. 102)*

Klein added a sentence at this point which might offer an explanation for Freud's
statement (1895, p. 331) that the mother is, amongst other experiences, the infant's
first enemy:

> Much of the hatred against parts of the self is now directed towards the
> mother. This leads to a particular kind of identification which establishes the
> prototype of an aggressive object relation. Also, since the projection derives
> from the infant's impulse to harm or to control the mother, he feels her to
> be a persecutor.
>
> *(Klein, 1946, p. 102)*

Bion took the containing aspect of Klein's ideas further, developing it as a
central line of his thinking by regarding it as a *mental function*. Taking the fear
of dying as the prototypic anxiety for which the initially helpless infant requires
help from outside, he wrote that the infant is driven to incorporate into itself a
representation of the experience between itself and the helping mother, its mouth
and her breast. Further, he theorised that what became an internalised model of
this crucial pairing became available for the processes we know as communication
and thinking. These ideas comprise the beginning stages of his theory of the
container–contained, which Bion introduced with a fascinating clinical example
in his 1959 paper, "Attacks on linking" (1959, see p. 312). It is interesting to note
that the term 'container and contained' (see 1962b, p. 90) and the shorthand term
for it (♀♂), echo the terminology used for a similar, but not identical, idea used by
Carl Gustav Jung in his 1925 paper, in which he described alternating patterns of
help afforded to one another by marriage partners.

Bion developed the idea of a containing function on the basis of his clinical
experience and by extending Klein's theory of projective identification, which
Bion felt illuminated a wider range of phenomena than those foreseen by Klein.
It is in the following passages that we most clearly grasp the clinical value of his
idea – the concept of a dynamic relationship between human minds based on the
acceptance of projective identification and a willingness to act as a flexible and
transformative container by treating projective identification as the earliest form
of communication, however much it may appear (or actually be the case) that the
primary aim is to be rid of raw, adverse experience. Here is Bion's beautifully clear
description of the process:

> As a realistic activity it shows itself as behaviour reasonably calculated to
> arouse in the mother feelings of which the infant wishes to be rid; if the
> infant feels it is dying it can arouse fears in the mother that it is dying. A well-
> balanced mother can accept these and respond therapeutically: that is to say

in a manner that makes the infant feel it is receiving its frightened personality back again but in a form that it can tolerate – the fears are manageable by the infant personality. If the mother cannot tolerate these projections, the infant is reduced to continued projective identification carried out with increasing force and frequency. The increased force seems to denude the projection of its penumbra of meaning.

(Bion, "The psycho-analytic study of thinking", 1962a, p. 308)

This early use of projective identification, which can be very forceful and hard to take, needs to be responded to as a priority and yet with relative calm by a mother who is required to perceive it as more than an obligation to meet a physical need with a material provision. If the mother cannot, for any reason, develop a psychologically informed and attuned response, rooted in her capacity to feel her own emotions, she is likely to be perceived as what Bion terms "an obstructive force", and internalised as such.

The projection of the infant's distress becomes an unconsciously container-seeking activity, based at first on a preconception that an object exists that can perform work – both to alleviate the excess of anxiety and to perform specific 'mental actions' on the feelings unbearable to the infant, and later, once this preconception has been met many times by its realisation in fact, based on its internalisation. What Bion means by the last point in the passage is that if the mother is experienced as an object that refuses such crucial help, there is (as Freud had indicated) a severe worsening of the infant's predicament. Sometimes in such situations infants can give up and withdraw in despair, but sometimes they can be observed to engage more actively in emotional 'hyperbole', literally the increasingly powerful throwing-out of the distress, with force, into the mother. It is not widely known that Freud had anticipated something of this as early as 1894 (Freud, 1894, p. 192). He wrote of the urgent crisis that occurs if the infant's mounting inner tension is not met by the required "specific reaction". The anxious tension under such circumstances, which in this chapter I equate with the lack of an adequate container for the anxiety, "increases immeasurably".

This, I believe, corresponds to the situation in the consulting room when the patient feels that her helper's repeated failure to understand her is felt to be due to the analyst's hardness of heart, and she reacts to this failure by redoubling her efforts to force the message home. Bion learned more about the container–contained process in the clinical situation from specific experiences of failure in its provision than he did from its successful workings. In 1959 he described something that he had learned from his own failure to contain something for his patient:

When the patient strove to rid himself of fears of death which were felt to be too powerful for his personality to contain, he split off his fears and put them into me, the idea apparently being that if they were allowed to repose there long enough they would undergo modification by my psyche and could then be safely reintrojected. On the occasion I have in mind the patient had felt . . . that I evacuated them so quickly that the feelings were not modified, but had become more painful.

(Bion, "Attacks on linking", 1959, p. 312; 1967a, p. 103)

Bion found that the 'ramping up' of his patient's emotions in the session was not to be understood simply as an attack on him, motivated by the patient's hatred, but as an understandable response to what was felt as the analyst refusing to take in pain-filled parts of the patient's personality. When he could stay with the situation, Bion came to see it as a reliving in the here and now of the patient's earliest relationship to a mother who, he believed, had repudiated her infant's primordial anxiety, treating the mounting uncontained anxiety as a sign of her infant refusing, stubbornly, to accept her 'good mothering':

> The analytic situation built up in my mind a sense of witnessing an extremely early scene. I felt that the patient had experienced in infancy a mother who dutifully responded to the infant's emotional displays. The dutiful response had in it an element of impatient, "I don't know what's the matter with the child". My deduction was that, in order to understand what the child wanted, the mother should have treated the infant's cry as more than a demand for her presence. From the infant's point of view she should have taken into her, and thus experienced, the fear that the child was dying. It was this fear that the child could not contain. He strove to split it off together with the part of the personality in which it lay and project it into the mother. . . . This patient had had to deal with a mother who could not tolerate experiencing such feelings and reacted either by denying them ingress, or alternatively by becoming a prey to the anxiety which resulted from introjection of the infant's feelings.
>
> *(1959, p. 312)*

How does a failure to be understood come to be a danger situation for the infant? Bion's response to the question is to suggest that a worsening situation arises in the following way. On top of the anxiety that remains unmodified, there is a new sense of dread in the already fraught situation caused by the feeling that the object has refused its understanding because it has so hated the experience of having been projected into that it has become an enemy. The presumed or actual suffering of the mother, and whatever internal object represents her, is felt to have turned her against her child as though she were no different from a tormented infant herself, and this spiralling predicament can become even worse in those instances where the mother does *in fact* have recourse herself, like an infant, to the forcefully evacuative form of projective identification, propelling her own uncontained feelings back into the child. It is under such conditions, if it cannot be arrested and reversed, that the whole of early mental development takes a pathological turn. If, however, a genuine and effective container can be found in another human being it becomes possible for the baby to build experiences in which an unobstructed openness and emotional availability to the normal use of projective identification can create a real sense of meaningful human contact. On this model it is the acceptance of normal degrees of communicative projective identification that itself produces the sense of true connection between human beings. The pressing need for a container for anxiety is evident in the anxiety situations occurring daily in the mother–infant relationship, and the analytic situation can be seen to arouse the same basic features and constitutes a later model of it.

I will now consider the role of the mother's attitude in being with her infant, which finds its counterpart in the analyst's willingness to be open to the use of the projective process by her patient.

Reverie: the mother as a projective identification-accepting object

Bion's use of the term *reverie* makes clear that the mother's willing acceptance of the need of her baby to project its elemental emotional experiences into her is an act of love and acceptance. Psychically it is her primary function for her child. Bion wrote of this in the following terms:

> when the mother loves the infant what does she do it with? Leaving aside the physical channels of communication my impression is that her love is expressed by reverie. . . . If the feeding mother cannot allow reverie or if the reverie is allowed but is not associated with love for the child or its father, this fact will be communicated to the infant even though incomprehensible to the infant. Psychic quality will be imparted to the channels of communication, the links with the child. What happens will depend on the nature of these maternal psychic qualities and their impact on the psychic qualities of the infant, for the impact of the one upon the other is an emotional experience.
>
> The term reverie may be applied to almost any content. I wish to reserve it only for such content as is suffused with love or hate. Using it in this restricted sense reverie is that state of mind which is open to the reception of any 'objects' from the loved object and is therefore capable of reception of the infant's projective identifications whether they are felt by the infant to be good or bad.
>
> *(Bion, 1962b, p. 35)*

Reverie is Bion's term for the mother's capacity to receive and to bear with her infant's evacuations of mental pain in order for some modification of the overwhelming rawness of them to take place – first of all in her mind, through her own transforming capability, and later as something that could be 'taken back', through introjective processes by the infant, where it can, with repeated iterations, instate and establish the child's own capacity for creating thoughts from emotional experiences rather than remaining at the mercy of physicalised, concretised events (referred to by Bion as 'beta'). In order to function with reverie – as described by

Bion and, on Freud's model, in order to perform the specific action – the mother needs to be able to manage, without breaking under the strain, the primitive feelings in relation to her infant that pull her towards excessive paranoid-schizoid and depressive anxieties and defences against them.

In the work that marks the beginning of Bion's theory of the container, "Attacks on linking" (1959, p. 312), there is a detailed discussion of the existence of normal degrees of projective identification. Just as we now recognise a normal use of projective identification in clinical practice, we understand that there are normal forms of the paranoid-schizoid and depressive positions identified first by Melanie Klein as occurring in the mental development of infants in the first year of life. Oscillations between these forms of anxiety and their associated organisations of defence were taken by Bion as being an important and perceptible part of psychic change and maturation. At times he used the signs for the dynamic relationship between container and contained ($♀♂$) and the oscillation of the positions (Ps $\rightleftharpoons$ D) as complementary terms, as though each of them reflected something of the other. These ideas can help practitioners to become more sensitively attuned to small shifts occurring in sessions between experiences of coherence–dispersal and persecution–depression. The two passages that follow, one from 1963 and the other from 1970, show how these ideas relate to therapeutic practice. They exemplify the twin aims that I have been exploring, defamiliarisation and truthful contact with the being of the patient:

> The patient may be describing a dream, followed by a memory of an incident that occurred on the previous day, followed by an account of some difficulty in his parents' family. The recital may take three or four minutes or longer. The coherence that these facts have in the patient's mind is not relevant to the analyst's problem. His problem – I describe it in stages – is to ignore that coherence so that he is confronted by the incoherence and experiences incomprehension of what is presented to him. His own analysis should have made it possible for him to tolerate this emotional experience though it involves feelings of doubt and perhaps even persecution. This state must endure, possibly for a short period but probably longer, until a new coherence emerges; at this point he has reached → D, the stage analogous to nomination, or 'binding' as I have described it. From this point his own processes can be represented by $♀♂$[3] – the development of meaning.
>
> *(Bion,* Elements of Psycho-Analysis, *1963, p. 102)*

And secondly:

> In every session the psychoanalyst should be able, if he has followed what I have said in this book, particularly with regard to memory and desire, to be aware of the aspects of the material that, however familiar they may seem

3 Bion's shorthand symbol for the container–contained relationship/function.

to be, relate to what is unknown both to him and to the analysand. Any attempt to cling to what he knows must be resisted. . . . 'Patience' should be retained without "irritable reaching after fact and reason" until a pattern 'evolves'. . . . Few, if any, psychoanalysts should believe that they are likely to escape the feelings of persecution and depression commonly associated with the pathological states known as the paranoid-schizoid and depressive positions. In short, a sense of achievement of a correct interpretation will be commonly found to be followed almost immediately by a sense of depression.

(Bion, 1970, p. 124)

The experiences described in the first of these passages led Bion to conclude that the terms he was using, 'container and contained', because they suggested a static picture of events, did not sufficiently reflect the interactions and changeability of the mutually altering forms indicated by the terminology and discernible in the analytic situation. By 1966 he was preferring to use the term 'container–contained', usually in conjunction with the Ps $\rightleftharpoons$ D oscillation. Britton felt that the term Ps $\rightleftharpoons$ D was itself too static, conveying as it did a similarity to the symbol for a reversible equation in physical chemistry. Just as Klein had considered that the two positions of anxiety alternated throughout life and could not be transcended, since integration and the hold on a good internal object were always relative and never complete, Britton modified Bion's formulation,

to represent the alternation between fragmentation and integration as an ongoing alternation throughout life, that implied progress and development. In this [represented by a diagram, $Ps(n) \rightarrow D(n) \rightarrow Ps(n+1)$], I suggested that there are successive states alternating between fragmentation and integration, *Ps* and *D*, which are incremental, the increment being represented by the letter *n*. As life repeats its cycles of *Ps* to *D*, and *n* represents the number in the lifetime series, the increasing value of *n* would be a measure of maturity. It is an unending struggle throughout life for the individual.

(Britton, 2010, p. 199)

Britton thus makes his version of oscillation of mental pain in the transforming container more capable of indicating something of the process of growth. He also allows the concept a closer application to other practical arts and, like Klein, reminds us that in these transformations what we cannot do is transcend the anxiety. In an earlier discussion of this, Britton explained the connection between this idea and the need for the practitioner to tolerate living with faith in probability:

So, that's where I am. I am about to leave you at Ps(n + 1), which is where I think I spend most of my time, and I would just like to say recently I have been thinking: What is it that makes Ps into something pathological or something developmental, and I think it has something to do with tolerating probability; with how well we tolerate the fact that we do not live in a determined and certain world, in physics nor anywhere else, and that we live in a probabilistic universe and our lives are probabilistic. How certain are we in our survival or the survival of our loved ones? You come to believe in survival, without actually knowing that to be the case, because otherwise you would be very anxious, because you don't know. You are therefore in that state of mind in which you are able to treat belief as if it is knowledge and certainty. This is not always the case and I think that can lead to psychopathology in which there is only a world in which there is either possibility, in which every possibility is a dreaded possibility, or absolute certainty and that makes the ordinary normative state impossible.

(Britton et al.*, 2006, p. 274)*

Britton's 'post-depressive paranoid-schizoid' position [Ps(n+1)] is, to my mind, a useful model for describing the process of *becoming informed from transformation of repeated cycles of depressive and chaotic pain*. In the clinical situation it helps us to bear in mind that a 'depressive position coherence' (what Bion terms → D) lending to our formulations a sense of conviction is transitory. Britton expressed something of this in 2018, updating slightly his concept of Ps(n+1):

> In psychoanalysis, as Bion asserts, we move from D (security) to Ps (patience) and back again. I would prefer to call it D (conviction) to PS (uncertainty) in a sequence of Ps(n) to D(n) to PS(n+1) to D(n+1) . . . each step including more information. Knowledge develops through epistemic crises, D to PS, which Bion called catastrophic change, the title of another paper given at a Scientific meeting in 1966.
>
> *(Britton, "Foreword", Bion, 2018)*

The analyst is required to undergo these unsettling oscillations through a therapeutic practice that privileges making contact with the being and the mind of the patient over the accumulation of psychoanalytical knowledge *about* him. To be consistent with these basic principles interpretive activity should be based upon the more immediate contact and not on the analyst's own second (and subsequent) order transformations.[4] It is a demanding version of analysis that requires the analyst to be capable of remaining open while undergoing disturbing oscillation in their work, tolerating fluctuations of doubt and conviction, chaotic persecution and depressing coherence, features comparable to those experienced by the contemplative thinkers discussed in Chapter 1. Britton's clinically relevant reformulation (Ps[n+1]) has a clear affinity to what I described earlier in dramaturgical terms as 'making strange the familiar' (*Verfremdung*).

In the following chapter I discuss the contribution of Bion's colleague, Donald Winnicott, to a psychoanalytic consideration of being.

4 See Bion, 1965, p. 137.

6

D. W. WINNICOTT AND THE BEING OF THE PATIENT IN ANALYSIS

> With the care that it receives from its mother each infant is able to have a personal existence, and so begins to build up what might be called a continuity of being. On the basis of this continuity of being the inherited potential gradually develops into an individual infant. If maternal care is not good enough then the infant does not really come into existence, since there is no continuity of being; instead the personality becomes built on the basis of reactions to environmental impingement.
>
> *(Winnicott, 1960, p. 595)*

Donald Winnicott, early in his career as a paediatrician and analyst, considered the being of the patient in analysis to be important. In this chapter I will discuss Winnicott's particular emphasis on being, expressed in his writings of the mid-1960s, at which time Wilfred Bion was developing his ideas in a similar direction but with a different emphasis. I will conclude the chapter with a beautiful clinically based description by Michael Parsons concerning the value of considering the 'states of being' of the human being as distinct from what we normally think of as 'states of mind'.

As a result of her work in editing *The Collected Works of D. W. Winnicott* (2017), Lesley Caldwell has noted that she became aware of the consistent interest shown by him in the being – and in particular the associated sense of aliveness and the continuity of existence – of the patient in analysis. Winnicott realised that to include ontology within psychoanalysis was to take a risk of being misunderstood by his colleagues. André Green (2010), in a late paper, "Sources and vicissitudes of being in D. W. Winnicott's work", whilst expressing respect for his clinical and theoretical contributions generally, seemed to have balked at the philosophical aspects of this direction in Winnicott's thinking. There is a tendency detectable in Green's paper to 'hive off' Winnicott's concern with being as something of a philosophical oddity connected with the author's personal existential struggles with mortality. In doing so there is, I think, a noticeable difficulty in quite taking seriously Winnicott's genuine interest in the subject of being *as a part of his psychoanalytic thinking*, in that Green appeared a little more inclined to *analyse* the interest, for example in its connection to ageing, than to understand it in relation to the overall context of Winnicott's work. That this might be so is perhaps indicated by a small but significant error in the original paper over the term *Dasein,* where Green renders this mistakenly as *das Ein* (a term falling recognisably within the psychoanalytic domain), rather than Heidegger's ontological signifier, which if it had to be partitioned would be *da sein* (to be there). The slip, occurring as it does at the juncture (in the linguistic sense) between the Freudian and the Heideggerian, is suggestive of a chafing between the two disciplines.

In my view it is possible to detect in Green's account something of this friction, a desire to maintain something of an 'official' (in the sense of an 'establishment') demarcation between the disciplines of psychoanalysis and philosophy, particularly existential philosophy. If this is so, it seems possible that it could in part be connected with a reaction to the outright repudiation by some existential writers and clinicians of the existence of the dynamic unconscious.[1]

Caldwell's 2018 paper,[2] "A psychoanalysis of being: An approach to Donald Winnicott", draws upon Winnicott's 1945 paper on primitive mental states and an earlier contribution on infant observation (1941), to show how his interest in being stemmed from a sustained interest in how the sense of aliveness and identity were formed from experiences in which the infant's physical sensation and incipient psychical experience were hardly differentiated, an interest shared by Bion. Caldwell writes:

> His extensive interest in the somatic indicators of psychical states, and the account of how the infant becomes a human being is an intensive study of the *conditions without which* the drives can never be accommodated sufficiently for the subject to begin to live a normal life (with all of the abnormal, psychoanalytically speaking, which that entails).
>
> *(Caldwell, 2018, p. 225)*

Both Bion and Winnicott found their inspiration for many of their ideas from Freud's pre-psychoanalytic (1894, 1895) formulations, in which, as we saw earlier, anxiety and its early management by the mother is the foundation for the inception of communication and thinking.

Winnicott's interest took him primarily in the direction of existential continuity and the sense of aliveness, whereas in the same period Bion's ontological interest took him in the direction of growth of the personality – its being and becoming – and the

---

1 Although Holzhey-Kunz (2014, p. 117) has shown how Sartre gives a place to the concept of the unconscious, formulating it in terms of self-deception and his concept of *mauvaise foi* (bad faith).
2 Original title "A psychoanalysis of being and communicating".

concomitant anxiety of turbulent truth with its potential for catastrophic change, and the importance in the analytic encounter of the relations of analyst and patient to truth and lies. He pursued these interests in *Transformations: Change from Learning to Growth* (1965a) and *Attention and Interpretation: A Scientific Approach to Insight in Psycho-Analysis and Groups* (1970).

The latter aspect of being, truth and lies, was an interest of Winnicott's too, in terms of what he termed the true and false self.[3] Both had been stimulated by the clinical descriptions of psychoanalytic inauthenticity made by Helene Deutsch (1942, p. 302).

The related but distinct ideas concerning the *being* of the patient, as considered by Winnicott and Bion, possess considerable overlap. Much would have been gained, and remains still to be gained, through cross-correlating their ideas on this subject – something for which Bion, had he attempted it, would have used the analogy of 'binocular vision'. I concur with Caldwell that it is unfortunate that Bion made no meaningful links in his writings with those of Winnicott, because it is in this area specifically that there are correspondences and affinities to be explored. Although Bion respected Winnicott as a colleague and read his work, it nevertheless remains the case that in none of his writings did he interact with Winnicott's ideas, mentioning only that he laid a different theoretical and clinical emphasis on the concept of regression.

It seems possible that any collaborative thinking on their growing interest in ontological aspects of analysis foundered on the rocks of the turbulent undercurrents of intergroup tensions, the kind of difficulties which, ironically, had been studied in depth by Bion in his work with groups in the 1940s. In spite of such tensions, Winnicott did acknowledge and make use of Bion's contributions,[4] and on the occasion of the presentation at the British Society of Bion's last paper before leaving for California he made a heartfelt comment to the meeting before the discussion of the paper, the title of which was "Negative Capability" (1967).[5] Following the presentation of his ideas, and before coffee and discussion, Winnicott, who as President of the Society was chairing the meeting, spoke movingly and directly to Bion:

> We seem to be in the process of learning new techniques. Dr Bion will I hope remember when he goes abroad that he is still a member of this Society and that we count on him to come back, and give these papers of this kind, which is one of a series, and it is a tremendous loss to us to have Dr Bion going, and he's just got to remember that we shan't forget him.
>
> *(cited in Bion, 2018, p. 33)*

Although Green (2010) had described Winnicott's interest in ontology as having occurred late on in his career, Caldwell (2018, p. 224) noted Winnicott's implicit

---

3 At this point the affinity of these concepts with the existential concern with authenticity in the work of Sartre is worth noting.

4 See, for instance, Winnicott, 1965, pp. 147, 191.

5 Published in Bion, 2018.

interest in the Being of the infant as early as his 1945 paper[6] on primitive emotional states. In that paper Winnicott had expressed himself with modesty:

> Primarily interested in the child patient, and the infant, I decided that I must study psychosis in analysis. I have had about a dozen psychotic adult patients, and half of these have been rather extensively analysed. This happened in the war, and I might say that I hardly noticed the blitz, being all the time engaged in analysis of patients who are notoriously and maddeningly oblivious of bombs, earthquakes and floods.
>
> As a result of this work I have a great deal to communicate and to bring into alignment with current theories, and perhaps this paper may be taken as a beginning.
>
> *(Winnicott, 1945, p. 137)*

Winnicott wrote of the original psychoanalytic method as dealing mostly with the patient's relations to his preconscious and unconscious objects, and its later extension to include the anxieties and unconscious phantasies belonging to them, including the picture held by the patient of his own inner organisation, elements revealed in some form, however partially glimpsed, through an interpretive understanding of the transference. Since the early 1950s we would add to these elements the emotional impact on the analyst and its countertransference influence. These processes were, he said, considered mainly in terms of whole objects in the inner world.

Just as ten years later Wilfred Bion, Hanna Segal and Herbert Rosenfeld were to describe their findings from their analysis of patients in psychotic states, Winnicott in this 1945 paper emphasised the significant departures from whole-object functioning in these patients. In that early paper he emphasised also that no significant modification needed to be made in the psychoanalytic method in investigating primitive states of mind.

> This work was a natural progression of psycho-analysis; it involved new understanding but not new technique. It quickly led to the study and analysis of still more primitive relationships, and it is these that I wish to discuss in this paper. The existence of still more primitive object relationships has never been in doubt.
>
> I have said that no modification in Freud's technique was needed for the extension of analysis to cope with depression and hypochondria. It is also true, according to my experience, that the same technique can take us to still more primitive elements, provided of course that we take into consideration the changes in the transference situation inherent in such work.
>
> *(1945, p. 138)*

6 Winnicott, "Primitive emotional development", 1945.

Winnicott believed that the individual's sense of aliveness and their awareness of a continuity of existence had to be founded upon and built from the *care* given to them by their mother. For Winnicott this provision allows the infant to come to feel themselves a being, through which their inherited potential to become what they can become can express itself. I believe that the root of this thinking can be found in Freud's early descriptions of the work done by the mother in orienting herself to address her infant's first experiences of mental pain and satisfaction. Like Bion with his theory of the container and the contained, Winnicott regarded the failure of these early interactional processes involving the external helper as catastrophic for the very being of the child.

Bion had referred to the infant's need to find a match in reality for its pre-conception that a container exists for its primordial anxiety, initially its dread of extinction. In the 1959 paper "Attacks on linking" he advanced specific hypotheses about the disaster posed by the absence of a relationship providing a transforming container for its dread, involving the formation of new and destructive internal agencies. Winnicott also regarded the care given to the anxious infant to be absolutely crucial to the survival of a self. In relation to the predicament of primitive anxiety, Winnicott wrote of the infant's vital need to find a 'holding' relationship[7] with the mother. Of this, Caldwell writes:

> [It] condenses the richness of the mother's provision for her infant which enables them to live an experience together and this in turn leads to the beginnings of the infant's personal aliveness.
>
> *(2018, p. 228)*

I will discuss briefly two elements of this, both of which have, I believe, profound implications for the practice of psychoanalysis and psychotherapy. The first is that Caldwell's way of expressing Winnicott's intention with his concept of holding brings out the importance that I discussed earlier in the book, in connection with the mode of being for which Heidegger used the term being-with (*Mitsein*). The phrase she uses, "to live an experience together" (2018, p. 228) when applied to the analytic couple, indicates an altogether more involved and intimate project for psychoanalysis than one based solely or predominantly on the exchange of knowledge and insight.

Holding and containing

It is not surprising that the term 'holding' is sometimes mistakenly taken as synonymous with Bion's concept of the containing function. Caldwell addresses this error as follows:

---

7 Winnicott's emphasis on the holding function became a central concern from 1960, with "The theory of the parent–infant relationship".

> The apparent interchangeability of holding and Bion's notion of containing contains a basic misunderstanding of their respective accounts of the life of the neonate since, for Winnicott, the earliest stages cannot include a mental object, a rudimentary ego, capable of engaging in the activities of projection and introjection that Bion's idea of the mother as container depends upon. For Winnicott this model of the mother belongs to a later stage.
>
> *(2018, p. 229)*

Caldwell locates Winnicott's concern with being in his emphasis on what she terms the 'living reality' of the baby, and, by implication, in the comparable living reality of the patient in analysis.

Bion and Winnicott both drew centrally on the correspondences between the analytic and the mother–infant couples, and they both felt these correspondences to reflect more than a conceptual analogy between the two relationships. On the matter of this analogy, before I take it further, it is important to sound a note of caution, both practical and theoretical.

A note on the analogy between the mother–infant situation and the analytic couple

In the case of analogy based on the perception of a close correspondence between aspects of the analytic situation and elements of the relationship between a mother and her infant, there are also features which differ significantly between the two relationships. This is in the nature of analogical relationships – they deal with commonalities arising between two otherwise different and contrasting situations, where the similarity is in *proportions* and not in 'things' themselves. In fact, whether or not an analogy between two domains in terms of the relationship between the abstractions 'container' and 'contained' is felt to be a useful analogy will depend on a number of factors that are outside the conceptual system of both the theory and the practical situations for which the analogy has been drawn. It is in relation to this issue that Hanna Segal warned that that although we can make use of such an analogy symbolically, we should not simply *equate* the parental function with the analytic one:

> The way I visualise it is that, at depth, when our countertransference is, say, in a good functional state, we have a double relation to the patient. One is receptive, containing and understanding the patient's communication; the other active, producing or giving understanding, knowledge, or structure to the patient in the interpretation. It might be analogous to the breast as containing and the nipple as feeding, or to the maternal/ paternal functions. This does not exclude our own infantile experience, since our capacity to perceive and contain infantile parts of the patient depends on our capacity to contain the infant part of ourselves. We must not, however, equate that analytic function with the parental function. We give over part of our

mind to this experience with the patient, but we also remain detached from it as professional analysts, using professional skills to assess the interaction between the patient and the parental parts of ourselves. In other words, we are deeply affected and involved but, paradoxically, uninvolved in a way unimaginable between an actual good parent and a child. When our countertransference works that way, it gives rise to a phenomenon called empathy or psychoanalytic intuition or feeling in touch.

(Segal, 1981, p. 86)

So, bearing this in mind, that the analogy between the mother–infant situation and that existing between the analyst and her patient is a descriptive symbolic relation and not an identity of relations, I will consider the affinity between the situation of anxiety in both relationships.

In relation to the prototypic anxiety, that of extinction, Bion[8] made the correspondence explicit when he wrote that the mother is required to accept the anxiety induced in her by her baby's intense cries and "to respond therapeutically". If she is able and willing to do this for her baby, she makes it possible for the infant, subject to a boundless and nameless dread, to receive back a personality that is frightened but bounded. Winnicott, however, did not consider anxiety, let alone its projection, to have a central role in the transactions of the mother–infant relationship. He did not attribute to the young infant an ego capable of taking part in the early exchanges to the degree considered by Klein and Bion, but that need not concern us in this context in which I consider their points of agreement.

Winnicott and the holding function

In Winnicott's model it is the exercise of the mother's holding function that makes possible the infant's ontological experience of continuity of existence – the term for which is *going-on-being*. Winnicott held that without this, the infant does not come to develop its potential as a human being, just as Bion considered that normal psychic growth cannot develop without the twin functions to which he gave the terms *container–contained* ($♀♂$; Ps $\rightleftharpoons$ D) and *alpha-function* (dreamwork-α). The concepts of both thinkers have a close basic affinity with Freud's early thinking in his 1895 "Project".

In this regard, Caldwell (2018, p. 229) notes that Bollas (see 2009, p. 35) refers to the performance by the mother of the holding function as her *act of psychic intelligence*, a term which, within the context of this book, corresponds closely, in spite of theoretical differences concerning the supposed integrity of the early ego, to what Freud termed the *work of the specific action* (1894, 1895) and to what Bion described as reverie, and, as I have just said, alpha function and the containing function. Bollas' emphasis that the mother's exercise of this function is an *act* accords with

8 Bion, 1962a, p. 308. And as "A theory of thinking" in *Second Thoughts* (1967a, p. 114).

Freud's specification that the mother's work of the *specific action*[9] has to be an action directed to the specific pathway of expressed distress – which itself produces the sense of a 'channel' or conduit for the pain – and not only work within her own mind *about* her child. In passing, it should be noted that this distinction, made in these terms, brings out another aspect of the difference between an experience and the transmission of knowledge.

Freud, it will be remembered from earlier in the book, emphasised that the infant cannot withdraw from internally arising tensions (1895, p. 297). These conditions, to which all human beings are subject, amounted to what Freud called *the psychical exigencies of life*. Transformation of the painful inner conditions can be effected only by an *act* from an external helper, an active *intervention* from the outside. He wrote that they "only cease subject to particular conditions, which must be realized in the external world" (1895, p. 297). The conditions for this realisation, as Winnicott and Bion both stressed, are those achieved for the infant by the mother.

Referring once again to Caldwell's paper, the mode of being which manifests as the sense of aliveness is, from a Winnicottian perspective, well expressed by Ogden (1991, p. 379) when he writes that it allows, "a state of aliveness without reference to either subject or object". This amounts to a proposition that it is maternal holding that makes it possible for her infant to bear the ontological experience of being alive in the world. I suggest that it is the specific requisite actions underlying what Bion refers to in his model of the container and the contained, and in what Winnicott terms 'holding', that find their ultimate effectiveness, and their grounding, in what from an existential perspective is the mother's unconscious openness to her infant's wordless experience of the abysmal ontological anxiety of non-being. This is what Sartre indicates by the term *le néant*. The experience of non-being is unbearable to the infant psyche.

Savery (2018), a daseinsanalytically oriented clinician, has suggested that the two concepts, 'holding' and the 'container–contained', are not incompatible but – in spite of the different conceptions of the role and significance of anxiety in the work of the two authors, and in spite too of their differing views of early ego-structure and discriminatory capability in the infant – that they are each related to the temporal dimension of the underlying process of anxiety and how it is attended to. Her suggestion is that whenever it occurs in an anxiety-situation that an unbounded ontological anxiety makes itself present, if it cannot be 'held' by the analyst in that moment, in a manner felt by the patient to hold them together, however momentarily, in order that depressive anxiety – in the form referred to by Bion as → D, meaning conjoined concern and coherence – can be felt by the analyst for both herself and the patient, then the 'specific action' (Freud, 1895, p. 318), which is a vital function, cannot be performed. In this statement, 'specific action' is the abstract theoretical term, the container-function is its embodiment in the helper's response to potentially traumatising anxiety.

9 See Chapter 3.

In Savery's view, where this combination of features can come together in a fraught situation between a couple, a 'held' configuration can evolve into a mutative one, in which the ensuing transformations can be modelled according to the terms of Bion's theory of the container–contained relationships.

It will be recalled from Chapter 3 that the universal condition of anxiety and the urgent need for it to be bound require the intervention from outside, the help of another. The need for the other, and the challenge of the psychical encounter with the other, and with the experience of difference that this inevitably involves, is also a core concern for both the psychoanalytic and the existential perspectives. As Caldwell expresses it,

> the very existence and the aliveness of an individual is constituted through the encounter with otherness, an otherness that is not there from the beginning but which emerges from the holding function.
>
> *(2018, p. 229)*

It is helpful at this point to be reminded of the contributions of Sartre to these central aspects of being.

Sartre: the Look and the being-for-others

In the latter part of *Being and Nothingness*, Sartre introduces the concept of a mode of being to which he gives the term *être-pour-autrui*. This idea indicates the importance of the inevitable reality that we are subject at all times to the uncontrolled perception of ourselves by others. The philosopher Arthur C. Danto (1975, p. 42) has referred to this mode of being as something of a torment. It is a pain not easily tolerated by the narcissistic organisation of the human being, as will be clear from the following two passages, one by Sartre and the other by Savery (2018):

> Due to the fact that I must necessarily be an object for myself only over there in the Other, I must obtain from the Other the *recognition* of my being. But if another consciousness must mediate between my consciousness *for itself* and itself, then the being-for-itself of my consciousness – and consequently its being in general – depends on the Other. As I appear to the Other, so I am.
>
> *(Sartre, 1943, pp. 260–1)*

> At this point the Other notices and looks at the narrator, who then understands that in *being-seen by the Other* he is no longer simply *not* at the centre of his own universe, but at that moment he is an object in that of the Other. Sartre describes how: ". . . through the revelation of my being-as-object for the other . . . I must be able to apprehend the presence of his being-as-subject".
>
> *(Savery, 2018, p. 47)*

The concept of the look stems from this aspect of the awareness of our existence *for* others. Savery (2018) has written of *être-pour-autrui* as a basic condition "to which we are all subjected ontologically, all the time, because we are visible to others and have an awareness of them even when we choose not to acknowledge them, and even when they are choosing not to look at us".

As Caldwell (2018) emphasises:

> The encounter with the other and with otherness is a major aspect of psychoanalysis but for those for whom this cannot be assumed, Winnicott insists that 'regular' analysis cannot proceed until it has been established, and that may require a long period. This statement will resonate with practising analysts and therapists who have discovered how difficult it is to establish communication with the patient whose earliest experiences in the mother-infant couple have gone badly awry. In such cases the capacity of the analyst to receive the profound emotional impact of the scattered early anxieties of the patient, many of which exist beyond words, will be paramount, and will often be of greater importance than being able to deliver interpretations.
>
> *(Caldwell, 2018, p. 229)*

This is an important statement with practical implications, one of which is the necessity to hold back from giving interpretations when there seems not to be enough of a patient with whom to make a connection with words. If Klein, Segal and Bion are correct in identifying scattered early anxieties with, to speak in structural terms, a scattered ego, then a particular quality of space and receptivity in the analyst will often be of paramount value in allowing a psychic space to emerge, one suited for an eventual coming-together of parts of a self to take place and some form of contact with an other to be at all tolerable.

It is in such a context that Caldwell quotes Winnicott as stating that being able to experience oneself as a human subject in relationship to others is *already* a significant achievement of mind and communication:

> When a human being feels he is a person related to people he has already travelled a long way in primitive development.
>
> *(Winnicott, 1945, p. 148)*

Both Winnicott and Bion urge us not to take the experience of an existing, living self as a 'given'. Both see it as a psychical achievement dependent on the existence of a couple.

Ahead of Bion, Winnicott had a sense of the potential for psychoanalysis to explore and to promote the being of the patient in analysis, together with the more traditional study of the conflicting emotions and instinctual drives. As Caldwell notes:

So, by 1945, Winnicott is already envisaging a very different project for psychoanalysis and for the analytic couple, one that prioritizes *the task of coming to be* over the centrality of conflicts originating in the drives.

(2018, p. 230, my emphasis)

Winnicott, therefore, was even at this stage moving away from a drive-based model, towards a recognition of the importance of being and becoming, an area taken up at the same time both by the existential philosophers and the approaches to psychotherapy based on their ideas.

Winnicott's emphasis on being has been continued by his students and colleagues in the British Psychoanalytical Society, where it forms an important line of thinking in the Independent tradition of British analysis. The following example of some work by Michael Parsons turns on his realisation that his patient, an artist, had made a distinction between states of mind and states of being.

States of being and states of mind

Parsons gives an account of an encounter which brought home to him the importance of the distinction between what ordinarily is referred to as a state of mind and what was described by a patient as a *state of being*. He reports that an artist came to him for help with his blocked creativity, asking for help in understanding what lay behind it, and behind the loss of his capacity to respond emotionally in his work. Parsons' recollection after the consultation had been that the artist's words had been that he had become "a maker of *things* rather than an investigator of states of mind":

> I remembered the impression that his words made on me. They seemed an interesting description of what being an artist meant to him, and there were echoes in them of what I think it means to be a psychoanalyst. But when I looked back at my notes, I found my memory was mistaken. He had not said 'states of mind'. He said he had become "a maker of *things* rather than an investigator of states of *being*".
>
> *(Parsons, 2014, p. 117)*

Parsons goes on to suggest that he assimilated the patient's words to the "apparently more manageable idea of an analyst as one who deals with states of mind". As a factor in this assimilation, he had considered the role of repression, but on that model it is not immediately clear what might have been the potentially painful impetus for that repression. One possibility, to speculate for a moment, is to take into account Strachey's formulation of how the analyst is unconsciously impacted by psychological danger situations (1934, p. 158). We might expect an analyst to be impacted painfully and personally at a deep level when being with an artist who expresses his acute pain at having lost his emotional responsiveness in his work and whose capacity to give birth to new creative ideas has dried up. If this experienced analyst had identified closely with the patient's description of the creative task shared by both of them, which he evidently had done, it seems possible that he had *also partaken of the mood of angst at the possibility of its loss*. In my view this is a clear and extremely helpful clinical example of the importance of the presence of the ontological in ontical descriptions of anxiety.

At the point of communication of the lost creativity and its expression in terms of *being*, (not 'state of mind') a potential 'transformation in O' may have been felt unconsciously to threaten an imminent breakthrough in both analyst and patient. Of what might this have constituted a conscious realisation? I suggest that it was a realisation of the ontological despair of losing the vital functions of creativity and potency, which lie at the heart of purpose and meaning for the artist and the psychoanalyst, and the recognition of the loss of these not as 'ontical losses' but as losses of being, of being what one *is*.[10]

"What happened to my first response?", asks Parsons. His answer:

> What this man actually said gave me a momentary sense, not just of under-standing, but of recognition. Then I let go of it, opting instead to deal with states of mind.
>
> *(Parsons, 2014, p. 117)*

In Parsons' account, the phrase 'opt to deal with' is noteworthy at this point. The everyday attitude for most of us, most of the time, I would suggest, is that a 'state of mind' is something that we *can* opt to *deal with*; that we can *choose* to, and that it constitutes something that can, in fact, *be* 'dealt with'. It seems to me that the 'letting go' of what the patient had in fact said, that it was a matter of *being*, had occurred precisely at the moment where what might have obtruded into the room and into the shared experience of both participants, was that something terrible could potentially happen to any artist, to any analyst, to any of us human beings, and deprive us of our creativity, our power to make and to achieve, to make and find meaning, to respond emotionally to our world and to one another in an alive way, and even to go on existing. For me it is a special moment that Parsons is describing with such honesty. We can find ourselves opting to know something in those terms, and to using thought and language suitable to that opting, which deflect us away from the ontological anxiety of that which we cannot in fact choose at all, cannot deal with, and to which we are all helplessly subject. It helps here to be reminded that our minds develop first and foremost out of such helplessness, in a situation in which it is the mother's presence and attunement, her emotionally informed being-with us, that transforms boundless inner dread into anxiety that can at least find some limits by being 'be-ed with' by a fellow human being who does not run away from us and their own anxiety.

---

10 Note that existentially this sense of losing 'being what one *is*' is a threatened loss not of *fixed essence*, a 'being-in-itself', but of *existence*, in the sense of Sartre's distinction, though it may contain a brush with the ontological anxiety that one might well not *be*, at all.

In the example Parsons uses his sense of being troubled by his momentary 'letting go' of what his patient was communicating to him, and he draws a number of conclusions. Thinking reflexively about his experience, he considers how it was the act of *recognition*, alongside the understanding, that had been behind the slip, behind – as he saw it – re-enacting something of the position of the patient in losing for a moment his own hold on being himself as an investigator of states of being.

It is one of the main methodological implications of this book that being an investigator of states of being is a much more demanding and potentially painful task than restricting the role to a study of states of mind. The former task cannot be tolerated and carried through unless the analyst can reach and sustain some contact with the ontological anxieties held in common with the patient because they are unavoidable anxieties of the human condition. Parsons' description is a clear example of this. I think it is exemplary how Parsons interrogated himself after the event and came to some penetrating insights. It is the very stuff of the mental work of being an analyst. In a moment I will come to what Parsons derived from his experience, how it informed him further. But my second reflection concerns the language that we all use, in which 'state of mind' is extremely common, and verging on the automatic in the English-speaking world. It is a serviceable enough term but it does predispose us more strongly in our thinking towards knowing-about and the ontic, than it does towards becoming attuned in contact with the ontological anxiety which is disclosive of the being of the patient.

In terms of language signification, the term 'states-of' with its empirical sub-context, effects a certain 'charming' effect on our subject matter, in that it introduces a hidden third element into the subject–object structure. (It is close to what Wittgenstein meant by a 'language-act'). What I mean is this: a 'state of mind' suggests a mind *has* its state, or that the mind is *in* its state. Both the 'has' and the 'in' constitute a third 'objective' element in the statement about a mind. The term *mood*, on the other hand, invokes more of a sense of being 'of' a mind. As well as indicating a condition of existence, the word 'state' can often conjure up a sense of something relatively *static*, an issue understood by both major translators of Heidegger's *Being and Time*, principally because the term *Stimmung*, important to Heidegger's explorations on how it is that anxiety reveals our being, can be rendered both as *mood*, or *state of mind*. In the chapter which features Michael Parsons' example of the artist, he makes the following point, similar to the one which I made earlier, about the 'static' sense invoked by the word *state*, even when it appears in the phrase *state of being*:

> The word 'state', in the phrase 'state of being', begins to seem too 'static'. Engaging with the work of Picasso, Braque, Schoenberg or Cage is not a matter of shifting from one position to another. What these creations do is to open up potential. They are avenues of movement and exploration.
>
> *(Parsons, 2014, p. 125)*

Questioning himself again, Michael Parsons felt that he could notice a desire of his own to opt to, as he put it, "deal with aspects of mental life that I could interpret".

It occurred to him that the phrase *states of being* "seems to encompass all levels of a person's subjectivity, including those experiences of self that cannot be put into words" (p. 119). He understood that he had realised this for a moment before moving away from it into a phrase having the meaning for him "those aspects of a person's intellectual and emotional condition that do have the possibility of going into words". With the achievement of this insight Parsons became informed from his experience of the need for his method to encompass the unknown, the unexpressed, and the inexpressible. He commented that the "habitual mode of analytic understanding leaves out what is not susceptible of verbal representation". We can obtain a misleading sense of mastery, he suggests, through our familiarity with the world of symbolic representation.

From this piece of work we are enabled to appreciate how Winnicott's inclusion of the realm of being can be translated into clinical practice, in a way that goes beyond the consideration of states of mind; and the principle of openness to states of being reflected in the analytic attitude recommended and exemplified by Parsons in his account can be seen to connect with the ideas of the previous chapters which apply existential principles to psychoanalytic practice and thinking. In the following section I discuss anxiety and being from a dramaturgical perspective, beginning with a re-evaluation of the concept of catharsis.

PART III

The dramaturgical dimension of psychoanalysis

7

THE DRAMATURGICAL DIMENSION I

Catharsis revisited

> Tragedy, then, is an imitation of an action that is serious, complete, and of a certain magnitude; in language embellished with each kind of artistic ornament, the several kinds being found in separate parts of the play; in the form of action, not of narrative; through pity and fear effecting the proper purgation of these emotions.
>
> *(Aristotle,* Poetics, *VI)*

Writing of tragic drama, Hans-Georg Gadamer (1989 [1960], p. 132) wrote, "What is experienced in such an excess of tragic suffering is something truly common". By this he meant that the drama pitches itself into the spectator in such a way as to bring about fundamental recognition of his or her inescapable finitude in relation to forces too powerful for them to master. The defining features of tragic drama laid out in the *Poetics* by Aristotle do not allow us to evade our fate through magical resolutions, *deus ex machina* appearances, or false conclusions in which all is made well by ending well. Gadamer related the construction and playing-out of dramatic tragedy to truth and the human condition.

> To see that 'this is how it is' is a kind of self-knowledge for the spectator, who emerges with new insight from the illusions in which he [or she], like everyone else, lives.
>
> *(Gadamer,* Truth and Method, *1989 [1960], p. 132)*

Experience of inner conflict, and the ways in which we harbour conflicting impulses and desires towards others, is defining of what it is to be human, and so it is not at all surprising that the myths and the tragic plays we create have human conflict at the heart of them. In working with, and presenting, the human condition and its conflicts using the forms and conventions of drama, it has proved possible to confront ourselves with some of the most unbearable, and otherwise unspeakable, atrocious, uncontainable and unthinkable aspects of our experience in the world.

Savery (2015), a theatre director and a psychotherapist, writing of the ancient Greek texts of theatre and myth, states that "they contain, in their very essence, characters with existential dilemmas who suffer the same anxiety, potentials, and fate as all other human beings, no matter how mythically or absurdly they are represented". Writing in a personal way of her experience as a theatre director, she wrote the following passage which brings out clearly the essence of the power of drama to express personally and intimately the shared human condition:

> In fact the more removed they were from my actual self and character, the more courageously I could imbue them with my own unresolved conflicts and deepest anxieties, under the guise of theatricality and metaphor. I came to trust these texts as containing human truths which could be relied upon for deep contemplation of myself and my relationship to others, and their connections to me through being human.
>
> *(Savery, 2018, p. 3)*

This deep contemplation is what Gadamer (1989 [1960], p. 131) called a 'tragic pensiveness', which is a form of mental pain that arises from the playing out of the tragic drama producing in the audience the conjoined emotions to which Aristotle gave the terms ἔλεος (*eleos*) and φόβος (*phobos*). These terms indicate complex identificatory emotions felt in relation to characters on the stage whose predicament is, by all the elements of the staging of the play, made to matter to the audience – a mattering that forms the existential and defining link in classical drama in which the communion of the audience with the imitation of action in the staging of the drama is integral.

In her dramaturgical and psychoanalytic study,[1] Maria Grazia Turri has clarified Aristotle's use of these terms as follows:

> Fear is about oneself, as Aristotle states: fear is felt by those who believe something to be likely to happen to them (*Rhetoric*: 1382b34). . . . Pity (*eleos*) is defined as "a feeling of pain caused by the sight of some evil, destructive or painful, which befalls one who does not deserve it, and which we might expect to befall ourselves or some friend of ours, and moreover to befall us soon". (*Rhetoric*: 1385b13–16). Pity, differently from fear, is felt about someone else, as long as the situation presents enough similarities to one's own conditions that one can imagine the same event might happen to him.
>
> *(Turri, 2017, p. 24)*

Although *eleos* and *phobos* are routinely translated respectively as 'pity' and 'fear', and thus given an 'ontic' rendering – that is to say pity of specific predicaments, fear of

---

1 *Acting, Spectating, and the Unconscious* (2017).

particular tangible entities – it is clear that dramaturgically and existentially Aristotle was also interested in them as ontological experiences. Rather than considering them as 'states of mind', suggests Hans-Georg Gadamer (1989 [1960], p. 130), they are to be taken in the context of classical drama existentially as "events that overwhelm man and sweep him away". *Eleos* and *phobos,* in this sense, are *states of being,* as described in antiquity by Lucretius as taking over and shaking the entire self, the bodily frame in resonance with its anxious heart – its *anxia corda.* The cold shiver mentioned by Gadamer in this respect brings us much closer to this, and to Kierkegaard's use of the terms 'Frygt' and 'Bæven'.[2]

In specifying the defining characteristics of tragic drama, Aristotle gave these emotions, and, in relation to them, a concept called *katharsis,*[3] a central position. In classical drama, the tragic fate of the characters cannot be evaded and its basic construction includes the experience of its spectators, who in their deep involvement suffer along with the protagonists of the drama. The *eleos* they feel is on behalf of aspects of the self and of the loved ones embodied in characters who are suffering their fates. They experience *phobos* because it could as easily be themselves. The combination of the two is the deep pensiveness in which the audience becomes connected intimately with the relationship between anxiety and fate in the human condition.[4]

Gadamer referred to the apprehension and relief induced by catharsis as involving a kind of renunciation of ourselves which brings about an eventual return through the theatrical process. Psychoanalytically, I take the 'initial renunciation' noted by Gadamer as a protective and appalled repudiation that any meaningful link exists between us and the fateful predicaments of the characters of the drama. In analytic terms, it reflects an urge to 'dis-identify' with them. On this view, it is *care* for the characters, *in the specific sense that their existence matters to us as fellow human beings,* that effects what Gadamer calls 'the return to ourselves'.

Of this insight, the philosopher Daniel L. Tate wrote:

> Torn outside ourselves by the power of the tragic events, overtaken by the misery and horror that they provoke, the cathartic effect enables the return to ourselves from this *ekstasis* in order to face the truth of what is. To admit, accept, and finally affirm this truth is the meaning of *katharsis.*
>
> *(1995, p. 46)*

To pursue this further requires an understanding of what Aristotle meant by *purging,* what he called "the proper purgation of these emotions", in the process of *katharsis.*

---

2 Generally translated as 'fear' and 'trembling', though a more apt rendering of his 'Frygt' is 'dread' or 'angst' rather than 'fear'.

3 Which we render as *catharsis,* a term which has accumulated additional meanings.

4 When an effective mix of fear and pity is required for this 'deep pensiveness' we are reminded of Bion, who wrote (1970, p. 123) that the analyst should wait before making an interpretation until an evolution takes place from having undergone mental pains belonging to both the paranoid-schizoid and the depressive positions.

Catharsis and the element of purgation

Referring to the role of purging, as an element of catharsis, Gadamer notes that Aristotle held that tragic drama brings about the 'purification' through purging of the combined emotions of pity and fear. Turri (2017, p. 17) has explored the consequences in both the study of drama and of psychoanalysis of the different perspectives flowing from the two main interpretations of what 'purification' means in Aristotle's writings. The question of greatest significance from a psychoanalytic perspective hinges on whether we take Aristotle's term to refer to an inner transformation of mental contents of, or to a evacuation from the mind of those of its contents felt as its pollutants. It is this latter idea that gives rise to explanations of catharsis that are more medical than theatrical. José Angel García Landa, for example, outlined non-dramaturgical notions of *katharsis* based on the idea that the release of unsettling emotions can function in the service of what might be regarded variously as forms of moral-emotional hygiene, emotional education, or homeostasis:

> pity and fear are raised up where they did not exist before, and are then released. This produces a kind of emotional education which will prevent them from overpowering the spectator in the circumstances of his real life. . . . Other theories we might call the 'safety valve' theories: pity and fear which have been dangerously pent up or repressed in the mind of the audience are excited by the means of pathetic and violent action, and are then released; this would seem to be closer to some related medical senses of the word catharsis.[5]

Such formulations seem thin, tame and lacking in complexity when compared to those explored by practitioners of theatre. Bertolt Brecht, in his "Short Organum for the theatre"[6] (1948), for example, wrote:

> How much longer are our souls, leaving our 'mere' bodies under cover of the darkness, to plunge into those dreamlike figures up on the stage, there to take part in the crescendos and climaxes which 'normal' life denies us? What kind of release is it at the end of all these plays (which is a happy end only for the conventions of the period – suitable measures, the restoration of order), when we experience the dreamlike executioner's axe which cuts short such crescendos as so many excesses? We slink into Oedipus: for taboos still exist and ignorance is no excuse before the law. Into Othello: for jealously still causes us trouble and everything depends on possession. Into Wallenstein: for we need to be free for the competitive struggle and to observe the rules, or it would peter out.
>
> *(Brecht, 1948, section 34)*

5 Universidad de Zaragoza (online text).
6 Brecht, 1948. Reproduced in *Brecht on Theatre: The Development of an Aesthetic.* (ed. and tr. J. Willett), 1964.

Here we not only see an entirely different meaning given to the concept of release, but a dramatist considering the element of dreamwork in theatre. Reflecting on the workings of dramatic tragedy, August Wilhelm von Schlegel (1807), the poet who translated Shakespeare's works into the German language, wrote in his essay "Ancient and modern tragedy", that the nature and function of tragic drama, *katharsis*, pity and fear had rarely been discussed in a satisfactory manner, and that it was not at all easy to do so. He wrote:

> It is somewhat surprising that such naturally compassionate beings as ourselves, beset by real misfortunes the effects of which we are helpless to remedy, should want to sadden our lives still further by the dramatic representation of imaginary calamities. Perhaps it will be suggested that we take pleasure in contrasting our own state of tranquillity with the upheavals caused by passion, just as a storm at sea can be watched with a reassuring feeling of security.[7]

Schlegel saw the applicability to this of the following lines from Lucretius:

> When stormy winds churn up the waves out on the open sea it is pleasing to stand on the shore and watch another's tremendous struggles; not because the sufferings of others are something to rejoice in, but because it is pleasing to see from what misfortunes you yourself are free.
>
> *(Lucretius, 50 BCE, De rerum natura, Book II, 1–4)*

Schlegel considered that Lucretius had intended these lines to apply to a detached and experienced philosopher of life, who in equanimity was capable of contemplating "the agitations of doubt and error with perfect serenity". But, he wrote tellingly, and very much in line with Aristotle's concepts (of pity and fear, purgation and *katharsis*, reversal and recognition):

> it is quite unsuitable to the spectator who responds feelingly to a tragedy. If such a spectator is really involved with the tragic characters, he will not be at all concerned with himself – or if he fails to be oblivious of himself, it is a sign that he is not deeply involved and that the tragedy is not achieving its end.

Those critics tempted to reduce tragic drama to a vivid or lurid spectacle of a catharsis of emotion in a more superficial sense, wrote Schlegel, might compare drama to Roman forms of visceral entertainment. This, he felt, would be an inadequate comparison:

> Perhaps it will be said that it is our need to be roused from the apathy of ordinary life by experiencing vivid emotions, whatever their nature may be

---

7 See in R. P. Draper, 2015 [1980], p. 102.

which has brought tragedy into being. I admit that such a need does exist. It has given birth to those animal combats which are such a favourite spectacle in many countries. The Romans carried the taste of this kind of thing so far that they took pleasure in watching men fight to the death with each other or with wild beasts, though these men were criminals or slaves who were not regarded as entitled to normal human rights. But we who are less callous than the Romans, and given to more refined forms of entertainment, only allowed exalted characters to appear on the tragic stage; and would we want these heroes and demi-gods to come down in to the bloody arena of tragedy, like common gladiators, simply to stimulate our jaded nerves?

(Schlegel, in Draper, 2015, p. 102)

These versions, then, and especially those explanations pointing to an *educative* or medical purpose, do not correspond at all to Aristotle's meaning. Moral education also is very far from the mark, and just as the intention of Shakespeare's works depart radically from that of the morality plays of the fifteenth and early sixteenth centuries, Aristotle's detailed and definitive writing on tragic drama places *katharsis* in a much more subtle and complex philosophical and psychological position. Tragic drama does not inculcate virtue, caution against pride through self-consciously arousing fear or teaching us pity, as José Angel García Landa notes in his catalogue of theories. He includes the possibility that a cathartic effect may be based on a kind of mimesis, an *imitation* by the members of the audience of the emotions played out by the characters on the stage, but Aristotle was suggesting much more than this in his use of the term 'imitation of an action'.

Gadamer asks some penetrating questions in the following passage:

But pensiveness is a kind of relief and resolution, in which pain and pleasure are peculiarly mixed. How can Aristotle call this condition a purification? What is the impure element in feeling, and how is it removed in the tragic emotion?

(1989, p. 132)

Gadamer asks fundamental questions about the mental pain evoked by tragic drama. What could be meant by 'purification' in such a context, he asks, and what is the 'impure' element and how could its removal be conceptualised? His answer to these questions comes close to the theories of Klein at this point. Painful feelings are regarded by the psyche as being capable of discharge, so that they are no longer experienced as being part of the self, which only wishes to be associated with good feelings. Mixed feelings are, in early states of mind, felt as contaminated or poisoned feelings. As we saw earlier, the principal protective measure under such circumstances is for a splitting to take place, separating good and bad experiences and relocating the unwanted elements elsewhere through projection. We see this process in the observations that Gadamer makes concerning the first reactions of the audience faced with the tragic misfortunes unfolding before them:

It seems to me that the answer is as follows: being overcome by misery and horror involves a painful division. There is a disjunction from what is happening, a refusal to accept that rebels against the agonizing events.

This form of splitting is what keeps us in ignorance. Because of certain classical aspects of the tragic form of drama, principally the harmonisation of its formal elements in an essentially truthful manner, two particular major components described by Aristotle enable a transformation of anxiety to take place. What I mean by this is that what would otherwise remain as an experience of unabated frozen dread is transformed by the play into what is, essentially, a different state of being. This I will describe in a moment, but first I will clarify the nature of these pivotal components which make the difference.

At the dénouement of the drama Aristotle identifies two specific elements – recognition, or *anagnorisis* (ἀναγνώρισις), and reversal, or *peripeteia* (περιπέτεια). What this means for the tragic hero is that there is a critical moment of recognition in which all that has been ambiguous or to which they have been blind becomes precipitously and dramatically evident. At this point all the events of the play become immensely turbulent and the character suffers a radical reversal of fortune, a turning which affects the audience powerfully because suddenly, in spite of warnings, the heroic character is revealed to us in all their frailty. Oedipus is pursuing his role, acting as the king, trying to overcome the truth of his existence through his blindness to it.

We, the audience, have already been occupying two positions. In one, we are involved in the drama, the imitation of the action is so compelling that we cannot help but be involved in it. As the same time, because we are aware before Oedipus of the truth that he is ignorant of, we occupy a comfortable position of security and knowing (K). At the moment of recognition we have a number of reactions. One is relief, but this is immediately dislodged. It is a temporary position, it is swept aside by the overwhelming impact of the play going into reversal. Because the salient messages are delivered by a messenger, and therefore are of the oral tradition, they have the power to stimulate the senses, and to thrust the audience member into a confrontation with their own vulnerable human condition. It is at that pivotal point that we identify with Oedipus as a real person. The splitting is arrested and we have a depressive, fellow-human-being feeling of pity (in the sense of pathos) and fear because we know that it could happen to us. We cannot occupy the separate, detached 'knowing position' anymore. Bion, from a psychoanalytic perspective, calls this moment $\rightarrow$ D, intending by this to show that such moments involve a shift towards a painful coherence of understanding bringing a willingness to embrace responsibility, remorse and an urge towards reparative action. This approach is an interesting perspective on the nature and purpose of dramatic tragedy.

This brings us to the question of truth, dramatic and psychical. From the discussion up to this point it will be clear that in the drama the characters are the vehicles through which the truthfulness of the dramatic actions has come to life. When, earlier, I referred to classical aspects of the tragic form whose key aspects need to be brought together in an essentially truthful manner, I was referring to Aristotle's conception of imitation of an action – a technical term of Aristotle's with a special meaning. Imitation (of action) in this context is not the same as in the psychoanalytic context, in fact it rather implies the opposite. Here it means a faithful repetition and rendition of something that truly has been going on, and for this to happen there have to be some invariants in the representation of the action, just as in a painting there have to be invariants that exist between the disposition of marks on a canvas and the situation depicted. The latter point was made by Bion in the opening lines of *Transformations* (1965a, p. 1), and by Bertrand Russell in terms of what makes language possible, in his introduction to Wittgenstein's *Tractatus Logico-Philosophicus*.

In tragic drama this core aspect of the representability of tragic actions, what gives the eventual recognition/ reversal its compelling truth, is that the six categories of the form – plot, character, thought, diction, song and spectacle – work together so that truthful correspondences are *catalysed* by and are *contained* in the drama, generating the deep sense that the characters are behaving in a real way. It is close to the moment of recognition that the reversal of the drama takes place; the action cannot any longer progress as it had done before the revealment. In other words, once recognition has taken place the play cannot fail to go into reversal. Neither can the narrative proceed in an orderly way, just as the royal household can no longer hold together as before; the one who considered himself the chosen one, destined to rid the land of plague, believing himself in possession of a strategy to evade his fate, is now aghast at facing all his projects gone awry.

We collide then into the frailty of our own human condition along with Oedipus, and furthermore we have a dreadful realisation that if this can befall the noble and the mighty, Agamemnon, Oedipus, Pentheus, what can happen to me, to us – the ordinary common human beings? Something enables us to remain with the unfolding drama in spite of the anguish caused by it. What is it? Until the fateful moments of reversal/recognition we in the audience have in a sense been complicit with the not-knowing (and the anti-knowing) of the chief protagonist and the other principal characters. In a sense we have joined him in his 'blindness' by means of the practice of division as discussed by Gadamer. Psychoanalytically, we recognise division in various different terms, including 'projection', 'splitting', 'splitting-and-denial', 'splitting-into-the-other', 'repression', and – importantly – 'disavowal'. Something of these processes is mirrored in the characters of the play, and the use and structure of these defences against psychic pain can be felt to alter dramatically in both the players and in the audience after the point of recognition/ reversal.

How does this set of defences itself become 'undone' when the central character, about whose predicament we have come to care, is himself undone? How do we come to see that what is reflected in what the characters at first ignore is a reflection of ourselves, and how is it that this becomes possible to bear, as a theatrical experience? How does it come about that, as Gadamer expresses it, the effect of the tragic catastrophe is precisely to dissolve this disjunction from what is. It effects the total liberation of the constrained heart. We are freed not only from the spell in which the misery and horror of the tragic fate had bound us, but at the same time we are free from everything that divides us from what is.

(*Gadamer, 1989 [1960], p. 131*)

Put in such terms, it can almost appear a form of magical transformation, and yet we can in theatre experience time and again that it is in fact achievable, an accomplishment demonstrating not only that theatre is a medium of communication, but that it is what Bion called a 'language of achievement'. It will be recalled that Bion meant this term, which he borrowed from the poet John Keats,[8] to refer to something common to all attempts in artistic endeavour to make contact, however difficult, with truth:

It is too often forgotten that the gift of speech, so centrally employed, has been elaborated as much for the purpose of concealing thought by dissimulation and lying as for the purpose of elucidating or communicating thought. Therefore the Language of Achievement, if it is to be employed for elucidating the truth, must be recognized as deriving not only from sensuous experience but also from impulses and dispositions far from those ordinarily associated with scientific discussion.

(*Bion, 1970, p. 3*)

Bion reminds us that we should not forget that language was developed "as much for the achievement of deception and evasion as for truth". A devotion to the exclusive use of medical terminology, or that of empirical science, can serve what he calls the 'language of substitution', and that what was required for psychoanalysis was an artistic language developed for the adequate expression of the passions, by which he meant full expression of the truth[9] of loving, hating and knowing relationships. It is worth considering therefore whether a dramaturgical formulation of catharsis and purging is more fertile for psychoanalysis than a medical model. Savery (2018, p. 21) takes this matter considerably further by taking Aristotle's concept of purgation as an instance of what the psychoanalyst Wilfred Bion (1959, 1962b) described as the projection of unbearable mental contents into an available emotional container. She has described, as I stated earlier, how the Greek myths and theatrical structures function as psychic containers for the worst

---

8 See Keats, 1817, for the letter in which he introduced the terms Negative Capability and Language of Achievement.

9 Truth in this context should be taken not as absolute truth, but as our human approximations to it, 'for all practical purposes', as Bion put it. Klein had said that all of our perceptions are 'varyingly veridical'; F. Bartlett had stated that all perception is construction, all memory the reconstruction of construction.

and most unthinkable aspects of human experience. Savery wondered why, when myths have shown themselves capable of expressing, as she put it, "the most dreadful of all aspects of the human condition and experience, from matricide and incest, to eating one's own children to placate the gods", the plight of the nymph Echo in Ovid's myth of Echo and Narcissus has so far little representation in the literature of psychoanalysis, a remarkable and heavily ironic omission[10] given the enormous degree of attention given to the clinical counterpart of Narcissus. This thesis has an implication for the study of myths for their psychoanalytical and existential meanings, as a lack of representability outside the myth, or of its dramatic elaboration within it, of one or more of its protagonists, may indicate a failure of the underlying container–contained mechanism. In theory, if this were true, it would imply a massive excess of dread wrapped up in the character.

Savery's application of Bion's theory to myth and drama takes us in an interesting direction in terms of the ideas explored in this chapter. In pursuing the theory of transformation of anxiety through its containment, she compares the kinds of predicament experienced by the mortal in the Greek myths, subjected to suffering at the whims of the immortal gods, with the helplessness of the small infant or child in relation to its powerful god-like parents. In quoting a passage from Ferry (2014, p. 20) in this regard, Savery shows us the difference between the experience of an audience member watching the drama from a detached viewpoint, and the experience of engagement with it:

> For the gods, time does not count . . . and this allows them both to endure and witness human passions with a superiority and from a vantage to which human mortals cannot aspire. In their sphere, everything is sorted out and settled sooner or later. . . . Our principal characteristic as mere mortals is quite the reverse. Contrary to the gods and the beasts, we are the only sentient beings in this world to have full consciousness of what is irreversible: the fact that we are going to die.
>
> *(Ferry, 2014, p. 20)*

This is a reminder that ontological anxiety, common to all human beings beyond any specific, tangible manifestation embodying it, is not shared by 'gods', whatever their tribulations at each other's plotting. In fact that is their defining feature and their *raison d'être* in the oral tradition and the written accounts of myths. They are the imaginary repository, so to speak, of that which to we can never attain as human beings in the world – freedom from the anxiety of not-being. As Ferry (2014, p. 20) states, "therefore nothing is definitive, or irreversible, or irremediably lost". Therefore if the gods were to be alone, without their mortal 'foils', their stories would not, by definition, partake of tragic drama.

---

10 An omission corrected in Savery, 2018.

Compare the situation with the description by the psychoanalyst Joan Riviere (1936) of a suffering mortal, the child in acute depressive distress:

> all one's loved ones *within* are dead and destroyed, all goodness is dispersed, lost, in fragments, wasted and scattered to the winds; nothing is left *within* but utter desolation. Love brings sorrow, and sorrow brings guilt; the intolerable tension mounts, there is no escape, one is utterly alone, there is no one to share or help. Love must die because love is dead. Besides, there would be no one to feed one, and no one whom one could feed, and no food in the world. And more, there would still be magic power in the undying persecutors who can never be exterminated – the ghosts. Death would instantaneously ensue – and one would choose to die by one's own hand before such a position could be realized.
>
> *(Riviere, 1936, p. 313)*

The persecutors that Riviere identifies are characters in the drama of the child's inner world held to be responsible for their suffering. In part they have this characterisation through being representatives of the child's own divided-off hostility, and in part they represent god-like figures of their world who respond with indignant retaliation[11] to any sign of independent agency felt by the child. Her vivid description brings out their essential god-like nature, they are felt to have magical power and they can never perish and neither can they be destroyed. The whole scene of the child's inner experience resembles the culmination of a tragedy.

This aspect of *inner tragedy* is clearly illustrated in the following passage by Riviere:

> As analysis proceeds . . . the analyst begins to see the phantasies approximating to this nightmare of desolation assuming shape. But the shape they assume is that of the patient, so to speak; the scene of the desolation is himself. External reality goes on its ordinary round: it is *within himself* that these horrors dwell. Nothing gives one such a clear picture of that inner world, in which every past or present relation either in thought or deed with any loved or hated person still exists and is still being carried on, as the state of a person in depression. His mind is completely and utterly preoccupied and turned inward; except in so far as he can project something of this horror and desolation, he has no concern with anything outside him. To save his own life and avert the death of despair that confronts him, such energy as he has is all bent on averting the last fatalities within, and on restoring and reviving where and what he can, of any life and life-giving objects that remain. It is these efforts, the frantic or feeble struggles to revive the others within him and so to survive, that are manifested; the despair and hopelessness is never,

11 Freud's 'Talion principle'. See for example Freud, 1913, p. 154.

of course, quite complete. The objects are never actually felt to be dead, for
that would mean death to the ego; the anxiety is so great because life hangs
by a hair and at any moment the situation of full horror may be realized.

(Riviere, 1936, p. 313)

Unconscious phantasies take an inherently dramaturgical form in the inner world.
The characters are animated versions of the entities we infer to be the part and whole
objects of that world, and they produce the kinds of anxiety described by Klein in the
two main configurations. These, as I have discussed, are the paranoid-schizoid position, in which the chief actor is the imperilled self, and the depressive position – in
which the central characters are loved objects put in danger by the destructive urges
of the self. This inner drama, with its character of the anxiety-situations comparable
to torments of the early myths (Savery, 2018), stems from the situation early in life
when, as infants, we first meet with unbearable, dreadful experience, and the need
for help with it. Both Freud's 1895 concept of the work of the specific action (*die
Arbeit der spezifischen Aktion*) and Bion's model of the container–contained (1962b,
p. 90) are ways of theorising on the requirement of the presence of an external other
"to bear what in the immediate situation is unbearable to the self, to take in the
experience and to suffer it in such a way that it may eventually be returned in a more
bearable form" (Savery, 2018, p. 19).

In Chapter 5 I showed how Freud's early writing on the role of the mother
in intervening into her infant's anxiety was developed further by Bion, with
his concept of the mother offering herself as a transforming container for raw,
indigestible experience. Transformation of anxiety by the mind of another
functioning as a living container for its unbearable aspects is possible, though by
no means always guaranteed, in the mother–infant couple, and an experience
with the same fundamental character occurs in the therapeutic situation of analysis, as Bion states. Savery is, in essence, adding that because (a) what Aristotle
identifies as the component of purging (purgation) corresponds to what from a
psychoanalytic perspective is projective identification, and (b) that this occurs
within a theatrical container, composed of the many interacting components in
the forms and functions of theatre, including those specified for the tragic form
of drama by Aristotle, the central process described by Bion happens also in the
transformations effected by drama. Savery writes:

> It seems that myth and theatre have both served as containers within which
> transformations in the form of catharsis (a purging feeling that enables expres-
> sion, thinking and some degree of resolution) can and do take place.
>
> *(Savery, 2018, p. 21)*

Returning to the nature and purpose of myth and drama, here is how Savery has
written of the relationships between myth, unbound dread, the container, and the
truth expressed and contained in drama.

If we consider myth as a container for such elements of the human condition as cannot be processed or tolerated, it goes some way to explaining the timelessness and universality of the ideas and truths contained within them. Freud's use of the myth of *Oedipus Rex* as a container within which pre-verbal and unconscious aspects of human relating can be transformed and thought about in the clinical situation is evidence of such a phenomenon. It is interesting therefore to consider which myths have *not* been taken up by psychoanalysis, and even more so to think about why only parts of a myth or characters within it have formed the objects of much psychoanalytic enquiry, while others have been largely ignored.

(Savery, 2018, p. 20)

Catharsis as taken up by psychoanalysis

In 1893, Breuer and Freud wrote of catharsis in relation to trauma, foreshadowing a concept, *adäquate Reaktion*, ('adequate reaction') which two years later, in the "Project", Freud worked into the concept of the specific action.

The injured person's reaction to the trauma only exercises a completely 'cathartic' effect if it is an *adequate* reaction – as, for instance, revenge.[12]

(Breuer & Freud, 1893, p. 8)

Catharsis is no longer regarded as important in psychoanalysis. Related historically to Breuer and Freud's pre-psychoanalytic use of it, and the associated term, *abreaction*, it formed a part of an earlier version of Freud's method, and has, like hypnosis and suggestion, undergone the fate of all terms which remind us of less sophisticated aspects of our own history. This may have occurred also through being regarded in its medicalised version as simply 'ventilation', or getting feelings 'off the chest'. Possibly it may also have been dismissed because it has been thought of as belonging, by contradistinction, to the methods of other treatment approaches, for example those belonging to the humanistic tradition or 'growth movement'. In my view it is also because the element of emotional discharge is, in Aristotle's definition of it, merely its initial phase, the term can become simplified as though it were the *whole* of it – a desire just to be rid of emotions, and 'that's that'. If catharsis is in this way reduced to *discharge,* the term becomes *contrasted* with reflection and thinking and, rather than an eventual aspect of comprehension, taking place through a mediated route. In my view it has been regarded mistakenly as referring only to a ridding of the psyche, or personality, of what is unwanted or unbearable.

In a line of argument spanning his 1894 draft, "How anxiety originates", his 1895 "Project for a scientific psychology", through *The Interpretation of Dreams*

---

12 "Die Reaktion des Geschädigten auf das Trauma hat eigentlich nur dann eine völlig 'kathartische' Wirkung, wenn sie eine adäquate Reaktion ist, wie die Rache."

(1900) and "Formulations on the two principles of mental functioning" (1911), Freud built a model of psychic functioning in which the growth of mental structure depended primarily on what devolved from mounting inner tension and anxiety, at first barely differentiated in terms of its fundamental forces. At first he included in this model the appropriately tuned responsiveness of the mother as its most essential and irreplaceable component, as I have outlined in Chapter 3.

As will be recalled by the earlier discussion of this model, it is the mother who, through being the infant's first satisfying 'object', becomes his first hostile object whilst being at the same time his sole helping power. All mental development thus takes place, insisted Freud at the time, in a couple, and in relation to a fellow human being. It is this fellow-human, the mother at first (later it becomes significant others) who notices the initial attempts of the baby to rid itself of feelings that are painful to him, who first responds in specific ways to alleviate the situation through an understanding of it, giving appropriate psychological help as well as practical provision. This essential central human process depends upon catharsis as its initial phase – following which the whole unfolding process as first described by Freud, and elaborated later by Bion (building on Klein) in his container–contained model, leads by complex identifications to the creation of an inner world. In the world of drama, Aristotle, in elucidating the definitive principles making possible the functioning of dramatic tragedy, pinpointed the role of *katharsis* as an essential component of its production.

For Freud, then, in psychoanalysis, and also for Klein and Bion in their later formulations of anxiety and its management, the 'ridding' component was never actually taken as an end in itself, however much an infant may be observed as wishing to achieve it, or acting in a way suggesting a belief that such a thing is possible. It is true that Freud referred to measures designed for "unburdening the mental apparatus of accretions of stimuli" (1911, p. 221), and that growth depends on whether painful experiences are faced up to, by making use of mental resources (including those recruited from and offered by others), or whether they are subject to powerful methods of evasion. Much of Bion's work developed from this distinction made by Freud between facing reality and evading it. Catharsis is a term that has undergone a deterioration of meaning in psychoanalysis in being made to refer more to an evasion of mental pain than to suffering it. I have tried to show how it is through an appreciation and understanding of its importance in Aristotle's thought that we can recover its full meaning for our psychoanalytic thinking. I argue that this is worth doing.

If we understand catharsis as discharge only, or abreaction, it is of little use to us. If, however, we take it as more than evacuative, it can be understood as a transformative process, taking place in the context of a container. This is the case in classical drama and, in a comparable form, in all meaningful human relationships, starting with the mother–infant relationship. Across these situations in which so much else differs, there is more than an analogy, there is an affinity in the basic principles of anxiety and its containment, in which the core Aristotelian insights which he investigates in tragic drama under the terms *katharsis*, pity and fear, recognition and reversal, correspond to what in psychoanalysis we formulate as projective identification into a willing human container for the unbearable elements of experience; the capacity for the helper, through being able to enter into complex identifications, to contribute to symbolisation and transformation of otherwise intolerable anxiety and raw affect; and the growth or otherwise of the personality depending on the availability and the uptake and the fate of all of these.

I now turn, in the next chapter, to another aspect of the dramaturgical, the way in which the familiar is made strange in order to reveal hidden forces and structures in human relationships and in the mind. This capacity of drama to raise questions about underlying truths, by way of the subversion of what makes for familiarity, is one which has relevance to the practice and theory of psychoanalysis.

8

THE DRAMATURGICAL DIMENSION II

Making strange the familiar

In this chapter I consider drama from a different angle in order to discuss ideas concerning the disruption, in the service of revealment, of familiarity and subversion of the appearance of 'naturalness'. I begin the chapter with a discussion of the way in which crises in the foundations of knowledge and belief are normally equated with a corresponding crisis of being. The reason I do so is that, as we will see, the theatre of Bertolt Brecht creates a setting in which pre-existing assumptions based on theatrical conventions are challenged in their core structure. The purpose is to use some philosophical ideas to form something of a backdrop for understanding Brecht's approach to theatre, which forms the heart of this chapter.

> The dramatic theatre's spectator says: Yes, I have felt like that too – Just like me – It's only natural – It'll never change – The sufferings of this man appal me, because they are inescapable – That's great art; it all seems the most obvious thing in the world – I weep when they weep, I laugh when they laugh.
>
> The epic theatre's spectator says: I'd never have thought it – That's not the way – That's extraordinary, hardly believable – It's got to stop – The sufferings of this man appal me, because they are unnecessary – That's great art; nothing obvious in it – I laugh when they weep, I weep when they laugh.
>
> *(Brecht, "Theatre for pleasure or theatre for instruction", 1935, p. 71)*

Because Brecht's theatrical methods work, as we shall see, to undercut those conventions of drama that through identification and empathy induce a sense in the audience of a natural order at work behind the drama, I will first discuss some epistemological aspects of the pervasive notion of 'naturalness'.

Crises in the foundations of knowledge and belief

Heidegger believed that the concept of naturalness served to conceal and distort a normally occurring type of crisis which stirs in the foundations of all defined domains of knowledge or belief. (BT, p. 9). Where such domains are exposed and delineated, he wrote, its "elaboration in its fundamental structures is in a way already accomplished by *pre-scientific* experience and interpretation of the region of being to which the domain of knowledge is itself confined" (my emphasis). Heidegger is writing of 'pre-ontological' factors in basic decisions concerning nomination, inclusion and exclusion in what are agreed as subject-areas in bodies of knowledge. Just as hidden interests may serve the choices of apparently 'natural' geographical features when drawing up territorial maps following wars or other disputes, the 'natural lines' of bodies of knowledge and belief may similarly be arbitrary in one sense, and interest-serving in another.

The way Heidegger set this out is as follows, and my purpose in doing so is to be found in the correspondences between formalised bodies of knowledge and the belief system of the individual, as discussed by Britton (1998). The core concepts resulting from the pre-scientific (or 'extra-scientific) establishment of the boundaries of a particular field of enquiry initialise, or pre-set, the guidelines for what it is capable of revealing. Heidegger's idea is that, once formed, the actual real growth of a domain of knowledge (or belief) depends less on how it deposits its findings in its particular 'containers' of formalised knowledge, *but instead lies in the flexibility and effectiveness of how it responds to the interrogation forced upon its structures, by the internal pressure of what its development throws up for it.*

In the latter case, a domain of knowledge could suffer a requirement to resist the development of its own propositions. In fact, Heidegger stated that if we are to consider the dimension of 'movement' in the sciences, it occurs in the *revisions* that are possible in the structures formed by – and which are also determining of – its core concepts, and this includes the scope for reconsidering what are in fact to be regarded *as* its core concepts. An important implication is that the level of development of a body of knowledge is revealed by its resilience in the face of pressure on its definitory structure exerted by new discoveries that stem from *how it is*. Most importantly, Heidegger states that the level of development (of a science) is disclosed by the extent to which it is capable of a crisis in its basic concepts, because this is what determines its capacity for growth.

The crisis in the foundation arises eventually in all organisations of knowledge and all systems of belief, suggests Heidegger. Unless recognition of crisis is evaded, the necessity is normally felt to place future research on new or extended foundations. These ideas from philosophy have an important bearing on my explorations in this book. It is enormously valuable to have Heidegger's particular way of describing these foundational crises in epistemological structures, and this of course includes the preconceptions and inclinations of theatrical audiences. It is precisely because the critical pressure he is describing arises from the consequences of how things have *come into being* and *how things are now*, and exerts itself upon the adequacy of that which proposes to *go on being* what it is. The questions, therefore, are predominantly *ontological* in nature. They pertain not only to functioning, but to existence.

After specifying foundational crises in various domains: mathematics, physics, biology, and what he called 'the historical and humanistic disciplines', Heidegger indicated the refractoriness of theology as a discipline in confronting its own foundational crisis. I include here his own characterisation of this failure because it offers a way to keep open the 'conduit of affinities' that I take to exist between Heidegger's ideas and the partially corresponding obstacles in the growth and development of the individual human being and its groups.

> Theology is searching for a more original interpretation of human being's being towards God, prescribed by the meaning of faith itself and remaining within it. Theology is slowly beginning to understand again Luther's insight that its system of dogma rests on a 'foundation' that does not stem from a questioning in which faith is primary and whose conceptual apparatus is not only insufficient for the range of problems in theology but rather covers them up and distorts them.
>
> *(Heidegger, 2010, p. 8)*

This failure, the failure of a subject discipline to face truthfully the crisis in its foundation by using and testing the concepts *at its foundation*, I see not only as an institutional lapse but as representative of the failure of all human beings to face their sternest test: in the ground of our being we are not as we think we are. One of the most valuable and enduring functions of theatre is that it can show us something of who and what we are, and I now turn to the ways in which Brecht altered drama with creative disruptiveness.

Precipitating an epistemological crisis dramaturgically

Between the wars, creative experimentation in the field of theatre was expanding in Europe. At the same time, structuralist ideas were taking hold in the fields of political theory, economics, literary criticism, linguistics, Lacanian theory, anthropology, epistemology, philosophy and psychoanalysis. The influence of these, along with Marx's ideology, had a profound impact upon Brecht's political theories which underpinned his practice.

The relationships between science, culture, the arts and indeed psychoanalysis at the *fin de siècle* are important in understanding the context within which Brecht sought to bring about social change through his theatre. During the late nineteenth century, widely accepted theological positions were being challenged through the evolutionary theories of Charles Darwin. As often happens (evidence of which we can see in the previous chapter) the anxiety provoked by this is discharged into, or sublimated through, artistic expression before both an understanding of the impact and emotional acceptance can begin to take place. We see in the movement of literary naturalism, founded by Emile Zola, a combination of exposure to the misery of the human condition, and a scientific detachment to observe and understand its impact upon the human subject. His novel *Thérèse Raquin* published in 1867, just eight years after *The Origin of Species*, analysed aspects of heredity and environment in its subjects who were drawn as 'real' characters while being observed through the microscopic lens of the scientist. Zola first coined the term 'naturalism' and his novel is usually credited as the first naturalistic literary work.

The naturalistic movement in theatre which developed from this was a dominant genre in the late nineteenth and early twentieth centuries. Presenting the human subject as real was central in the works of naturalistic playwrights such as Strindberg and Ibsen. The genre also explored the impact of heredity and environment upon the human subject and, in particular, upon the mind. These plays focused on exposure to the sudden responsibility upon the human being for her subjective existence in and for the world which had previously been able to be absolved through the relation to an omnipotent god. This provoked existential anxiety, to which the audience were exposed through a new theatrical form, in which the 'fourth wall'[1] is effectively removed and the audience feels they are sitting in the room with these actual characters. The juxtaposition between being drawn in and identified with the characters and, at the same time, observing them as subjects in an experiment (like rats in a laboratory) while watching the effects of certain stimuli upon them, placed the audience members in interesting and often paradoxical, ambivalent, contradictory positions. For the actors, truth was uppermost in their ability to perform these fully fleshed out characters, giving rise to a new approach to acting taken up by Stanislavsky. His method, through which characters are given a psychological and physical history with which the actor must fully engage, involves drawing upon parts of himself and his own emotional memory. From a psychoanalytic perspective this may be likened to the interplay of what are termed 'internal objects' in the unconscious inner world of the patient, as they can be observed in the transference to be called from the 'wings', as it were, to take centre stage under particular emotional conditions, and there to play the main role in shaping what goes on in the unfolding relationship to the analyst.

We can see the impact of these new forms upon thinkers and other artists and especially upon psychoanalysis, which was having its birth at this time. The philosophies of Nietzsche, the music of Wagner, the works of painters like Kandinsky and Picasso, and the understanding of the material world as structured and formed through the actions of human beings lays the foundations upon which Marxist and structuralist theories developed. They attempt both to understand and to break through the false consciousness that what is, is somehow 'God-given' and natural.

There was a growing willingness amongst thinkers to expose received and unquestioned 'facts' and 'truths' (including their own) presented as 'natural', to an exacting

---

1 A 'term of art' in the study of theatre, the fourth wall refers to the abstract, non-material boundary, experienced consciously only when breached, between actors on stage and the audience.

and unsparing deconstructive type of intellectual enquiry, in which the underlying structures of language and ideas were themselves subject to investigation.

It is the investigation of the whole character of those events which present as, or are made to appear, 'natural', unremarkable, and commonplace in their 'everyday-ness' that are so interesting and so relevant to the study of the themes explored in this book. As will be clear from the quotation at the beginning of the chapter, by the playwright and theatre director, Bertolt Brecht, it is possible to bring a perspective to theatre in which the audience's tendency to form identifications with the characters of a play is replaced by relative detachment from the emotions of their predicament. Later in the chapter I will say more about such identificatory relationships with characters and situations, as it proves extremely useful to be able to use such a concept to consider principles which allow transitions between the domains of psychoanalysis and those used by the dramatic arts.

Brecht sought a method which would bring about this relative emotional detachment in his plays. I begin the chapter by describing his approach, which began as a method to agitate and to break through existing social and political structures with their sense of natural inevitability, using dramatic effects which both disrupted and revealed their underlying structures of power and influence.

In the 1920s the German theatre director Erwin Piscator (1893–1966) extended the boundaries of dramatic structure and performance to include startling politically charged effects. He created a different kind of theatrical space, one which challenged the structures of society and the conventions of drama itself. Piscator, with his confrontational methods, put to the forefront the socio-political aspects of human life to be challenged and examined through his drama.

Piscator, and after him Bertolt Brecht, found ways of turning down the volume, so to speak, on the emotional dimension of drama and the audience's personal identification with it. Whereas for classical drama an *identification* with the action of the characters is central to its workings – through its characteristic functions of catharsis, recognition and reversal – the form of this new approach, which became known as epic theatre, later to be renamed dialectical theatre, was suited to its specific function of emphasising social contradiction using a different kind of acting, and also by making use of political satire and mixed-media commentary on the action.[2] In a speech given in March 1929,[3] Piscator commented on dominant theatrical and social trends, saying, "In lieu of private themes we had generalisation, in lieu of what was special the typical, in lieu of accident causality". This sentiment, expressed in this way, corresponds closely to Proust's discussion of *l'habitude* and Heidegger's '*das Man*', which I explored in Chapter 2.

---

2 This is not to say, however, that in modulating the degree of emotional commonality between audience and actors, Brecht's plays lacked the emotional power to move their audiences deeply. His later work in particular, for example *The Caucasian Chalk Circle* (1944; tr. and perf. 1948) and *Mother Courage and her Children* (1939; perf. 1941), included alternations of both cathartic and distancing methods. Whilst this undoubtedly has its purposeful elements, he sometimes could not help writing into his plays the emotional drama of the common human condition, perhaps almost in spite of himself.

3 See Paget, 2004, p. 397.

Piscator formed a collective in Berlin in the late 1920s to develop his politically aware form of drama. It was belonging to that theatre company that encouraged the young Bertolt Brecht to develop his own approach to acting. It contrasted with the form and workings of tragic drama in that Brecht was concerned to interrupt those processes that would otherwise operate to bring about in the audience an emotional participation with the actions of the characters of the drama. The aim was to promote instead a degree of separation suited to observation and critical examination. He found ways to get his actors to understand the necessity to suspend their own normally un-self-conscious movements and their inclinations to act in a way that promotes emotional identification, taking the aforementioned method of Stanislavsky and the recommendations of Aristotle to its fullest potential – a process that, unless checked, leads almost to 'being' the enacted character in such a manner as to convince the audience that they *are* the character. Brecht wanted to bring about a distinctly different dramaturgical attitude both in his actors and audience because he wanted them to retain, and to sustain, a separateness between them and the action, and also between the operation, whilst watching the drama, of the observing and critical intellect and the play of emotions.

Why did he want his audiences to hold back their emotional responsiveness to the characters? It was because his primary purpose in theatre was to stimulate a critical awareness of the political process through an explicit revealment of its workings.[4] It was important therefore to find modes of conveying the action which pushed the audience out of their normally receptive position into another, unfamiliar attitude, so that they could adopt a critical perspective in order to recognise dynamics of power, injustice and the exploitation of human beings individually and in groups. Like Piscator, he envisaged theatre as a force for social and political change. Unlike Piscator in his early career, Brecht emphasised less the agitational propagandist element, preferring instead to surprise the audience out of their everyday state, by using the *Verfremdungseffekt* – making strange the familiar. This method will be described in detail, and with its relevance to psychoanalysis, later in the chapter.

An important epistemological principle was important to Brecht in bringing this about. He wanted his audiences to remain aware of the difference between representation and that which was represented. It was keeping this distinction alive that was so important in countering the slide into the reification of 'naturalness'.

Brecht held that dramatic theatre enabled human relationships to 'come into view' but, through our own identification of ourselves with them, something highly specific and important belonging to the characters eluded our grasp. The price of meaningful emotional participation through the cathartic process, mainly because of the necessary element of identification, was the loss of distance for critical thinking concerning the particularities, differences and

---

4 And exposing, on stage, the means of production of activities and not just their smooth 'agentless' processes.

contradictions involved. Both perspectives cannot be held at one and the same time by the audience.[5]

In his "Short Organum" (1948), he referred to the passivity that may be induced in audiences by repeated emphasis of drama that relies heavily on emotional identification. He wrote of the substitutions, to and fro, between worlds containing inner contradiction and those meant to be received as wholly consistent and coherent. He meant that if an realistically inconsistent world becomes rendered through drama as though it were consistent, natural and inevitable, then it fails thereby to apprehend the field of human relationships.

If an effect of emotional identification with characters in a play is to efface the unique separateness and historical conditions of the other, how can dialectical theatre suspend this powerful human tendency, which dramatic tragedy employs and mobilises as part of its own appropriate aims? The epigraph by Brecht at the beginning of this chapter captures the question perfectly. In his "Short Organum", Brecht asks:

> Where is the man himself, the living, unmistakeable man? . . . It is clear that his stage image must bring him to light. . . . Such images [stage images] certainly demand a way of acting which will leave the spectator's intellect free and highly mobile . . . a process which leads real conduct to acquire an element of 'unnaturalness', thus allowing the real motive forces to be shorn of their naturalness.
>
> *(Brecht, 1948, sections 39–40)*

Brecht's theatre and artistic praxis

Another important strand in what Brecht was trying to bring about through theatre, albeit with a less directly confrontational attitude than his colleague Piscator, is that of something known as artistic praxis. This is the application to art of Marx's encouragement for thinkers not to halt at interpreting the world but to consider how to bring about change. Brecht later renamed his epic theatre 'dialectical theatre', to reflect the link between his approach to drama and the ideas of Hegel and Marx. Brecht found ways of directing that subverted the production of effects normally employed by actors to produce emotional identification in the audience, identification which in many instances contributed to naturalistic adoption of unquestioned social and political codes. To put this in another way, Brecht wanted to explore and to put forward theatre that ran counter to trends in art where the hidden assumptions functioned smoothly to conceal socio–political *praxis* and to render it instead both as natural and as historically inevitable *process*. He sought methods to reintroduce history where it had been effaced by historicism, that is to say the hidden assumption that historical events are governed by natural laws independently of human designs and actions.

---

5 In a manner analogous to the impossibility in small particle physics of an observer locating simultaneously the position of an electron and determining its momentum: the aspect of complementarity described by the physicist Niels Bohr.

The specific handling of this in dialectical theatre has to be different from tragic drama, as the following passage by Brecht makes clear:

> The 'historical conditions' must of course not be imagined (nor will they be so constructed) as mysterious Powers (in the background); on the contrary, they are created and maintained by men (and will in due course be altered by them): it is the actions taking place before us that allow us to see what they are.
>
> *(1948, section 38)*

What is being emphasised is the subversion of the seemingly natural in the service of revealment – the disclosure, that is, of the concealed dynamics and structures behind the normally accepted but incomplete narrative. The ways in which Brechtian theatre is effective in unmasking for its audience the influence of otherwise hidden agencies of power and vested interests have real significance for psychoanalysis and psychotherapy informed by existential philosophy.

Methods for countering the generic and the 'naturally familiar'

I will now consider (a) Brecht's approach to opposing generification of the human character, and (b) his method for undoing familiarisation and revealing underlying structure. Both were important to him in his passionate personal and political philosophy and in his expression of it in the development of dialectical theatre.

Firstly, then, Brecht (1948, section 40) asks with some passion, "Where is the man himself, the living, unmistakeable man, who is not quite identical with those identified with him?" He is asking how it is that we can find the real unmistakable person behind the generic persona that we are invited to accept, to find a way to bring out differences and contradictions in human characters and not to submit to the common smooth generalising and anonymising tendencies. The generalising attitude of Proust's *l'habitude* effaces the fact that in spite of (and concealed by) our human capacity for sympathetic identification, not everybody has the same experiences of being a person. It is an attitude with which Picasso disagreed passionately. In an interview with Simone Téri, in March 1945, he said:

> What do you think an artist is? An imbecile who only has eyes, if he is a painter, or ears if he is a musician, or a lyre in every chamber of his heart if he is a poet, or even, if he is a boxer, just his muscles? Far from it: at the same time he is also a political being, constantly aware of the heart-breaking, passionate, or delightful things that happen in the world, shaping himself completely in their image. How could it be possible to feel no interest in other people, and with a cool indifference to detach yourself from the very life which they bring to you so abundantly? No, painting is not done to decorate apartments. It is an instrument of war.
>
> *(Picasso, cited in Elliott et al., 2016, p. v)*

His 1907 painting *Les Demoiselles d'Avignon*, not exhibited until nine years later, depicts five nude prostitutes seen by Picasso on the street known as Carrer d'Avinyó in Barcelona. When unveiled before colleagues his painting was met by attitudes of repulsion and horror because the work departed so radically from, and was subversive of, the conventional style of female representation. The women in the painting held a confrontational attitude, as did the painting itself. Its abstract aspects jarred with the observers' expectations of passively possessible eroticism. In place of feminine passivity inhering in images taken as representing familiar and 'natural' objects of erotic possession, perhaps with eyes lowered in a seductive pose, most of the women are looking straight *at* the viewer of the scene, their potential consumers – a reversal of the familiar and conventional division between voyeur (consumer) and the gazed-upon (consumed). It is as though each one is saying to us, "I see you standing there seeing me as an object, but I am a subject in my own right, and I see you and take you as the object of my own look".

Pablo Picasso (1907), *Les Demoiselles d'Avignon*

Another defamiliarisation effect in Picasso's painting is the juxtaposition in two of the faces of the women of human and animal elements, in one of the ears and a nose. The baboon-like nose elicits its own associations of primitiveness, perhaps reminding male viewers disturbingly of their own primitive being, but so does the intentional offsetting of harmony in the facial features. The empty or blinded eye belonging to one of the figures is ambiguous and particularly open to interpretation. The muscular and geometric angularity of the Amazon-like naked forms subverts easy categorisation of the body in normative terms of gender discrimination, as well as bringing an aggressivity to the whole picture and to the dynamic relation between viewer and painting. It truly is, in painting, a making strange of the familiar. A more vivid experience of that effect requires the full colour image or, better still, to stand before the actual canvas.

Just as painting, then, is not limited to a representation of characters who would, unambiguously, recognise themselves in a mirror, and art is not simply decoration, theatre is neither confined to entertainment nor to rest at simple depiction in its specific imitation of human action. There is, however, a tension at the heart of art – a conflict between showing us what we already know and revealing that which we would prefer not to know. This applies to the transformations effected by our three main perspectives – psychoanalysis, existential philosophy and theatre, and the tensions therein.

Gadamer (1989) addressed this by reference to Aristotle, who reminded us of the difference between natural science and the study of the human being in the following terms:

> Human civilization differs essentially from nature in that it is not simply a place where capacities and powers work themselves out; man becomes what he is through what he does and how he behaves – i.e. he behaves in a certain way because of what he has become. Thus Aristotle sees *ethos* as differing from *physis* in becoming a sphere in which the laws of nature do not operate.
> *(Gadamer, 1989, p. 312)*

Ethos (ἦθος) refers to how human beings find themselves being and acting in their particular unique circumstances, whereas *physis* (φύσις) denotes an inherent, dispositional quality to them, taken as stemming from their 'nature'. At first sight Gadamer's remarks concerning laws of nature and laws of human conduct seem incompatible with the use of the term 'scientific spirit' by Brecht – a spirit which he wishes to retain in his theatre so that the audience is enabled to exercise their critical faculties and their political consciousness on the material of the drama. That particular contradiction vanishes if we bear in mind that Brecht (1948, section 40) is not referring to conventional scientific theorising *about* the human being in terms of the 'laws' of natural science, but to an unsentimental critical analysis, nonetheless scientific in its spirit, of what in Gadamer's interpretation are the "human institutions and human modes of behaviour which are mutable, and like rules only to a certain degree". Chief amongst these modes are the dynamics of power and the structures that arise from them.

To address such questions in theatrical terms, Brecht introduced the concept of the actor's 'stage image'. It is the stage image presented by the actor, he says, that must bring the actual person, the person himself, to light. In other words something of the real being has to be brought to light by effects of the acting that counteracts emotional identification with his actions, and any psychological tendencies to see the actor as depicting 'a type of person'. In other words, active steps have to be taken to counter effects which normally serve to promote emotional identification to the extent that the character is made familiar and can be felt to be 'just like' another, or ourselves.

Brecht used his theatre, as I have described, to awaken his audiences even from emotional sensibility, shaking them out of *ahistorical* understandings, and sharpening their consciousness of personal and political specificity. He employed a method for revealing underlying structures of power and influence concealed behind the familiar narrative.

From the psychoanalytic perspective, in terms of disclosing human drama in the consulting room, this approach of Brecht's with its primarily 'non-identificatory' emphasis can be thought of as alternating in the mind of the practitioner, moment by moment, with a contrasting but complementary attitude corresponding more to the stance of Aristotelian drama, according to which a degree of emotional identification and role-immersion is necessary. Perhaps the transition to each of these 'dramaturgical positions', so to speak, takes place as a departure in one direction or the other from the 'flow' of the analyst's primary attitude of reverie, in which the practitioner is equally open to the patient's projections of ontic and ontological anxiety and all the objects and parts of the self bound up with the former. Reverie, in this sense, which I consider a state of being, is like the evenly suspended attentiveness recommended by Freud – a basic position of repeated return for the analyst to re-establish the vital 'uncertainty principle' with her patient, shortly after specific experiences in the consulting room have been to some extent understood and given a temporary form.

The characteristics of reverie and negative capability are more suited to an attunement to something unique of the patient, and of the relationship, in which the suspension of the analyst's emotional identification, as well as their memory and desire, aids a more intuitive grasp of that uniqueness. The practitioner needs, I am suggesting, the freedom to allow somewhat 'Brechtian' moments – of *dis*-identification with the dramatic forms that are appearing in the transference relationship, with room in the method for some detachment from the drama in which they figure as a central character. They also, I suggest, need to be mobile enough to experience oscillations into something analogous to 'Aristotelian' moments. At such points the analyst can let themselves feel, as discussed by Heimann (1950), the emotions that they need to undergo to get a feel for the forces of characterisation that are an inevitable part of being a participant in, as well as an observer of, transference and countertransference.

I suggest that it is through being willing and able to go through such oscillations that the analyst can learn from what is, essentially, both an existential and a dramaturgical experience of the analysis. These processes are not only challenging, they are extraordinarily interesting and illuminating. Through immersive experience in such experiences the practitioner becomes wiser to their workings by having been repeatedly recruited into the dramatis personae and productions particular to the patient, through intricate and projective processes identifiable only through emotional identification with the patient and his inner objects (characters). Identification with the emotions and parts of the self of the patient is known as 'concordant', or homologous, whereas that which is in relation to the patient's internal objects or characters is termed 'complementary'.[6] This is a distinction that becomes useful when considering psychoanalytic methodology in relation specifically to moments in which ontological anxiety is encountered in analysis.

For now, however, I will stay with Brecht's method, with its aim, in dramatic performance, to retain the audience's capacity for effective detachment and critical thinking. At the same time, he wanted to apply his defamiliarising method to characters and events, "stripping the event of its self-evident, familiar, obvious quality and creating a sense of astonishment and curiosity about them" (Brecht cited in Eriksson, 2011, p. 68). Stimulating wonder and curiosity was as important to Brecht as promoting critical thinking; in fact the two can be mutually enhancing.

Brecht's idea of reproducing, faithfully, the raw roughness of his characters, allowing them to retain their internal contradictions, was expressed in his insistence that the actor's 'stage image' should itself carry these same contradictions and roughnesses. Another way to put this is to say that certain 'invariants' in the representability of dramatic action, what Aristotle called the imitation of action, have to be maintained in spite of the many transformations[7] that are permissible between the stage image and the character to be portrayed in the action. This is how Brecht describes the central idea:

> It is clear that his stage image must bring him to light, and this will come about if this particular contradiction is recreated in the image. The image that gives historical definition will retain something of the rough sketching which indicates traces of other movements and features all around the fully-worked-out figure.
>
> *(Brecht, 1948, section 39)*

In the same passage he likens the situation to someone who, standing in a valley gives voice to speech expressing many mutually conflicting views and opinions,

6 For this distinction of Helene Deutsch (1926), and its relation to modes of identification in countertransference, see Racker, 1968, p. 134.
7 This structural way of putting it allows us later to compare the dramaturgical situation with various modes of representation in the other perspectives of this book.

with its echoes in the valley confronting us starkly with all the untidy contradiction. This is a good poetic image of what Brecht hoped to achieve. Following it in his 1948 "Short Organum" is a beautiful description that was preparatory to introducing the *Verfremdungseffekt* – his method for allowing room for critical thinking through the defamiliarising of what is presented as unremarkable, natural and already well understood.

> For it seems impossible to alter what has long not been altered. We are always coming on things that are too obvious for us to bother to understand them. What men experience among themselves they think of as 'the' human experience. A child, living in a world of old men, learns how things work there. He knows the run of things before he can walk. If anyone is bold enough to want something further, he only wants to have it as an exception. Even if he realizes that the arrangements made for him by 'Providence' are only what has been provided by society he is bound to see society, that vast collection of beings like himself, as a whole that is greater than the sum of its parts and therefore not in any way to be influenced. Moreover, he would be used to things that could not be influenced; and who mistrusts what he is used to?
>
> *(Brecht, 1948, section 44)*

Keith Langsdale, the director of a production of Brecht's *The Caucasian Chalk Circle* gave the following description, which brings out nicely how practical measures can aid in this defamilarisation:

> I always felt that there was an Asian influence in it. Some of this comes from images I looked at that struck me – for instance an image of a Japanese bridge. Another part of it comes from the fact that Brecht admired the presentational quality of the Chinese theatre. And in the setting of the play itself – the Caucasus – there is historical reference for it because of the number of cultures that have conquered the region throughout the ages. *But what it really boils down to is that it always seemed, to me, like the most interesting way of making the world of the play separate from us.* The costumes make the characters separate from our reality, *so that we cannot casually identify with them and their story.* Part of what Brecht said about theatre is that it should have some distance, and this gives it some distance for us. *Looking at the play, our audiences will see a world where the elements don't always fit together the way you'd expect a world to fit together; the costumes help to establish these incongruities. This is all meant to pull the audience back from the play – to give them some critical distance.*[8]

8 Interview with Liana Thompson on his direction of the UMass production of *The Caucasian Chalk Circle*, University of Massachusetts-Amherst Department of Theater (emphasis added).

Brecht's *Verfremdungseffekt*: making strange the familiar

Brecht's principal dramaturgical effect which, as he put it, "allows us to recognize its subject, but at the same time makes it seem unfamiliar" (1948, section 42), was an experimental approach to acting which he introduced in Berlin between the wars, at the Theater am Schiffbauerdamm. The name he gave to this technical recommendation which 'makes strange' the familiar taken-for-granted-ness of events, was the *Verfremdungseffekt*, after the German term for alienation and distancing, *Verfremdung*. This concept, as I will consider after describing Brecht's method in theatre, turns out to have an important affinity with the fundamentals of the psychoanalytic method.

We saw earlier how Proust and Heidegger both drew attention to the ways in which we reduce the unique individual freshness of experiences to generalised conceptions – Proust with his concept of *l'habitude* and Heidegger with the terms *das Man* and the 'everyday'. Both terms point to the same underlying reality, which is that for the most part we interpose (and impose), between ourselves and real phenomena, a general and anticipated version of what we have seen, and expect to see. Such a 'reading ahead' mode, predicated as it is on the sensorial, determines what we experience more than that which is actually present to us.

In theatre, Brecht was particularly aware of the implications for what we could call a 'naturalisation' effect, which, as well as constituting an aspect of Heidegger's '*das Man*', is a core component of all perception. Accordingly, he set out to undermine it, and his principal reason for doing so was to counter the inherent tendency for drama to reinforce a form of 'false consciousness', particularly in Marx's use of this term. This connection is evident in the following passage, which makes clear also Brecht's central aim of developing drama which fully includes, and does not allow the smoothing-over, of *inconsistency* and contradiction:

> This technique allows the theatre to make use in its representations of the new social scientific method known as dialectical materialism. In order to unearth society's laws of motion this method treats social situations as processes, and traces out all their inconsistencies. It regards nothing as existing except in so far as it changes, in other words is in disharmony with itself. This also goes for those human feelings, opinions and attitudes through which at any time the form of men's life together finds its expression.
>
> *(Brecht, 1948, section 45)*

Brecht's initiatives also encouraged a freshness of perspective and an openness to the element of surprise and discovery which, as I say, links in the psychoanalytic perspective with Freud's concept of evenly suspended attentiveness, Bion's use of negative capability and his recommendation to heighten the role of intuition by means of the relative suspension of the operation of memory, desire and (apperceptive) understanding.

The requirement to adopt a naïve openness to observing phenomena was described by Brecht in the following comparison with the scientist, Galileo:

To transform himself from general passive acceptance to a corresponding state of suspicious inquiry he would need to develop that detached eye with which the great Galileo observed a swinging chandelier. He was amazed by this pendulum motion, as if he had not expected it and could not understand its occurring, and this enabled him to come on the rules by which it was governed. Here is the outlook, disconcerting but fruitful, which the theatre must provoke with its representations of human social life. It must amaze its public, and this can be achieved by a technique of alienating the familiar.

(Brecht, 1948, section 44)

This statement, to "transform himself from general passive acceptance to a corresponding state of suspicious inquiry", used by the playwright in relation to the art of acting, describes well the attitude recommended by Freud and by Bion, as well as expressing what existential therapists know as *epoché* and 'bracketing' (Spinelli, 2007).

It was clear that Brecht meant to make his audience work. Repeatedly they were placed in an uncomfortable position of having to adapt themselves to the shifting dramatic structures produced by Brecht's 'making strange' devices. It made them think – about *motive* forces in particular. As he stated, in his approach it was the intellect that had to be "free and highly mobile", less so the emotions. The principal intellectual process was that in the development of the drama it was the suspension of some motives and the substituting of others which provoked the audience members into reflecting on the structure of the play and, ultimately, that of society itself. Brecht wrote that such a process

leads real conduct to acquire an element of 'un-naturalness', thus allowing the real motive forces to be shorn of their naturalness.

(Brecht, 1948, section 44)

Because of its affinity with, and relevance to, the field of psychoanalysis, I will reproduce Brecht's sections 35–7 of his "Short Organum".

35: We need a type of theatre which not only releases the feelings, insights and impulses possible within the particular historical field of human relations in which the action takes place, but employs and encourages those thoughts and feelings which help transform the field itself.

36: The field has to be defined in historically relative terms. In other words we must drop our habit of taking the different social structures of past periods, then stripping them of everything that makes them different; so that they all look more or less like our own, which then acquires from this process a certain air of having been there all along, in other words of permanence pure and simple. Instead we must leave them their distinguishing marks and keep their impermanence always before our eyes, so that our own period can be seen to be impermanent too. . . .

37: If we ensure that our characters on the stage are moved by social impulses and that these differ according to the period, then we make it harder for our spectator to identify himself with them. He cannot simply feel: that's how I would act, but at most can say: if I had lived under those circumstances. And if we play works dealing with our own time as though they were historical, then perhaps the circumstances under which he himself acts will strike him as equally odd; and this is where the critical attitude begins.

(Brecht, 1948, sections 35–7)

Some psychoanalytic reflections on the above

Section 35 above requires no significant transformation in its wording to bring out its correspondence with psychoanalysis, for which (borrowing the playwright's words) we also require a setting suited not only to the release of the feelings, insights and impulses possible within the field of human relations in which the transactions take place, but one which employs and encourages those thoughts and feelings which help transform the field, the structure of the relationship to the analyst itself. The next section holds a parallel to a hazard that exists in our listening to the patient, that of the generalising tendency that, unannounced, creeps in whenever we perceive our patient more as a generic confirmation of our pre-existing theories than the unique individual that we have never really, until that moment, met before. This facet of the basic psychoanalytic attitude will be discussed later under the shorthand term 'memory and desire'. The condition of impermanence referred to by Brecht in the text is of real importance both to psychoanalytic and existential forms of therapy. The over-reliance on empathic understanding can lead us to minimise the differences between the experiences of the other and those with which we are familiar. Similarly, when Brecht speaks of identifiable structures as acquiring 'a certain air of having been there all along', which implies the taking hold of a knowing attitude, this can also become an obstruction in being open to new discoveries in therapeutic work.

In this regard Freud (1912a, p. 112) cautioned against both expectations and inclinations in imposing their own structures on those of the patient's communications of themselves. The psychoanalyst's precocious 'knowing' is a major obstacle to the evolution of the real action of the analytic encounter and the unfolding of the transference relationship. In that situation, the characters on the stage are those of the patient's inner drama, which for convenience we call the 'objects' of their world. When we read Brecht's words, "He cannot simply feel: that's how I would act, but at most can say: if I had lived under those circumstances", we recognise the 'he' as the person of the analyst, in the 'there but for the grace . . .' sense of the patient as a fellow human being. The method of listening that Freud recommended gives equal weight to those elements for which the patient, by contrast, wishes to be taken as a narrative, temporal structure. In that generally preferred and more psychologically comforting structure, the theory of cause and effect is, with its associated sense of blame taking precedence over responsibility, paramount. I will say more about this tendency shortly.

If we regard Brecht's initiatives as constituting a dramaturgical version of what Bion, following Keats, called a 'language of achievement', what the drama accomplishes for its audiences bears some correspondence to the shift actualised with the patient in the therapeutic situation, whose sense of familiarity with their experience of themselves and the other is challenged and upset in being exposed to a new and unforeseen interpretive context. In both settings the predicament is one of being exposed regularly to the challenge of the familiar made suddenly unaccountably strange (which is an inevitable consequence of contact with the unconscious), a challenge which has either to be addressed or evaded. There is something important to be learned from either choice.

At a fundamental level, in the way of listening requisite in psychoanalysis, the analyst has to bear fully the anxiety of unfamiliarity, even *of* herself *to* herself. It is here that Brecht's words have such significance:

> if we play works dealing with our own time as though they were historical, then perhaps the circumstances under which he himself acts will strike him as equally odd; and this is where the critical attitude begins.
>
> *(Brecht, 1948, section 37)*

The playwright Enda Walsh felt that, for him, the necessary unfamiliarising effect could be obtained by focusing away from the verbal content of the drama:

> The play isn't about words. It's not about information. It's about what goes on between the characters, and the way they *use* the story. A lot of the time, I want to turn the volume down on all these words, and just trace the characters' emotional connection to what it is they're talking about.
>
> *(Enda Walsh, interview in* The Times, *2 August 2008)*

Freud's evenly suspended attentiveness as a *Verfremdungseffekt* in psychoanalysis

The principal method of psychoanalysis – listening with an evenly suspended attentive attitude – brings a comparable 'making strange the familiar' effect to what otherwise would remain a narrative-based conversation,[9] replete with assumptions and supportive not only of psychic defences but also of the everyday mentality that

---

9 Where what Freud called the 'primary process' is converted into 'secondary process', one consequence of which is to introduce 'narrativity', a temporal structure of cause and effect to what, when deconstructed using evenly suspended attentiveness, can be seen more as a 'palimpsest'. (Etymological note: ad. Fr. narrativité: the quality or condition of being or presenting a narrative; (the action or process of) story-telling.) Disclosure of the unconscious pattern is made possible by a deconstructive process, of which evenly suspended attentiveness is an instance. It also has the effect of making strange what would, as narrative, be familiar to both analyst and patient. This, incidentally, is why the ordinary conversational mode is *not* the mode of psychoanalysis.

I have been describing as that of the Heidegger's concept of the 'they-self' (*das Man*) and what Proust called *l'habitude*. Listening with evenly suspended attentiveness subverts the 'required reading' and preferential hearing of speech, its familiar and practised narrativised contours in which temporal order and the categorisation of subject and object, self and other, are generally not meant to be questioned.

These everyday attitudes tend to become structured in a concealed way in language, where they create shared conventions and defences against anxiety, both ontic and ontological. In fact, it is in the nature of psychic defences to become organised in such a way as to make the strange familiar.

The two basic methodological principles of analysis – encouraging the patient to associate freely without all the time having to speak logically and coherently, and the recommendation that the analyst should listen as far as possible with the attention suspended evenly, without selection according to what is preferred or expected – have the overall effect of making strange the otherwise familiar and routine use of language as a narrative-based conversation. The use of the couch introduces a *Verfremdungseffekt* into the situation, as does the altered pattern of 'turn-taking' in psychoanalytic discourse, the way it departs from ordinary social conversation.[10]

An important consequence of Freud's introduction of a *Verfremdungseffekt* in the defining method of psychoanalysis is to allow the 'deep structure' of the free-associative mode of communication to emerge from its concealed background in ordinary speech. Crucial polarities are thereby disrupted in a disturbing way for both participants, chief amongst them the commonly accepted idea of cause and effect. The concepts of blame and historical explanation are thrown into question by the significant difference between psychoanalytic discourse and everyday speech. So too is the common way of allocating human *agency* in terms of personal pronouns, so that all firm statements by the patient concerning who is held to have done what, and to whom, are rendered less definite and fixed through being listened to with evenly suspended attention. This latter feature works both ways, in that the patient listening to the analyst with a loosened attention comparable to that of the analyst is thereby opened more than is usual to hearing undefined attributions of agency. Murderous urges, for example, may arise as a subject in the analysis, and through analytic listening these and other impulses become open to being heard without immediately deciding *who* possesses these feelings and against whom they may be directed. In this way the *directionality* of human impulses to action is allowed, at first, to be indeterminate, in order to facilitate their deeper nature. Another way in which an analyst may introduce a quiet and subtle version of 'making strange the familiar', perhaps on occasion inadvertently, is by drawing attention to a particular word or phrase used by the patient, when doing so leads to a disruption in 'received meanings' – a very common occurrence in therapeutic work. Such an intervention is not itself interpretive, it is indicative – but the turbulence released in such situations may eventually become ripe for interpretive consideration, once the dust settles.

10 This pattern may be represented as: A, A, A, A, B, A . . . in contrast to A, B, A, B, . . .

The past presented, the past examined

Dramatic tragedy brings past events into the vividly lived and played-out world of the performance with full emotional import. The epic theatre of Brecht retained a perspective on the past *as* the past, in order to maintain a distance for critical reflection. Brecht (following Goethe and Schiller's 1797 essay on the subject) considered that the epic poet presents the event as totally past, while the dramatic poet presents it as totally present. That this is so is consistent with the cathartic and identificatory emphasis of the latter, in which the emotional impact is very much experienced in the here and now of the drama. Retaining distance is a defining feature of Brechtian drama, essential to its primary purpose of maintaining a critical lens on the unfolding theatrical presentations, but this does not mean that the element of emotional investment and the role of catharsis is totally banished in his work. Where it does appear, in his later work, it is brought in expressly to render the subsequent distancing, with its critical analysis, all the more effective, when the moment arrives, for us having identified closely and compassionately with the characters in their terrible predicaments.

It must be remembered that Brecht avoided fixity. He experimented with his dialectical theatre and the philosophical ideas that underlay it throughout his relatively short career – from his early inspiration and collaboration with Erwin Piscator in Berlin in the late 1920s, through later exile after 1933, six years in the USA, and East Germany, until his eventual return there to establish the Berliner Ensemble. Highly original later works included *Mother Courage* and *The Caucasian Chalk Circle*. These plays in particular were notable for a development of his work in which he included scenes in which the audience would be bound to enter into compassionate identification with the characters – figures who nevertheless contained internal contradictions which prevented easy and casual identifications – the better to prepare the way for a subsequent switching of his dramaturgical 'lens' to give a deeper critical insight into the specific and historical conditions underpinning their predicaments.

In *Mother Courage and her Children,* written in 1939 and performed two years later, there is a build-up in the play to a climactic scene where Kattrin, the daughter of Mother Courage, becomes alert to a situation of great danger to them all. Because she cannot speak she tries desperately and with great urgency to bring this to the attention of the others, by starting to bang and bang and bang on her drum. As an audience we are completely drawn in, because in this moment Brecht invites us to perceive the danger; to empathise with Kattrin for the fact that she cannot speak; to feel protective towards Mother Courage and her children. We end up feeling for everybody. But then, from a drama perspective, it becomes very interesting. Brecht does not rob us of the emotion, but he allows it for a very short time and then he shifts his lens, so to speak, and we are suddenly plunged into a very different perspective, which is – rather than being-with the characters in the play – that of trying to understand exactly what has happened; and he tries to reveal something to us of the workings of it, its 'praxis' in human action with motives uncovered. We are then invited to take a scientific perspective on it, and to deconstruct it – and we see that Brecht is trying to explain and reveal something quite different, which is: what has brought about the conditions that have made this happen, rather than for us to stay in that cathartic response where we feel the combination of pity for the character and fear for ourselves, as characteristic of dramatic theatre.

His claim that virtually all the emotional identification with characters that we find in classical drama was prevented by his distancing and defamiliarising effects, was truer of his theory than his practice. Often he did not quite do what he claimed to be doing, and in many of his plays we are encouraged to empathise with his characters, so in a sense Brecht plays with us, intuitively as a playwright – by allowing us to get very close, which we do when we see, in *The Caucasian Chalk Circle*, the mother who is desperate to save her son, and we feel for her; we are invited to share her cause and her suffering. But, straight after the climactic scene, Brecht uses his very specific techniques – such as third-person narration – and the focus is changed to put us into a scientific perspective in relation to all that has gone before. This dialectical relationship is part of the dramatic form, as well as the philosophical underpinning.

In their purposeful disruption of familiar and comfortably reassuring structures, the methods discussed in this chapter from the perspective of theatre reveal not only specific human conditions of fear and danger, with their historical and individual formation, but also the anguish that belongs to those ontological aspects of our being in the world. These, in contrast with more specific fears, cannot be 'managed', 'coped with' or even ameliorated substantially through understanding. Theatre and psychoanalysis in certain of their forms may enable us to confront these human conditions together with as much truth as we can muster, and to at least become more aware of our individual and collective use of the inevitable domiciliating tendency, uncovering it where we can. The beautifully spare *Waiting for Godot* of Samuel Beckett takes from us all sense of homeliness in the world on the stage and leaves us without protection in considering our existence, alone-together, in contemplating what it is we are waiting for. The next chapter returns us to anxiety, and how its ontological forms and their associated modes of being may be addressed in practice, with the perspectives developed so far in the book that give an important role to the experience and defences against the ontological.

PART IV

Psychoanalytic understanding as becoming informed through being

9

FROM KNOWING TOWARDS BEING

> We must therefore consider further the gap between O and knowledge of phenomena and transformations of O. The gap between reality and the personality, or, as I prefer to call it, the inaccessibility of O, is an aspect of life with which analysts are familiar under the guise of resistance. Resistance is only manifest when the threat is contact with what is believed to be real; there is no resistance to anything believed to be false. Resistance operates because it is feared that the reality of the object is imminent. . . . The point at issue is how to pass from 'knowing' 'phenomena' to 'being' that which is 'real'.
>
> *(Bion, 1965a, p. 147)*

How can the practitioner 'shift' in their working attitude towards an awareness of the being of the patient, and how does knowledge intercede in the transition? How, and in what form, do intimations of the being of another reach us 'outside' knowledge? A third question arising from the other two might be: Once a *form* has become developed out of the awareness of something of the being of the other, how might it be addressed in speech so as to further the growth of understanding and that of the patient's capacity to be real with this understanding, and if speaking with fidelity of this transformation should prove too threatening to the individual, in terms of existential anxiety or perhaps also in a crisis precipitated in the foundation of already existing knowledge, how might the analyst detect the resistance stirred up by these anxieties?

Addressing these questions in a way that is relevant to therapeutic practice is the aim of the two chapters in this section, beginning in this one by considering the shift necessary in the analytic attitude of giving priority, in the clinical situation, to modes of being over states of mind. To the extent that such a thing is possible, I go on to suggest that the return to knowledge subsequent upon what we could call 'dwelling with being' is best described not as knowledge *about* the patient, or insight *into* him, but a becoming informed of his particular being in his worlds, inner and outer.

In terms of the 'directionality' of the relationship between knowing and being, it needs to be understood that I am not taking the $\rightarrow$ sign to mean the same in the two expressions K $\rightarrow$ O and O $\rightarrow$ K (which I consider later). The shorthand expressions are not symmetrical or reversible, in that I use K $\rightarrow$ O to refer to a *movement of emphasis* in the practitioner, from a preoccupation with knowing about the patient towards an attitude of openness, before engaging in interpretive activity, to what may be experienced of their *being*, but the directionality implied by O $\rightarrow$ K, on the other hand, does not refer to a shift of emphasis in attitude, but is used instead to indicate a particular form of knowledge only available on the 'return' from the domain of being and becoming.

This movement (O $\rightarrow$ K), in which intimations of 'O' may become known from brief contacts with being (evolutions) I call *becoming informed,* to distinguish it from the conventional use of K to mean apperception. The purpose of using the term is to enable me to discuss an ontologically related version of the K-link, one that indicates a fluid, transitional process and not a fixed entity to be entered, as it were, into a cumulative mass of knowledge 'about' the patient. In this 'formula', it should be appreciated that 'O' does not 'turn into' 'K' – the domains remain separate – but the 'K' function is informed by an intersection, or a 'brush', with the domain of being. Another way to put this is to say that O $\rightarrow$ K indicates the possibility of becoming informed from the way one is struck (*Betroffenheit*) by a contact with the ontological, and thereby "Won from the void and formless infinite", as Milton wrote in *Paradise Lost* (Book III, line 12).

I begin by considering the unbridgeable gap between what *is* and how we come to have any knowledge of it at all, a characteristic of the world that, in the realm of language, led Ludwig Wittgenstein to develop his 'picture theory' of meaning, and which Werner Heisenberg in the field of physics and Ronald Britton in psychoanalysis have explored in terms of *models*.

Conceptual models

In the analytic setting the interpretive side of our activity is guided by our implicit philosophy of what knowledge *is*. Britton considers that we think, inside and outside the consulting room, in models, and that the use of models not only pertains to our investigations *into* the mind, they seem also to be an intrinsic part of the functioning *of* the mind.

> I am suggesting that we think initially and inescapably in models, whether as scientists, psychoanalysts, patients, or babies. I am asserting that we think in models, whether we are conscious of it or not, and when we believe that we are dealing directly and only with facts or theories we are probably in the grip of an unacknowledged model. Thinking in models has enormous advantages for us as a species, in representing the unknowable world in a form in which we can locate ourselves and with which we can engage. But it also has disadvantages for us whether as natural scientists, psychoanalytic theorists,

practising analysts, or simply as individuals. We can become in Wittgenstein's phrase the fly in the 'fly bottle' of our own model, with its own language from which philosophy might have a part to play in rescuing us.

(Britton, 2015, p. 145)

I begin with this passage, and these associations, to make explicit an aspect of the attitude that can remain hidden in our work, one that has to do with all matters concerning the relations between the language of our interpretations, the implicit categories of inclusion and exclusion implied by them, and the supposed underlying realities for which that language has been formed. This set of principles, many of which are likely to remain implicit, I will be referring to as an analyst's *practical epistemology*[1] – the philosophical substrate of his analytic attitude.

Such implicit or explicit principles concerning the understanding of the nature of our understanding, are I believe, a cardinal aspect of philosophy in the practice of our analytic work. A grasp of the key principles of epistemology, together with the basic principles of structural linguistics, can help the analyst to be aware of the pitfalls of reifying our conceptual 'maps', in other words the mistake of treating ideas as identical with the territory they aim, transiently, to describe. In practising our art we need to be aware of the two central epistemological principles that the physicist Werner Heisenberg (1958) emphasised in regard to all scientific enquiry. Following Wittgenstein, he stated that we can only use words to describe processes for which we can form pictures (Heisenberg, 1930, p. 10) – in other words, for what can serve the function of analogy. In case we fall prey to the mesmeric potency of words and ideas, Heisenberg went further – he said that we must retain the awareness that how things strike us in our science is not reality itself, but how it appears under our particular method of enquiry into phenomena. This insight from the physicist, that sounds a note of caution about over-objectifying phenomena, is significant in how I conceive of our therapeutic method in its approach to knowing and being in the psychoanalytic situation. It is relevant specifically to that form of understanding for which I am using the language of 'becoming informed by being-with'.

The phenomenological dictum, 'back to the things themselves', *(zurück zu den Sachen selbst!)*, can be a useful reminder of something achievable only as an approximation, because 'the things themselves' are inaccessible directly. They cannot in principle be known, but only 'known of' through a being-with relationship – a relationship of being to knowledge that I am calling 'being informed by being-with'. In order not to be trapped within the concreteness of reification – of taking ideas as things, as Britton's earlier comment reminded us – scientific investigation requires a philosophical perspective in which an awareness of the structure of language is essential. If we do not observe this, we find ourselves asking, for example, what *is* light *really*? Is it ultimately a wave, or is it a particle? Since science does not

---

1 Following the use of this term by the American analyst James Gooch (see later).

deal with reality directly, it *is* neither, and in a sense it is both, and 'it' will no doubt present differently in future, as yet unconceived experiments too.

An important thing to realise about the analogy-function of models is, as has been recognised since at least the sixteenth century,[2] that they refer not to *things* in the world, but to *relationships* – and further, to relationships between relationships (Bateson, 1972, p. 153). Of this, Bion wrote:

> It has to be understood that the importance of the analogy lies not in the two objects which are compared (for example, a breast with a penis), but with the link made between the two. Speaking psychoanalytically, what we are concerned with is the relationship, not the things related. This is close to the view of the pure mathematician who will say that he is dealing with the relationships of objects.
>
> *(Bion, 1990, p. 86)*

Freud too understood the importance of models. In the following quotation from *The Interpretation of Dreams* he suggested that certain steps in thinking about our minds can only be taken with the help of analogies rendered in pictorial terms.

> The mechanics of these processes are quite unknown to me; anyone who wished to take these ideas seriously would have to look for physical analogies to them and find a means of picturing the movements that accompany excitation of neurones.
>
> *(Freud, 1900, p. 599)*

As Heisenberg also clarified, this requirement for analogical models is not limited to what Freud called "unknown mechanics" of mysterious processes. Even processes that are quite well understood will still require pictorially based models for communication between practitioners, and he made the point that such models are not made redundant by mathematical formulations offering relatively high degrees of precision. He added a corollary, an 'uncertainty principle' in the realm of knowledge, concerning the lack of fixity in our *use* of words, even from occasion to occasion, to map the meaning of human emotional experience.

> Any concepts or words which have been formed in the past through the interplay between the world and ourselves are not really sharply defined with respect to their meaning: that is to say, we do not know exactly how far they

---

2 OED: ad. L. analogia, a. Gr. ἀναλογία equality of ratios, proportion (orig. a term of mathematics, but already with transf. sense in Plato), f. ἀνάλογ-ος adj.: see analogon. Cf. mod. Fr. analogie. 1557 Recorde Whetst. C ij, "If any one proportion be continued in more then 2 nombers, there maie be then a conference also of these proportions that conference or comparison is named Analogie".

will help us in finding our way in the world. We often know that they can be applied to a wide range of inner or outer experience, but we practically never know precisely the limits of their applicability.

(Heisenberg, 1958, cited in Tauber, 1997, p. 136)

Applying Heisenberg's insights to the use of language in the analytic situation, we need, with each of our patients, to become accustomed to how – for that unique individual – particular terms have come to mean what they have, through the marking and binding of conjunctions and contrasts that have made sense for *them*. The differences between such verbal signifiers, though they may have the same signs (words) as the ones which we may use, they might indicate for the patient a 'different difference' from that with which we are familiar. Once we begin to be acquainted with how a particular individual tends to use language, it is the 'differences that make a difference' specific to that person to which we become attuned, and increasingly so as we pay more attention to what makes for a discrimination or a similarity in their idiolect[3] than we do in ours. Nevertheless, even when we are forewarned with the preceding arguments about language, Heisenberg's second note on limits of representability is also relevant:

The concepts may, however, be sharply defined with regard to their connections . . . a group of connected concepts may be applicable to a wide field of experience and will help us to find our way in this field. But the limits of the applicability will in general not be known, at least not completely.

(Heisenberg, 1958, p. 92)

It is not only of value to the practitioner to sharpen their awareness of their implicit theory of knowledge in doing their day-to-day work with patients – it is completely indispensable if the aim is to include what I have so far described as the ontological perspective of our patients' experience, in other words, of their relationship to the analyst and to themselves in terms of their being and not only of their knowing. Because this is so, it becomes of the utmost importance to develop a sharpened sense of the *constraints* within which words and concepts can be used effectively, for communication of mood and experience, and where there is a boundary between their articulation and the uncertain formlessness which is a necessary and unavoidable part of the encounter. The study of the underlying nature of language itself – including an awareness of the importance of models, and the function of analogy in clinical thinking – is a worthwhile addition to the resources of the analyst in attempting to recognise the patient's modes of expression of anxiety. The following illustration of some of these principles is taken from a supervision.

3 I discuss idiolects later, in Chapter 10.

Clinical illustration

Mrs L, an artist who had moved to England from a European country partly in order to pursue treatment for her depression, had been in four times weekly analysis for the past five years. Her analyst, normally very capable of waiting patiently for her patient to feel ready to convey her feelings in the session, had, in a particular moment, been felt by her patient to have 'jumped in' a little too swiftly in making an interpretation. The analyst, Dr P, had intuited – perhaps correctly – that her patient felt herself to be disappearing into a void, but when this was offered as an interpretation of that experience, Mrs L said to Dr P that she felt she had not been heard.

Mrs L's mother tongue was not English, and it appeared that this had played a part in how she had experienced the interpretation of her state in that moment. She had indeed experienced herself as disappearing, but her most immediate and acutely felt need had been for signs of her analyst's presence, and it had been precisely this feeling, which may have been close to what Winnicott meant by the infant's sense of 'going-on-being', that had somehow been disrupted by the analyst's particular choice of words, or perhaps even the act of speaking at all. Had speaking itself, particularly in a language not her own, been experienced, *in extremis*, as an unbearable 'gap' for the patient? The session had continued, with Dr P listening to her patient's account of what had just happened between them. Once her analyst was able to hear this fully, the patient said that the words "Be not afear'd" had come to her mind – Caliban's words from Shakespeare's *The Tempest* – and on further exploration her associations to Caliban's predicament could be understood as expressing her own experience of feeling an 'outsider', with no language of her own to make herself understood. It also occurred to Dr P that since her patient was familiar with the play, the rest of Caliban's speech might also have felt salient to this patient, who seemed so often to long for the appearance of a bountiful providing and nurturing breast.

> The clouds methought would open and show riches
> Ready to drop upon me, that when I waked
> I cried to dream again.
> > *(Shakespeare, c.1901,* The Tempest,
> > *Act III, Scene ii)*

The experience was available for reflection by both patient and analyst, leading to an understanding of a profound underlying yearning – the unrequited longing for a breast that would nurture the patient and for an experience of reverie, and this was able to be illustrated most clearly because the feeling of being missed is made more obvious when the analyst uses a different language from the patient's mother tongue. It is in fact the case at times for all patients, even when it is the 'same language', because their unique experiences, like their words, can never be generalised: we should remember that if the language of analysis becomes that of '*l'habitude*', and '*das Man*', it is not 'the same language' any more, even if patient and analyst were both to speak the same tongue. The primordial experiences can, before words are found for them, however, be 'be–ed with' and felt to have been 'touched on' by both parties, as the above vignette illustrates. Openness to this experience is close to what Bion intended by his use of the term maternal reverie.

Betty Joseph, who had worked closely with Bion in clarifying the methodological importance of this particular principle, considered, as Michael Feldman and Elizabeth Bott Spillius have observed,

> that the interpretations that are most likely to lead to psychic change are those that are anchored in the transference and countertransference; that is, in the analytic relationship as it is experienced by patient and analyst.
>
> *("General introduction" to Joseph, 1989, p. 5)*

This basic principle is part of my method, one that I find myself willing to make explicit in my work. I will discuss it as an aspect of the analyst's personal philosophical assumptions regarding knowing and being – a practical epistemology that forms the core of what I have been calling the analytic attitude.

Practical epistemology

Each practitioner holds, explicitly or implicitly, a personal philosophy informing their work, and it is bound to include ideas bearing on the distinction between the realms of knowing and being. I have been suggesting that the practice of analytic work is likely to be deepened if the analyst looks further into their thinking on these matters.

For myself, I follow the first principle that for real contact to be possible between myself and my patient, and for growth and learning in the analytic situation to become based upon it, I need to be open to anxiety in all its forms, and also to the scrutiny of my patient. I accept for this reason, as well as for reasons intrinsic to enquiry itself, that the psychoanalytic relationship is in every case turbulent and conflictual. The pursuit of understanding, as well as bringing relief and deepening curiosity, is also messy, prone to reversals, shadowed by doubt, uncertainty, hopelessness and hidden danger, and in the face of these hazards both analyst and patient need to find the resources necessary to bear the process, often over a long period of time. I find that premature closure, especially finding an 'explanation', is the most commonly sought protection against the anxiety of openness to the unknown and the partially known. It is for these reasons that I have been emphasising the central role of anxiety – the anxiety of being in the world and of being open to finding out who we are in it – and of openness to the experience of being with it (reverie). The epistemology underlying Bion's use of the term negative capability has become a part of my daily work, as has the capacity to use the dramaturgical concept of 'making strange the familiar'. The distinction between the ontological and the ontic, rooted in the phenomenological philosophy of Heidegger, has also become an integral part of my personal epistemology.

It has become an intrinsic part of my working attitude firstly to take anxiety as disclosing what is real in my patients, and to take seriously my own anxiety in the same way, and also to be open in the consulting room to the workings of the dramaturgical and existential dimensions of the experience. I find that it is the characteristics of care, patience and openness that are of most help to me in discovering and bearing truths, and to continue developing a method capable of uncovering what is, and has needed to be, hidden in the lives and the minds of my patients.

The American analyst James Gooch referred to the fundamental attitude of his analyst, Bion, towards the understanding of understanding. It was he who described this attitude as a practical epistemology, a mental characteristic that he had experienced first-hand in the consulting room. He meant the way in which Bion conducted himself in all matters of interpreting and understanding during his time in analysis with him. I include Gooch's perception of his analyst's attitude to knowledge to illustrate this. In an interview at the C. G. Jung Institute of Los Angeles, in 2011,[4] he said:

> One of the things that struck me from the very beginning was Bion's very early on [making] interpretations about my omnipotence, which I had got [for] 2 years of my classical analysis except there was a dramatic difference. And that is, that I do not recall one single incidence in which Bion made that interpretation in which he did not interpret what he *guessed* and always made it clear [that] he couldn't read my mind, he wasn't *telling* me . . . it was his speculation. He would cite the evidence, if there were evidence in the session, but he would often say something like "well, I can't tell from what you said why you would need to be reduced to omnipotence, but my experience is that people are feeling helpless about something when they are in an omnipotent state of mind". Invariably, I would know what I was feeling helpless about even if there weren't evidence in the material of the session. So I found every one of the interpretations scored, whether he could cite the evidence or whether all he could say is "I don't know what it is but I suspect you are feeling helpless about something".
>
> *(Culbert-Koehn, 2011)*

It strikes me as a description of an analyst at work in the mode of being I discussed earlier as Heidegger's 'being-with', the expression of an authentic basic attitude of care in the specialised sense (*Sorge*) of attending to the handling of knowledge in its relationship to the patient's existence.

> I can't tell you how different that experience was. . . . It felt so different; that he [Bion] was really *with me* and tried to help me understand . . . and whatever it was I was feeling helpless about, to grow the capacity to stand that.
>
> *(Culbert-Koehn, 2011)*

---

4 With Dr JoAnn Culbert-Koehn.

Gooch added that Bion had respect for what could be gathered as evidence available to both parties to the encounter. Moreover, he felt that he could discern in Bion's voice, when he did speak, that his analyst was being with his patient, and with himself, in a very real way,[5] albeit that he was still functioning within the bounds of being an analyst.

> I increasingly could feel in the music, and the dance, the cadence . . . the timbre of his voice that he was speaking to me from his heart; that he had to be having an emotional experience himself to be speaking to me that way. So even though he wouldn't tell me what his associations were, it was clear that he was in touch with something within himself that had been evoked by me.
>
> *(Culbert-Koehn, 2011)*

Being receptive to what could impact both analyst and patient in the immediate present of the analytic session was not simply a methodological preference of Bion's, it related to his growing theory (Bion, 1965, p. 48). He came to feel that only experiences that could 'evolve' into the immediacy of the relationship could be made available for psychoanalytic exploration,[6] and that all other interventions tended to effect transformations in the realm of knowledge only: knowledge about knowledge.

In the case of *knowing about knowledge*, the representability effected by such transformations (transformations in K) possesses the allure of being, as Heisenberg put it, based on ideas that appear "sharply defined with regard to their connections". Although we may find these easier to apply in the analytic encounter, and, as Heisenberg says, they may "help us to find our way", they only help us to find our way amongst ideas that are already familiar to us: transformations in K are the basis of the faculty of apperception, which William James defined as to "unite a new perception to a mass of ideas already possessed, thereby to comprehend and interpret it". It was to dissuade us from this everyday, efficient yet generalised kind of observing that Freud (1912a, p. 112) recommended that we "simply listen",[7] without 'listening for'.

Practically speaking, it means we tolerate doing much of our work without an 'anchor', so to speak; we allow ourselves in the analytic situation to be moved around by forces and by dimly perceived dramatis personae, without steadying ourselves, often even surrendering to dizzying uncertainty concerning what, in fact, constitutes 'ourselves' as observers and participants in the drama of the

---

5 And see Bion, 1970, p. 28.

6 Note that this is not a recommendation, nor should it be taken as one, for the analyst to share with the patient, 'intersubjectively', her emotional reactions to them. This was not a part of Bion's method.

7 "'He should withhold all conscious influences from his capacity to attend, and give himself over completely to his "unconscious memory".' Or, to put it purely in terms of technique: 'He should simply listen, and not bother about whether he is keeping anything in mind'" (Freud, 1912a, p. 112). Earlier, in 1909, in his discussion of 'Little Hans', he had described the attitude as: "We will suspend our judgement and give our impartial attention to everything that there is to observe" (1909, p. 23).

evolving and lurching transference, and this turbulence is a consequence of being willing to bear negative capability.

We can appreciate the correspondences between Bion's emphasis, when he reminds us that the patient that we see tomorrow is a patient we have never seen before, and that of Proust when he shows us that, in meeting a friend whom we know, we may not in fact truly be meeting them as they *are*. They both in their distinctive ways highlight that we may be paying more attention to stored images and ideas of the friend than being open to a fresh perception of the real person who is being there, right in front of us. They point to the fact that it is the normal, habitual operation of our own minds that forms the obstacle between us and our patient as a consequence of attention as it normally operates in the everyday world – a function which, as Freud noted (1911, p. 220) , meets phenomena half-way.

As Proust expressed it, "In the end . . . each time we see the face or hear the voice it is our own ideas of him which we recognize and to which we listen", and, as Freud reminded us, our ordinary listening tends to be a 'listening out for', in which our anticipation and our preferences play a large part.

> This, however, is precisely what must not be done. In making the selection, if he follows his expectations he is in danger of never finding anything but what he already knows; and if he follows his inclinations he will certainly falsify what he may perceive. It must not be forgotten that the things one hears are for the most part things whose meaning is only recognized later on.
> *(Freud, 1912a, p. 112)*

There are two aspects here, in this passage of Freud's, of relevance to our psycho-analytic attitude if we are to be with the real patient in the immediate present, and for our interpretations, when we formulate them, to take proper account of *this* patient, in this moment, not a generic one, and not a previous image of him, or a wished-for version of him. The first I have dealt with already at length, and in different but complementary forms of language – it consists of becoming aware of, and then suspending – as far as is humanly possible – the influence of expectations and inclinations, of *l'habitude* and its everyday mentality, of memory and desire, to some extent even the act of categorising. The second component is cultivating the capacity for *waiting* – which Freud understood as listening without knowing. Simply listen, he said, though this is far from simple.

Short illustration: listening anew

Mrs H, who had been in psychotherapy for two years, was a young woman who for as long as she could remember had found it difficult to have her own voice heard. One day she shared with her therapist, Mrs C, that before beginning her therapy she had never felt listened to, and that she had realised recently that she herself never really listened to others. Instead, she understood, she anticipated what they might say in order that she might think of a response to have ready. This had the effect that she was never truly able to relate to the experience of the other, isolating her and increasing her social anxiety. She arrived to one session with some genuine excitement, having found herself being truly available to her son as he spoke to her of his problems in relating to his girlfriend. Rather than anticipating the 'required reaction' she felt that she had been available to listen to him and to communicate her care in doing so. They had, she said, shared an encounter that had been richer, and had made them feel closer than she could recall. In this she demonstrated how, having internalised something of the relationship between herself and her therapist, she could draw upon this new configuration of being in the world.

Simply listening is as uncommon in our daily lives as simply sitting, or just waiting, and in my experience it is not a simple matter even in a fifty-minute hour. Nevertheless, it is in my view a valuable element of the analytic attitude to regard all spoken interventions as just that – interventions. What are they interventions *into*? The short answer is that when I make an intervention, I am stepping into *silence*. On the whole, I tend not to intervene when the pattern of communication in the encounter seems to be emerging without any resonance, or 'echo' of the real person, or when a pause occurs in which there is the sense that I may, by invitation or otherwise, be stepping into a required role. I feel it is especially important not to intervene simply to 'sound like' an analyst (see later). Excessive silence is unnatural and is generally counter-productive in analysis, but the kind of quietness that I am describing is necessary to 'catch the drift' of communication that is unconscious, of opaque states of mind and states of being, one's own and those of the patient.

A note on the analyst's feeling for silence

> "But doctor, can't you do anything?" – I remember being asked – "Don't you do anything besides talk?"; and I said, "Yes, we are also silent". There is a place, even in ordinary speech, for silence.
>
> *(Bion, 1976)*

The philosopher Ivan Illich, in an essay, "The eloquence of silence", quoted Baltasar Gracián, who wrote that "silence is frequently misinterpreted but it is never misquoted". He spoke of the varieties of silence in his address to prospective missionaries learning Spanish:

> Words and sentences are composed of silences more meaningful than the sounds. The pregnant pauses between sounds and utterances become luminous points in an incredible void.
>
> *(Illich, 1956, p. 41)*

Illich believed that using a language in a humane and mature way meant to shoulder personal responsibility for its silences as well as for its sounds. He wrote of the "gift of the rhythm, the mode, and the subtleties of its system of silences", as well as its co-ordination of sounds. He considered also that some people have a special gift for learning the silences of others, noting that some missionaries, for whom his essay was first written, "never come to speak properly, to communicate delicately through silences. Although they 'speak with the accents of natives' they remain forever thousands of miles away." The relevance of Illich's words to our field requires no clarification. Silences must be acquired, suggested Illich, 'through a delicate openness to them', their pauses and hesitations, their rhythm, expressions and inflections; "their durations and pitches, and times to be and not to be".

> First among the classification of silence is the silence of the pure listener, the silence of deep interest. This is threatened by another silence – the silence of disinterest and indifference.
>
> The silence of patience is when you listen quietly to the sickness report of the elderly or the injured. The silence of love is when the involved are exploring possibilities of togetherness, albeit through mere visual locks. This form is emphasised further when in company of others.
>
> In the silence of prayer courageous words of request begin hesitatingly but progress steadily. The silence of obedience is beyond bewilderment and questions; it is a silence beyond the possibility of an answer. The silence of triumph bears the smug heaviness of "I told you so".
>
> *(Illich, 1956)*

To these varieties of silence, Illich added the silence of apprehension, such as we might feel while awaiting a verdict, and one final, terrible one: "The deadly silence has neither the deadness of a stone, indifferent to life, nor the deadness of a pressed flower, memory of life. It is the death after life, a final refusal to live". Distinct from the deadly silence, Illich understood a silence of finality – "one which has said everything because there is nothing more to say, a silence beyond a final 'yes' or a final 'no'". Wittgenstein's last proposition in his *Tractatus* is of such a kind: "Whereof we cannot speak, thereof we must be silent".

If as analysts we "speak with the accents of natives" but remain "forever thousands of miles away", we will introduce into the relationship a discernible lack of resonance and depth in what, from an existential perspective, I have been calling the being-with relationship. This can come about not only through the patient's unconsciously or consciously driven *mauvaise foi*, which I discuss at length later in this chapter, but also that stemming from a particular attitude in the analyst, which I will now discuss, whose determination to be 'seen-as understanding' and to be 'seen-as knowing' the patient, may sometimes conceal his unconscious desire *not* to be with the reality of the patient, and himself.

Vignette: reading silences

Mr N, a technology consultant, had been in analysis for three years. He was successful in business, was an active sportsman, but close relationships never seemed to last more than a few months. Although he filled his time in various social groups, mostly revolving around sport, both participating and spectating, and was generally gregarious, I could tell that he was a lonely man. His relationship with me was the only one in which he spoke at all personally to anybody, but he seemed to have to act as though this was not the case, and that his life satisfied him fully. He began his Tuesday session in a lethargic and dispirited mood. It seemed that he had become demoralised overnight since seeing me the day before. He began several times to speak, but each time he gave up and 'petered out', saying eventually, "I don't know what to say". He said that whatever he tries to do, it is not enough. He shrugged and was silent. When, after a lengthy silence, he spoke again, it was to suggest that something I had said to him had led him to say to himself, "What is the point of trying, if all he does is complain about what I am not doing?" I recalled that the previous day he had, following an especially full and active weekend, given me a list of the activities that gave him pleasure and a sense of purpose, but he had been left with a sense of 'something missing', in spite of his attempts to 'talk up' his satisfaction with his activities, both on Sunday night, to himself, and on the Monday morning to me. I had interpreted that in spite of all the good things he told us about, he nevertheless seemed to feel that he lacked something important in his life. Even after all that he had told me, I felt that he had not been able to get away from the realisation that he had unmet needs. I interpreted that my words might have felt to him, either at the time or later, as an inner accusation that he was inadequate and worthless.

To feel supported in trying to make changes, in the moments in which it was actually his own feeling that this was necessary, my patient did need to feel the presence of an inner helper, someone who accepted him as he was and yet would assist him to develop along his own lines. Lacking this, and so far having felt unable to internalise his analyst, all he had to go on was a critical and carping figure, founded on his experience of his mother, which seemed both to complain that his life was sadly lacking while at the same time providing nothing whatsoever to galvanise him. To him it felt that his object preferred him to remain stuck, so that it could never have a shortage of complaints and criticisms.

We gained a degree of freedom from this object in the session, and a measure of thinking, when I put to him that he felt trapped by being unable to feel he had any alternative source of information concerning himself than this unfriendly character, which I also seemed to have become. Mr N said he needed to feel somehow that I was more powerful than his bad object, but on reflection he reconsidered the term 'powerful'. It should, he said, come about that he would turn to me, or something of me in his mind, as somehow more influential. Influence seemed a more promising direction for him in that moment than power. The problem, however, was that he felt me to be a helpful person for him when I was physically present, but in my absence in his outer world I was absent from the inner, and this, in turn, stemmed from his fundamental uncertainty as to whether I retained anything at all of him while he was away from me. This was a difficulty, and a doubt in relation to his objects, of long standing, ever since he was a baby. It helped to be able to put it into words today, and after a very lengthy silence Mr N said, simply, "I understand this". After another silence he said to me, "I don't know what to say".

It was the particular quality of the silence, and then his six words – the same six words with which he had begun his session – that enabled me to say to him that it was not the same 'not knowing what to say', at the end, as at the beginning. He replied that he felt that I had understood this, because I had taken him in, and therefore had read his silence, and understood him – at least on this occasion. The session ended at this point, following which I found myself listening, as it were, to my own silence as I sat there after Mr N had left. I was alone, and I was able to 'hear' my own feeling at my understanding being acknowledged by my patient. I realised then, in hindsight (or more to the point, 'hind-hearing'), a new aspect of the situation, namely that if his silence at not knowing what to say at the start of the session had *not* been distinguished from that at its close, he would have been left vulnerable to his know-it-all inner object saying, quietly into his ear, "see, it ends as it begins, and you still have nothing interesting to say".

Being, acting-like, and being-for-others

The distinction between knowing about psychoanalysis and living an analytic relationship applies to the analyst and patient equally. James Gooch felt the distinction to be at the core of his analyst's psychoanalytic attitude. Bion had asked him whether he was emphasising the importance of appearing like a father, or of actually *being* one. It seems that Gooch had been woken up to the difference articulated by his analyst.

Earlier I discussed the ideas of Proust and Heidegger concerning the habit of 'behaving like a father', or 'behaving like an analyst' – a practice articulated by the respective concepts of those writers, *l'habitude* and *das Man*. The latter, Heidegger's mode of 'the everyday', is reflected prototypically in the phrase, 'to be a father (for instance) *one* behaves *like this*'.

The ontological question asked of Gooch reminds us of Sartre's illustration of his concept of *mauvaise foi* (bad faith), as expressed in the following passage:

> But what are we then if we have the constant obligation to make ourselves what we are, if our mode of being is having the obligation to be what we are? Let us consider this waiter in the cafe. His movement is quick and forward, a little too precise, a little too rapid. He comes toward the patrons with a step a little too quick. He bends forward a little too eagerly; his voice, his eyes express an interest a little too solicitous for the order of the customer. Finally there he returns, trying to imitate in his walk the inflexible stiffness of some kind of automaton while carrying his tray with the recklessness of a tight-rope-walker by putting it in a perpetually unstable, perpetually broken equilibrium which he perpetually re-establishes by a light movement of the arm and hand. All his behaviour seems to us a game. He applies himself to chaining his movements as if they were mechanisms, the one regulating the other; his gestures and even his voice seem to be

mechanisms; he gives himself the quickness and pitiless rapidity of things. He is playing, he is amusing himself. But what is he playing? We need not watch long before we can explain it: he is playing at being a waiter in a cafe. There is nothing there to surprise us.

(Sartre, 2013 [1943], p. 82)

Sartre's writing captures beautifully the performance of the imitation, and it is a description in which we can all recognise something of ourselves. The passage uses hyperbole and repetition to great effect with no less than seven instances of 'a little too muchness' in the waiter's actions. The excess of the performance draws our attention to the intended synthetic quality that we are meant to experience as 'waiterliness', the very model and essence of the assumed fixed identity. *There is nothing,* as Sartre says, *to surprise us.* If the mask slipped, then there would of course be something to surprise us. We would perceive in that moment a real person hiding within a practised role. The actor-waiter might, should his own real and individual love (and hate, and knowledge) of his work, and his own contradictions and idiosyncrasies become visible, feel such a slip as a *falling* (out of role) and a failing (to play the part); the patient in analysis in a comparable moment could experience directly, and with immediacy, a truthful contact with what is real, whether jarring, threatening, discordant or in tune with his idea of himself. So, I would add, might the analyst.

It was particularly in this sense that Bion was concerned with truth, a psychoanalytic conception of truth, recognising that the absolute truth of anything – what Heidegger referred to as 'objective presence' – was unreachable directly. Nevertheless, accepting that constraint, which is the gulf between knowing and being, Bion retained the notion of the truth of an emotional experience as central to his work. In a talk given in São Paulo in April 1978, he said:

Although it may seem theoretical, or even philosophical, I find it easier to fall back on the feeling that I am called upon to make the person familiar with a particular aspect of truth.

(Bion, 1980, p. 126; 2014, vol. 8, p. 375)

He felt that for all practical purposes most people would know what he meant when he said that

one becomes part of a distinguished company of scientists, painters, musicians and other artists; they are all attempting to display some aspect of the truth. I say 'all'; I mean all those who belong to the distinguished company. Imitation musicians, imitation painters and scientists there are in plenty. There is something unsatisfactory about the imitation, and if it is unsatisfactory to oneself it doesn't require a great deal of imagination to suppose that it would be unsatisfactory to a patient who is in a desperate situation.

(Bion, 1980, p. 126)

Helene Deutsch (1942, p. 303) gave an example of a young woman patient, impressions of whom were described to her by another of her patients, a man who had met the woman at a social event. The man had found the young woman interesting and stimulating, and superficially attractive, but he had intuited that there was something wrong with her, even though he had been unable to find evidence for this. The young woman had struck Deutsch herself as being almost, but not quite, real. In spite of appearing quite compelling as a personality, her observation too was that something indefinable was awry, and she too had felt unsettled in her company. Moreover, the young woman produced art which had a peculiarly *imitative* quality:

> the drawings showed much skill and talent but there was also something disturbing in them . . . her teacher had been impressed by the speed with which she had adopted his technique and manner of artistic perception, but, he had frankly to admit, there was an intangible something about her which he had never before encountered, and he ended with the usual question, 'What is wrong?' He added that the girl had gone to another teacher, who used a quite different teaching approach, and that she had oriented herself to the new theory and technique with striking ease and speed.
>
> The first impression these people make is of complete normality. They are intellectually intact, gifted, and bring great understanding to intellectual and emotional problems; but when they pursue their not infrequent impulses to creative work they construct, in form, a good piece of work but it is always a spasmodic, if skilled, repetition of a prototype without the slightest trace of originality. On closer observation, the same thing is seen in their affective relationships to the environment. These relationships are usually intense and bear all the earmarks of friendship, love, sympathy, and understanding; but even the layman soon perceives something strange and raises the question he cannot answer. To the analyst it is soon clear that all these relationships are devoid of any trace of warmth, that all the expressions of emotion are formal, that all inner experience is completely excluded. It is like the performance of an actor who is technically well trained but who lacks the necessary spark to make his impersonations true to life. Thus the essential characteristic of the person I wish to describe is that outwardly he conducts his life as if he possessed a complete and sensitive emotional capacity.
>
> *(Deutsch, 1942, p. 303)*

We are left with an impression of the difference, in the realm of being, between the adaptation to the look of others, the performance of the self that is *mauvaise foi*, which as the description above shows can be very skilful. When it is so, the imitation may fool some of the people most of the time, or even all the people some of the time, and yet it lacks the spark of real life that animates the being of what Sartre calls the 'being-for-oneself'.

Perhaps, in such situations, it is the way in which the personality is contained by the performance, and that the imitative performance is contained by its surrounding personality, that leads to the lack of emotional depth and 'resonance' in the way that it is carried out. From a psychoanalytic perspective, the projective process may play a decisive role not only in generating the act, but also in 'priming' the other to receive it, in just such a way as to mesmerise them into accepting it, an effect discussed by Bion in his early studies of groups:

> Now the experience of counter-transference appears to me to have quite a distinct quality that should enable the analyst to differentiate the occasion when he is the object of a projective identification from the occasion when he is not. The analyst feels he is being manipulated so as to be playing a part, no matter how difficult to recognize, in somebody else's phantasy – or he would do if it were not for what in recollection I can only call a temporary loss of insight, a sense of experiencing strong feelings and at the same time a belief that their existence is quite adequately justified by the objective situation without recourse to recondite explanation of their causation. From the analyst's point of view, the experience consists of two closely related phases: in the first there is a feeling that whatever else one has done, one has certainly not given a correct interpretation; in the second there is a sense of being a particular kind of person in a particular emotional situation. I believe ability to shake oneself out of the numbing feeling of reality that is a concomitant of this state is the prime requisite of the analyst.
>
> *(Bion, 1961b, p. 148)*

Bion's way of referring to the aspect of depth was to refer to the two-dimensionality of a *trompe l'oeil* painting, one whose main effect functions by, so to speak, realising its own preconception to give a counterfeit conception of three-dimensionality, a deception of depth:

> The truth. What does it look like? Who wants to be confronted with a *trompe l'oeil* representation of Paradise? Such confections are pardonable to an agent selling us our earthly home, but not for our eternal home – our Self.
>
> *(Bion, 1980, p. 126)*

Enacting the two-dimensional picture of the 'pseudo-essence' of a waiter-persona falls a long way short of being real. Insofar as we are able to wait, in evenly suspended attention, and to hold back from falling for a 'waiterly' presentation of the other, or of oneself, a pattern can emerge – one that is suited to 'catching the drift' of the real patient in relation to a real analyst. In São Paulo in 1978 Bion spoke of his experience of the moment in which, as I would put it, the being of the patient evolved into an experience of the analyst's *becoming informed* of him:

part of the progress from O – when you know nothing whatever about the patient – and one tenth or one hundredth of a second later when you begin to have an idea of who or what has entered your consulting room. A minute later the shadowy impression might become more solid, 'three-dimensional'.

(1980, p. 127)

If, through excessive anxiety, in our role or for any other reason, we interpret before having 'caught the drift' of the patient's being, we do so without being informed by what Illich understands as the "rhythm, the mode, and the subtle-ties" of their silence. Though *we* may interpret with the "right accent", we too are likely to be many miles away from them. Sometimes when we do this, and most practitioners stray into this tendency at times, the subsequent associations of the patient may contain unconscious traces of having spotted that we have taken a short cut to understanding them, often with a cryptic reference to the 'waiterliness' of our behaviour.

Clinical illustration

The patient, Mr C, a university lecturer in the second year of his four times a week analysis, reported to his analyst, Dr L, in a monotonous and 'dutiful' voice his thoughts from the previous day. Analytic sessions in which dream material was brought held a special dread for this man, and accordingly, anything relating to a dream that felt real, fresh and 'of him' tended to be recycled the next day devoid of living spark. What had the previous day been a vivid dream about a cat roaming freely amongst pigeons, with all the scope for mayhem suggested by that scene, was brought back today as 'deliberations on the analysis', with a reference to "that pigeon thing I remember telling you about". The adjunct 'thing' was used habitu-ally by this patient to make routine the potentially dangerous uniqueness of any experience, a habit with which the analyst was familiar. In the session discussed in supervision it was also apparent how the patient used the limiting word 'just', and the tag 'really' together to engender a similar dulling of the sense of the reality of the utterance as a whole. "I was just thinking about that pigeon thing again really".

After speaking of the 'pigeon and cat thing', there followed a long, generalised rehashing of the dream, peppered with some psychoanalytic jargon, together with recollections of some of the previous day's interpretations. There was little or no discernible anxiety, and no emotional resonance. The analyst was left troubled by her awareness that she could find nothing to say.

The patient said that he had "had another think about the cat and pigeons thing. Perhaps some idea of a sort of disaster about to happen, but it didn't". "Perhaps it was about dependency really", he added. Dr L did not at the time hear the fleeting reference to an impending disaster. In its surrounding context it did not stand out for her. Feeling her mind to have been dulled, Dr L felt that she had to say something, to remain awake perhaps, or to make some sort of impact on her patient. She found herself making what later seemed to her a generic and uninspired interpretation, to the effect that Mr C felt dependent upon her and anxious about the forthcoming weekend separation, that perhaps the little pigeon was having to go unfed. Mr C's nods and sounds of agreement felt similarly routine, and unconvincing. The truth, on the other hand, could have risked putting the cat amongst the analyst's pigeons. As it was, they all took off and she was unable, in that moment, to stay with him. If this was so, the hackneyed and generic remarks of analyst and patient could be understood as a jointly mounted defensive barrier against something frightening to both, a phenomenon that I will discuss later under Bion's concept of 'column 2' statements. The basic principle at work is that by making a routine interpretation, both members of the analytic couple are kept away from what Klein termed the 'point of urgency' in the session, and from what Strachey called a mutative interpretation – one conducive to promoting a psychic change.

At the end of the session reported, Mr C told his analyst that he had been helping his daughter with revision for her school examinations before coming to his session, but that they had both become stuck when they did not understand a question. When Dr L interpreted that they had both become stuck in the analysis, Mr C replied, "The text book had all the answers in the back." I think this extract shows a kind of experience that arises frequently in an analysis, in which both participants are anxious about a more direct contact, feeling it to be dangerous. It is at times like this that we tend to reach for the relative safety of ready-to-hand 'textbook interpretations', something that this patient seemed, unconsciously, to perceive.

I will revisit this issue in the closing chapters when I discuss the difficulty for the analyst in being with the patient, and how James Strachey considered the sense of imminent danger as an adverse influence on the analyst in being on the verge of making an interpretation likely to precipitate change. Such observations are, in fact, an uncomfortable reminder of just how much of our time is spent in the everyday attitude, and in an unconscious attitude of shielding ourselves against incipient anxiety. It requires a particular mental discipline, involving some strain, to remain aware of the insights of Freud, of Bion, and of Heraclitus, who – as Feldman (2009, p. 233) reminds us – wrote that "no man ever steps into the same river twice, for it is not the same river and it is not the same man". Genuine discovery of the real patient in analysis depends upon the analyst being able, at least for some of the time, to retain such an attitude of mind. Feldman used the dictum of Heraclitus in describing the difficulty experienced by analysts as they move between staying with the 'flow' of the evolving session and taking a moment for reflection on that process. It is important to realise that the kind of practical epistemology being explored in this chapter prioritises formulations based not primarily upon the faculty of apperception and recognition, but on clinical intuition.

A note on intuition

Concerning intuition, Immanuel Kant implied the existence of an intuitively available version of what, eventually, would become summated and unified by what he called 'the synthesis of the understanding'. His concept of the 'manifold', described by Bertrand Russell in his introductory pages to Wittgenstein's *Tractatus* (1921, p. xii), suggests something that might form the grounds of our faculty of intuition, a nascent unity of sorts, prior to perception proper. One interpretation of Kant's idea of the manifold is that it refers to the very first intimations of the presence of invariant features, of constantly conjoined elements in a pattern, before the mind has yet had time to form a construct – an overall idea of the meaning of the pattern in terms of its pre-existing categories. Kant referred to a 'sum of particulars' existing before they became constituted as a 'synthesis of understanding'. I am suggesting that Kant's idea helps us consider the difference between *awareness* and *sensibility*. If this is right, that these ideas have some affinity for psychoanalysis, we would expect such a 'partial unity', a manifold, to be only dimly perceptible, if at all – unless, that is, there was some reason to create conditions favouring intuition over normal perception.

Before what Kant calls the synthesis of understanding, which can be very rapid, analysts may, if they explore Bion's procedure of suspending aspects of memory and desire, set aside for a while the main functions which in the everyday world make for speed and efficiency of processing material from the senses, and instead slow down to allow a more receptive and uncertain openness to prevail – a sensibility not only to the unconscious but also to the presence of hidden ontological anxieties. Proceeding in this way allows us to let the impressions of the patient strike us in their own way, unobstructed as far as humanly possible by our own categorising processes. Methodologically this amounts to a call for slowness as well as openness. The combination allows more of a feel for all the 'chords', as it were, that are happening at the same time – the 'synchronic' (or the paradigmatic) dimension, which contains elements likely to go undetected if the quicker type of attention is placed along the time dimension, in which cause and effect and narrative become the driving forces. This is what could be called the 'diachronic' (syntagmatic) dimension, by analogy to linguistics. Feldman quotes Bion to make this latter point in his own way.

> Bion suggests that if, by steadily excluding 'memory and desire', the analyst does become more receptive to the patient's communications, he will find in the patient, in any given session, an 'increased number and variety of moods, ideas and attitudes'.
>
> *(2003, in Feldman, 2009, p. 74)*

This is an important comment by Feldman, particularly in view of the significance I gave earlier to mood, as it appears in the existential-phenomenological perspective of Heidegger. It will be recalled that, from that perspective, it is mood – particularly the mood of anxiety – that discloses being, and it is receptivity to mood (reverie) that permits what Bion calls transformations in O. This is the point of intersection of the being of the patient with the openness of the analyst to becoming informed by that experience of being-with. I now turn to the difference between mental growth and the accumulation of self-knowledge.

It is important to remember that accumulation of self-knowledge is *not* synonymous with psychic growth. For a hermeneutic method to promote growth, it requires a spirit of exploration that effects the transition from K (which is knowing about phenomena of the self) to 'becoming' or 'being' that self. Bion's project in the last decade of his life was to explore how to use openness and interpretation to effect this change, to promote interpretive work of a kind suited to helping the "transition from knowing the phenomena of the real self to being the real self". In suggesting this extended potential of the psychoanalytic method, Bion was aware of the received wisdom, which was that such change took place, if at all, outside the parameters of the analysis itself.

> If I am right in suggesting that phenomena are known but reality is 'become' the interpretation must do more than increase knowledge. It can be argued that this is not a matter for the analyst and that he can only increase knowledge; that the further steps required to bridge the gap must come from the analysand; or from a particular part of the analysand.
>
> *(Bion, 1965a, p. 148)*

Around the time that Bion was including being and becoming in his analytic attitude, in the mid-1960s, a marked divergence appeared between the psychoanalytic and the existential approaches to therapy. The ideas of Sartre in particular were taken up by existential therapists in a way that opposed the concept of transference and denied the existence of the dynamic unconscious in mental life, and partly in response to this psychoanalytic writers and practitioners separated themselves from the existentialists. It was a false division based largely upon a mixture of prejudice and a misunderstanding of the complexities existing in psychoanalysis and existential philosophy. There is in fact a form of the unconscious accepted by Sartre, and consistent with but not identical to the axioms of psychoanalysis, but it is not often acknowledged by existential therapists in the UK.

One approach to psychotherapy, developed by Holzhey-Kunz in Zurich, avoided this polarisation and enabled the investigation of states of being as well as states of mind. As I illustrate in the next chapter, the daseinsanalytic method as practised by the Swiss analyst Holzhey-Kunz and her group is unique in bringing together, in the same method, psychoanalysis and the philosophical sensibility for the existential modes of being described by Sartre and Heidegger.

In the next chapter I will consider the relevance for clinical practice of differentiating between *knowing* and *becoming informed*, in order to think about how this distinction can orient us to the point of contact between the separate realms of knowing and being in the psychoanalytic experience. The aim will be to explore possibilities for interpretive activity that opens the way to ontological anxiety and experience.

10

BECOMING INFORMED FROM BEING (O → K)

You must be able to think back to streets in unknown neighbourhoods, to unexpected encounters, and to partings you had long seen coming; to days of childhood whose mystery is still unexplained, to parents whom you had to hurt when they brought in a joy and you didn't pick it up (it was a joy meant for somebody else); to childhood ill-nesses that began so strangely with so many profound and difficult transformations, to days in quiet restrained rooms and to mornings by the sea, to the sea itself, to seas, but it is still not enough to be able to think of all that.

You must have memories. . . . But you must also have been beside the dying, must have sat beside the dead in the room with the open windows and the scattered noises.

And it is not yet enough to have memories. You must be able to forget them when they are many, and you must have the immense patience to wait until they return. For the memories themselves are not important. Only when they have changed into our very blood, into glance and gesture, and are nameless, no longer to be distinguished from ourselves – only then can it happen that in some very rare hour the first word of a poem arises in their midst and goes forth from them.

(Rilke, 1989, p. 91)

These lines from Rilke indicate clearly the difference between knowing and being informed through being. The distinction forms the basis of this chapter. I will be asking the following questions: What are the implications for therapeutic practice of the ideas developed over the course of the book? How can the way of listening that is specific to psychoanalysis, and the formulations and interpretive activity that follow, be extended in such a way that we are informed sufficiently of the being of the patient before offering an understanding? So far, in beginning to address these questions I have been developing the idea, central to the daseinsanalytic approach of

Holzhey-Kunz, of an ontological philosophical perspective as a valuable inclusion in our analytic attitude. Holzhey-Kunz came to this realisation through combining a Freudian psychoanalytic approach with the insights of Heidegger and Sartre, not only to address the being of the patient, but also to take fully into account *the inherently philosophical nature of their strivings to understand,* which is the philosophical counterpart to Britton's insight into the function of models, with which I began the previous chapter—that in the domain of K they not only pertain to our investigations *into* the mind, they seem also to be an intrinsic part of the functioning *of* the mind. The inclusion of the ontological into psychoanalysis shows this also to be true of what we could call the psyche's philosophical function.

The inclusion of a philosophical dimension into psychoanalysis has been discussed too by Britton (1998, p.2) in his investigations into the mind's *belief-function.* He suggests that what he calls 'incursions' into philosophy may arise not solely from the personal inclinations of the analyst but because psychoanalysis "necessarily finds itself exploring the areas of mental life that have been the concern of philosophers, theologians and poets". He quotes Bion (1967a, p. 152), who wrote that "The psychoanalyst's experience of philosophical issues is so real that he often has a clearer grasp of the necessity for a philosophical background than the professional philosopher". Bion noted that relationships between the implicit philosophical perspective of the analyst and the findings of formal academic philosophers had sometimes approached contact with one another, but most often that it was without full recognition. Without quite recognising it himself, Bion had, in a 1973 discussion of some of his early clinical work, come close to making an explicit link between a patient's anxiety about the existence of holes and gaps, and a philosophical anxiety belonging to the human condition.

Everything is full of holes: a case of neurosis or a disabling philosophical sensitivity?

Because Holzhey-Kunz had developed a method giving priority to the ontological anxiety of her patients she was able to recognise that Bion, in one of his clinical accounts, had come close to recognising the existential significance of his patient's special sensitivity. Such a sensitivity, if not recognised in its existential perspective, can lead to an exclusive preoccupation with concepts of psychopathology, which had in fact been a feature of Bion's original formulation, as well as those of Freud and his Viennese colleagues, who, as we will see later, had also described similar instances of the dread of holes.

Bion's clinical example, of great interest to Holzhey-Kunz because of its clear relevance to psychoanalysis under a philosophical perspective, concerned a man

---

1 Published subsequently in 1954 as "Notes on the theory of schizophrenia", *International Journal of Psycho-Analysis*, 35: 113–18.

who felt intensely persecuted by the awareness that his socks were made up more of holes than material. Bion had first introduced the clinical description in a paper[1] presented at the IPA Congress in London, in the summer of 1953. As we will see, he revisited it almost exactly twenty years later, in a talk given in São Paulo (Bion, 1990, p. 21) with new understanding and from an entirely different perspective. It was that description that Holzhey-Kunz had recognised as the point at which Bion had come much closer to an understanding of the ontological source of anxiety than had Freud, *in relation to a similar set of ontic fears.*

Bion's patient had suffered an extraordinary and disabling dread stemming from the observation that his socks consisted of a series of holes knitted together. His original formulation, along the Kleinian lines of interpretation that he and his immediate colleagues[2] were exploring, was that his patient suffered from excessive splitting processes robbing him of the capacity for verbal thought and leaving him at the mercy of severe primordial anxiety. This anxiety, thought Bion, found representation in unconscious phantasy life, as the horror that he had, in his mind, torn out both his own penis and that of his analyst, leaving no possibility for a 'breast' relationship to his analysis. This, suggested Bion, left him feeling that no interesting food for thought could arise, but all that remained was a concrete physical scene, and a sense of a physical hole and a sock but no meaningful symbolic relation, either on the plane of feeding or of creative intercourse.

Bion reported that in 1915 Freud had described three comparable cases (1915, p. 200). One was one of Freud's own patients, another was mentioned to Freud by a colleague, Viktor Tausk, and the third was a case treated by Rudolf Reitler. In each case a dread of holes was the common feature. Freud and the other Viennese analysts had focused on specific phantasies based on somatic and sexual aspects – Tausk's patient appeared to have held the phantasy that every hole was equated with the vaginal aperture and Reitler's had, it seemed, made a concrete equation[3] between the sock and the penis, such that taking it off and putting it on reproduced in his mind the consummated sense of masturbatory action.

Bion's earlier account of his patient, presented at a conference in London in 1953, placed the emphasis on the psychopathological state of the patient, but when he revisited the matter twenty years later, he illustrated his revised perspective by inviting his audience, as a 'thought experiment' to contemplate a tennis match played at dusk in which the diminishing illumination made possible a perspective on the net alone. His description has the effect not only of reminding us of Freud's comments on the value of analytic 'night vision', "to behold like the eye of the burrowing mole", as he states in verse in a letter to a childhood friend,[4] but also the

2 Herbert Rosenfeld, Hanna Segal, and Klein herself.
3 See Segal, 1957, p. 393 on such 'symbolic equations'. And, same author, 1978, p. 316: "A part of the ego becomes identified with the subject and as a consequence, the symbol is equated with the thing symbolized. The symbol does not represent the object, but is treated as though it was the object".
4 "Epithalamium by a Homerian of the Academía Española", letter from Sigmund Freud to Eduard Silberstein, 2 October 1875 (Boehlich, 1992, p. 137).

Verfremdungseffekt of Brecht, the creative possibilities released by 'making strange the familiar', potentials for exploration made possible by that perceptual shift.

Bion's mental exercise was a marriage of both principles that enabled his listeners to set aside their normal perspective to enable them to shift to a *similar position to that of the specially sensitive patient* in a startlingly non-pathologising way. It was an exercise that originated from, and exemplified, a philosophical perspective on clinical phenomena. Here are his instructions to his audience, given in a manner that reminds us of Freud's references to dark-adapted vision:

> We dim the intellectual illumination and light, forgetting imagination or phantasy or any once-conscious activities; first we lose sight of the players, and then we gradually increase the darkness until only the net itself is visible.
>
> *(Bion, 1990, p. 21, Lecture 3, São Paulo)*

What was it that Bion felt his imaginary twilight tennis could help his audience to discern concerning the suffering patient? He suggested to his colleagues that if we can bear to abandon our 'normal' position, and become oriented, like the patient, to experience the collection of holes at dusk, we can come closer to their unique experience and being, which may be a special sensitivity to realities from which the analyst is shielded:

> it is possible to see that the only important thing visible to us is a lot of holes which are collected together in a net. Similarly, we might look at a pair of socks and be able to see a mass of holes which have been knitted together. Freud described something of this kind, but said that the patient had a phobia which made it impossible for him to wear socks. I suggest that the patient did not have a phobia of socks but could see that what Freud thought were socks were a lot of holes knitted together. If this is correct, terms like 'phobia' in classical analysis do not do justice to the facts, and in particular do not do justice to the extreme capacity for observation which is natural to some patients . . . this kind of patient has a visual capacity[5] which is different, making him able to see what I cannot see. What I think, with the light of my intelligence, brains, knowledge, experience, is a pair of socks, he can see is not. We should reconsider this domain of thought, because as psychoanalysts we must be able to see that it is a pair of socks, or a game of tennis, and at the same time

---

5 Following the thinking in this book, I would maintain that the *visual* analogy used here by Bion is misleading despite being convenient. Instead I favour strongly Holzhey-Kunz's way of describing the special sensitivity, such as the one described here by Bion, as the patient's *Hellhörigkeit*, a term closer to the auditory than the visual, with its etymology of 'clairaudience'. Ultimately I would argue for the special sensitivity to be considered apart from *any* directly sensuous channel, instead 'locating' it in the non-senuous intuitive contact with the relations not so much 'representing' the ontological as 'making it present'.

to be able to turn down the light, turn off the brilliant intuition, and see these holes, including the fact that they are knitted, or netted together.

(Bion, 1990, p. 21)

This exercise, with its affinity to the principles of negative capability, the suspension of memory, desire and (apperceptive) understanding, and Brecht's 'making strange the familiar', was the precondition and the preparation for an 'intersection' between the different worlds of the patient and the analyst – for suspending what is known and making contact with the being of the patient, in which what the patient was in touch with, the analyst was not. It possesses a third, and more concealed element. The exercise draws our attention to the special sensitivity of the patient, and to the need for the analyst to be similarly attuned, to the presence of what is not. The patient is highly attuned to absence, and is painfully aware of what is *not*, when we are more likely to perceive what *is*. The full expression of the characteristic of negative capability is openness to the perspective of lack and absence, irrespective of the disturbance caused by the sensory deprivation associated with that state of mind. This state I discussed in the opening chapter of the book as the apophatic method of contemplation – understanding obtained by way of absent properties, in the absence of evidence from the senses.

The idea is not to abandon for ever our "intelligence, brains, knowledge, experience", as Bion put it, but we do need to be prepared to do so for a while in the session, in the service of not only 'seeing the patient who is seeing the holes', but to be fully with him in experiencing these holes and the unique ways in which they are knitted together in the experience of the patient. It is this methodological principle to which I will be returning in the final chapter.

Holzhey-Kunz (2014, p. 219) noted that what struck Bion in the anxiety about the world of holes was not a view of neurosis, corresponding with Freud's preoccupation with similar case material, but that his patient was especially raw and sensitive to what could be considered, were it not so traumatising to the patient, "a special observational gift". I find this description, and Holzhey-Kunz's way of interpreting Bion's insight very interesting, in that it can serve as a prototypic example of what can be derived from it in terms of the special philosophical sensitivity in some patients to *other* forms of ontological anxiety, and which can be discerned to exist within more discrete and therefore more readily identifiable fears. From Holzhey-Kunz's theoretical perspective, which is known as *daseinsanalytic*, it is the traumatising sensitivity of the patient to the ontological realm that would provide a therapeutic focus, but not however to the exclusion of a more 'classical' psychoanalytic understanding of unconscious forces, phantasies and defences.

Methodologically, the two separate perspectives on the 'anxiety of the holes' return us to the epigraph that appears at the very beginning of the book, on the importance of the rift, what R. Allen Shoaf called "the impassable fissure between knowing and being". I will now consider this from the perspective of clinical technique and the psychoanalytic attitude.

In Holzhey-Kunz's approach, and in the line of thinking that I have been developing in this book in relation to a model based on the work of Klein and Bion, we would need to be informed of the state of being of the patient by tolerating the anxieties presented by being with him in his anxiety of lack, absence, hiatus, insubstantiality – in short, the 'lacunary', in which there are no determinate values or objects. It is where the object relations models of Klein and Bion meet the daseinsanalytic method of Holzhey-Kunz. In the anxiety of the ontological there are no ready-to-hand psychical objects.

> The stocking's hole-ridden fabric becomes so deeply threatening for the patient because the truth dawns on him through this ontical perception that on closer inspection the supposed compactness and constancy of all things and so the entire world turn out to be an illusion. Only someone who is ontologically sensitive can have the experience with such a harmless item of daily use as a stocking of essentially living in a 'lacunary' world into which the anxiety that was already defined by Kierkegaard as 'the nothing of anxiety' can intrude at any time.
>
> *(Holzhey-Kunz, 2014, p. 221)*

The patient seen from the perspective described by Holzhey-Kunz, therefore, is not functioning under the protection of the defences we discussed earlier as those of Proust's 'l'habitude' and Heidegger's 'the everyday', which, in psychoanalytic terms might include a defensive organisation developed from, and kept in shape by, systems of denial, repression, splitting, and the use of various forms of projective identification. In a sense, such defences, when effective, could be seen as depending on the dramaturgical use of projective identification in casting others in the world in roles that correspond to required arrangements amongst those of the inner world, in such a way as to redistribute anxiety itself. The patient described by Bion, and as he is considered by Holzhey-Kunz, does not have this capability. Instead, he is unshielded from the ontological, and may fear, or be at risk of, insanity as a result.

It is interesting to contemplate the kind of interpretation that might be given to a patient suffering from such an anxiety, in the light of the formulations being considered in this chapter. On the ideas put forward in Freud's (1915) paper on the unconscious, the Viennese analyst might put an interpretation to Tausk's patient along the lines of, "You appear to feel you cannot dress in the ordinary way which you would like to, because it feels so troubling to you that in pulling on the material of your socks you are really stretching apart a woman's vagina". Reitler could be imagined as interpreting to his patient that he equated putting on and removing his sock with his masturbation, about which he felt anxious. Whilst on a symbolic level such interpretations of bodily-based unconscious phantasy may in a sense be 'correct', they can be seen as omitting the patients' ontological sensitivity to a deeply unsettling kind of truth, one that includes the analyst even though the two participants will not share every component of the experience. In the absence of, or defence against, such awareness of the ontological domain, there is an increased risk of giving interpretations that are 'over-saturated' or even trite.

By 1973 Bion was clearly aware of his patient's heightened sensitivity to onto-logical anxiety. Whatever his patient was showing from the standpoint of his psychopathology, he was also from the ontological perspective expressing his sense of pain at the *lacunity* of life itself. Whereas we may not share with the patient their specific (ontic) fear of holes in the socks, or of any unconscious phantasy belief or entity that may be associated with the vastness of the angst, what we *do* share with the patient is the deep sense of *hiatus* in life, which is exactly what is meant by this more profound sense of the lacunity of our world, *indicated* by holes. To put it suc-cinctly, in the final analysis these terms refer to a shared unconscious anxiety arising from the universal dread of non-existence. It is what Sartre is pointing towards with his concept of *le néant*, his term for the absence of existence.

To reiterate: whatever we might observe in terms of psychopathology in our patients, we would not want to ignore the patient's awareness of a kind of truth which pertains to the human condition, and lacunity *is* such a perception of truth, one which, incidentally, accords with the discoveries of small particle physics – where everything is, in fact, mostly nothing.

Maintaining awareness of the domains of knowing and being as separate

Although it is customary in the literature of psychoanalysis to read of the importance of synthesising, integrating and harmonising different views, there are good theoretical and practical reasons for maintaining a clear distinction between the major domains considered in this book. That is to say: (a) epistemologically, a distinction between Bion's K and O, with its clinical implication of a difference between accumulated knowing-about reality and becoming real, and (b) existentially, that between the ontic and the ontological conditions of, respectively, fear and anxiety.

Bion's recommendations on the suspension of memory and desire, for exam-ple, were advanced as a means to reduce the 'bleaching out' effect of sense-based thinking that keeps the ontological at bay. In the philosophical area, the ontological quality of anxiety tends to be eclipsed by the more commonly understood ontic forms, as has been discussed earlier. Relevant to this is a recent contribution by Birksted-Breen (2016, p. 38), who posits a relationship between two qualitatively distinct modes of functioning of the analyst's mind which, though it is 'bi-ocular', so to speak, it is not 'binocular'. In other words, her model emphasises *not* a com-bined functioning of two vertices – one a more focused analysing faculty and the other a distinct faculty of reverie and negative capability – but rather an analytic atti-tude that maintains – and I would add recognises the actuality of – their separateness as a permanent distinction. This gap, considered by Birksted-Breen to be important to foster in the psychoanalytic situation, corresponds closely with that existing in Bion's model between the domains of K and O, and to the rift to which I refer in this book as existing between the analyst's contact with knowing and being.

In the language of the dramaturgical perspective, an observing attitude which favours 'making strange the familiar' (*Verfremdung*) will also make it more likely that such apparently 'out of context' impressions will make themselves known in the therapeutic situation. The feeling of unhomeliness that has to be tolerated by the analyst under such conditions, which Bion has considered as a type of catastrophic anxiety, can seem close to feeling on the brink of madness. Birksted-Breen (2016, p. 38) in the concluding remarks to her paper on bi-ocularity, writes of this as a "necessary madness" for the analyst. The experience is unavoidable if we accept the rift between knowing and being as relevant to psychoanalytic practice.

A conclusion from these clinically derived ideas from Bion and Holzhey-Kunz is that, in their respective terms, working in the K domain and that of the primarily ontical, is not sufficient. Concerning this, Bion wrote:

> A psychoanalyst must be able not only to see something which is apparently a game of tennis, but also be able to move to a different vertex and see this same game from that position; he could then see what the patient who could not wear socks could see. Similarly, it might be possible to move the vertex and get nearer to being able to see what an artist or a theologian sees. It depends on a certain flexibility of mind of all of us who concern ourselves with the human mind. This can be seen to be difficult. . . . This means that the domain of present-day analysis is much wider than that known to classical analysis.
>
> *(Bion, 1990, p. 21)*

Expanding the domain of psychoanalysis to include the ontological, the being of the patient and the anxiety that belongs to it, which includes that of the analyst, can contribute to a widened sensibility that allows us to join psychoanalytic insight with a mode of interpreting attuned to furthering the capacity of the patient to do more than know about themselves, but to become who they actually are.

I began exploring this line of thinking in the earlier chapters by pursuing Bion's later theory of technique, expressed through his ideas concerning distinct domains of K and O, and as the book comes to a close it is possible I think to see why that line of development requires the inclusion of the perspective of existential philosophy, as Britton and Holzhey-Kunz discerned. This component, combined with Bion's recommendations on 'memory, desire and understanding', and reverie, offers – according to this model – a way of access to brushes with the ontological experience of the patient, moments of contact, however brief, in which something of their being is disclosed.

From knowing to being informed

I have not yet found the time to have a word with my female side.

(Freud, 1897, pp. 290–1, letter to Fliess, 29 December)

The distinction I draw between knowing and becoming informed is based on the fact that something has to be made present, or to be tolerated as present, *before* it can be represented. As Camus said, "experience cannot be constructed, it must be undergone", and while it is being 'undergone', or "be-ed" as Bion put it, it is not being known. It is perhaps close, in Winnicott's language, to the realm of experience that is "incommunicado" (1965, p. 187).

The human capacity for understanding one another requires a distinction to be made between two fundamentally different attitudes, which I will indicate with the terms: 'penetrating / apprehending / organising', on the one hand, and 'receiving / allowing / comprehending' on the other. It should come as no surprise to learn that it is the latter attitude with which I associate the foregoing discussions of (a) reverie, (b) negative capability, (c) the *being-with* relation, and (d) interpretation principally as making-present; and it is to the former mode that I associate apperception, categorisation, explanation, and interpretation primarily as representation. I take the two attitudes as alternating within the analyst rather than as co-existing, just as earlier (p. 176) I considered the psychoanalytic counterpart of the Brechtian dramaturgical attitude to be in complementary alternation with the Aristotelian one.

In some languages, German and Dutch for example, different words exist for the different modes outlined above, whereas in English no clear distinction is made. I will make use of a grammatical form, not commonly used in psychoanalytic discourse, that can be used to effect a similar shift of meaning within the terminology of knowing. It is the distinction between knowing and being informed. From this point of the book I refer not to the analyst knowing the patient, but *being informed* by being-with the patient. Following the work of Heidegger in *Being and Time*, it involves an attitude in which attunement to mood, particularly the mood of anxiety, which is most disclosive in itself of the being of a person, takes precedence over the comprehension of specific – in his terminology, ontic – experience. In the field of analysis and psychotherapy it is sensibility to this dimension that is the defining feature of the daseinsanalytic expansion of the psychoanalytic attitude as introduced by Holzhey-Kunz.

A linguistic note on being informed by phenomena

The distinction between knowing and becoming informed (by being-with) relates to the qualities involved in relating to things and relating to persons. Linguistically, the term *informed*, in the phrase 'I was informed', is an example of a part of speech called a 'participial' adjective, unlike *knowing*, which is an example of the present participle. I will clarify why this is so important for my purposes because it explains why it makes a difference to say – rather than 'I know X' (with an implicit implication that I possess something of X) – 'I have been informed' or 'I am becoming informed' through my experience of, or with, X. This mode of language de-emphasises the subject–object split, because it 'subjectivises' the object and invariably refers to persons and not to things. In daily analytic work our own syntactical choices impart particular psychological qualities, sometimes unintended, to the communications.

Choices of different modes of expression in giving interpretations can communicate emotional distance, but more crucially they can affect whether the patient feels treated as a subject in their own right. Clinical experience shows us not only what a numbing effect it has on an analysis when we objectify our patient, but also sometimes the surprising appetite held by some patients, and some analysts too, for a scientistic[6] way of relating.[7]

The analyst's idiolect

We are all sensitive to idiolects – personal variations in the use of language – particularly those forms that imply that we have done something or that we keep on doing the same thing. This is particularly true of those who are in a mode of being in which blame and responsibility cannot be differentiated. In such cases the patient will hear us differently if we say, "I think that you keep pushing me away whenever you feel me to be getting close to you", compared to an interpretation when put thus: "I can see you keep finding yourself, for some reason, feeling that we are too close, it seems to become so uncomfortable that you feel you need to do something about it".

The past participle (the '-ed' form of the verb), as in 'informed', or 'closed' (as in the example) is used to express how a person is *affected* by something. The reference to the patient's experience of repeatedly 'finding themselves' in a particular position is to render 'finding' as the principal verb instead of their 'doing' something to their analyst, and in many cases it helps us in the choice of linguistic mode for the giving of interpretations. Earlier I wrote of this in existential terms as *Befindlichkeit*, which for Heidegger means, roughly, 'being in the mood in which we (in our being) are found'. This mood of the patient relates to their own unique way of experiencing the analyst and the setting of the analysis, and our patients' feeling of being understood depends in large part on having their subjective viewpoint respected when interpretations are made to them of what it is that their analyst feels them to be doing or feeling in any moment.

Evolution

The being of the patient, as we encounter it in the consulting room is without form, but it gains its 'own form', a transitory one distinct from the form we give it, when, as Bion puts it, it "enters the domain K when it has evolved to a point where it can be known". At this point the evolved elements of being are available for 'knowledge

---

6 A distinctly self-conscious and forced, 'waiterly' (compare Sartre) way of performing the role of scientist.
7 Bion (1992, p. 244) has discussed this preference in relation to psychology, and elsewhere (e.g. 1959) he has written of the unconscious hatred of emotion and the corresponding preponderance of inanimate elements in thinking resulting from the destruction of alpha-function.

gained by experience', rather than 'knowledge gained by reference to *memory* of experience' (K_a), a mode of becoming that I am calling *being-informed* (O → K_i).

What I am emphasising is that when something has evolved from the domain of being – at first indeterminate[8] as to whether we should consider it as 'part of the analyst' or 'part of the patient' – so that it 'condenses' and 'precipitates', as it were, into the session, the ontological anxiety common to both members of the pair is stirred, with the potential too for both participants to be altered, in their being, by the contact. I want to emphasise that being informed, as contrasted with knowing, is not, linguistically or actually, a term for how a subject 'operates' on an object, it is a phrase indicating instead a phenomenological *mode of being* – specifically that of a relation to phenomena as 'being-with' (*Mitsein*). If the analyst is unable to bear the anxiety that stimulates their own dread of non-being, or any other ontological anxiety, they will be very likely to provide a more 'procedural' response.

It is a fact of clinical practice that ontological anxiety tends to mobilise, as a defence against its full and open recognition, features of the psychoanalytic method itself. When this happens the analyst may discover only in hindsight that they have their own defensive organisation with that of the patient to 'manage' the anxiety,[9] commonly through various forms of action, rather than risking the imminent danger of remaining open to it.[10]

Interpreting from becoming

The way that I have come to understand the relationship between being a container for anxiety and what I have been considering throughout the book as the patient's suffering from their being, is as follows. In moments of anxiety undifferentiated in terms of its physical, psychological and ontological aspects, something of the patient's being, from which they suffer ontologically finds, through communication of self with self, an incipient form of containment through being converted into what we refer to as an 'object' of their world, in interaction with the self and with other internal objects. On this model, the creation of mental objects arises from the casting of basic raw feelings (β) into the existing psychic structures with their content as represented in the form of the unconscious dramas that we term phantasies. If doing so fails to contain the current anxiety, there is an intolerable sense of escalation, as discussed by Freud, and the person then stands in urgent need of a helper to function as an external container. As a helpmate in this specialised sense we are required to remain open to, and responsive to, the anxious person and to bear the feelings stirred up within us. It is only through this process, I maintain, that we become informed

---

8 This is an instance of the central place I give in my thesis to *doubt*.
9 See Chapter 11. It is in this context that the analyst, and/or their patient, reverts to what I will later describe as 'column 2' procedures, following Bion's use of the term as a column in his Grid.
10 Rupert King (2018) in his research on Heidegger and psychotherapy has posited openness as a central dimension of therapeutic work, irrespective of modality.

(K_a) of the being of the patient – becoming informed, that is, by contact with what Bion termed transformations in O – as distinct from knowing *about* him (K_a).

Rather than being detected mainly through the senses, the mood of anxiety is intuited. It is sometimes, as Bion suggested, first conjectured phenomenologically from other communications. The most salient[11] anxiety of the patient, at what Klein called the 'point of urgency' in the session, is not detected principally through sight, smell, taste – or even through hearing – even though the combined musical dimensions of hearing come closest to furnishing a sensory channel for it.

Once picked up, communication of the nature of this anxiety back to the patient depends on the analyst finding words, and these rely on models that derive from commonly held (sensuously derived) experiences of being in the world. The 'knowledge component', in the approach I am exploring here, based upon negative capability and suspension of memory and desire, differs from its usual application in many fields where observation is central by being drawn not from cognition but by being *informed by being-with* the patient.

From a philosophical perspective it involves understanding from *attunement to mood* (*Stimmung*) as contrasted with apperception, and gives priority to a mode of thought that is rather more 'meditative' than calculative and categorical. In *Discourse on Thinking*, Heidegger considered that the peculiar ubiquity of the calculative mode

> consists in the fact that whenever we plan, research, and organize, we always reckon with conditions that are given. We take them into account with the calculated intention of their serving specific purposes. Thus we can count on definite results. This calculation is the mark of all thinking that plans and investigates. Such thinking remains calculation even if it neither works with numbers nor uses an adding machine or computer. Calculative thinking never stops, never collects itself. Calculative thinking is not meditative thinking, not thinking which contemplates the meaning which reigns in everything that is. There are, then, two kinds of thinking, each justified and needed in its own way: calculative thinking and meditative thinking.
>
> *(Heidegger, 1969, p. 46)*

Interpretation is a core component of the practice of analysis, which I take as a contemplative therapeutic practice and a hermeneutic art that gives priority to exploration over explanation. The importance of maintaining this distinction – between the exploratory and the explanatory – cannot be underestimated in understanding the distinction followed throughout this book between psychoanalysis and talking about psychoanalysis.

Understanding from being informed is similar to writing what we are discovering rather than writing what we know. In working psychoanalytically from such a

---

11 Note: this is not necessarily the most intense, or the most obvious anxiety.

position and making it the fundamental basis of interpretation, the being and the becoming (the growth) of the clinician is part of the total situation of an analysis (see Parsons, 2014, p. 143). Recently, Thomas Ogden (2016, p. 1) wrote that every now and then he has to write in order to discover what he has become. Similarly, in the analytic situation, every now and again our patient, at the point at which we interpret to them what we have heard of them, gains an impression of what we have become. From this it follows that if we can dare to allow our basic interpretive activity to spring from becoming informed, rather than knowing, we surrender the aim of mastery over phenomena and are equally exposed alongside our patients to the shock and the challenge of personal discovery, to share and bear witness to discovery, and to the extent that this may in important moments be possible we may be able to develop a practice capable of harnessing psychoanalytic insight to furthering the capacity of the patient to be real, which is the growing point from which I began to write this book. It is my firm belief that exploring this possibility thoroughly can help emancipate our method from its debasement by its participation in the age-old myth of oracular truth, an activity that leads inevitably to the aggrandisement of analysis and prevention of the growth of the patient as a being-for-him- or herself.

At this point it is I think important to sound a note of caution. I am discussing these ideas from a practical standpoint. It could be assumed that exploring and following the technical aspects under consideration will lead inevitably and smoothly to openness and growth in the therapeutic encounter. With the potential for beneficial consequences of this process for realisation and change, however, comes turbulence, mental pain and *resistance* to both. As Britton has pointed out, the main function of the container–contained relationship is not amelioration, it is transformation. Growth based upon the potential for transformative change is not to be confused with becoming calmed and settled. There is an inevitable sense of trouble in what Bion calls a 'symbiotic relation' between container and contained. Intuitive awareness of its presence creates difficulty for both participants of an analysis in their capacity and willingness to be there, together. The particular difficulty for the analyst is the subject of the next chapter.

11

ON THE DIFFICULTY FOR THE ANALYST IN BEING WITH THE PATIENT

[O]ne might start from the question of what happens, in general terms, in the analyst in his relationship with the patient. The first answer might be: everything happens that *can* happen in one personality faced with another. But this says so much that it says hardly anything. We take a step forward by bearing in mind that in the analyst there is a tendency that normally predominates . . . it is the tendency pertaining to his function of being an analyst, that of understanding what is happening in the patient. Together with this tendency there exist towards the patient virtually all the other possible tendencies, fears, and other feelings that one person may have towards another.

(Racker, 1968, p. 134)

In this chapter I consider, in the light of the ideas that have so far been explored in this book, the difficulty for the analyst of making contact with the being of the patient. The main difficulty for the analyst, behind all other difficulties, arises from the fact that the success of the patient in making use of the most basic method of communication, often the only one available, depends entirely on being able to make an emotional impact and to observe that they have done so.[1] This understanding had been foreshadowed by Freud in 1917 when he brought together two complementary statements on the centrality of anxiety and transference. Firstly (1917, p. 411) that the problem of anxiety holds the central place in the study of unconscious mental life, and secondly (1917, p. 417) that in the transference relationship everything becomes "concentrated upon a single point – his relationship to the doctor". It is the intensity of this concentrated impact that produces one area of challenge and difficulty for the analyst. James Strachey, at the end of his

---

1 This insight, fundamental to the practice of psychoanalysis, stems from the detailed clinical observations of Bion (see 1959, p. 312), building on Klein's work.

1934 paper on mutative interpretation, indicated a specific aspect of this problem, hinting that the analyst senses the danger of becoming, through playing it out against the patient, a damaging part of their own personality. I will consider this as the anxiety of the analyst, conscious or unconscious, at the prospect of abrupt and uncontrolled shifts in their own being or becoming in the analytic situation. Because working with anxiety and transference opens up a valuable but risky way of access to the opaque workings of the mind, those who do this lonely work with its hazardous materials require what Bion (1977) referred to as the analyst's necessary "supply of capacity".

As I have made clear in the first chapter, and also those in Part II of the book, the need to be able to impact another human being derives from the foremost reality of anxiety, that it requires, and therefore seeks, a home in the heart and mind of another, to make it bearable at all, prior to the understanding. The origins of this insight can be found as early as the first century BCE, in the verses of Lucretius, and later in the work of Kierkegaard, in *Fear and Trembling*. Because of this fundamental fact, the need of our patients to be able to affect us, and to know that they have done so, is at the heart of clinical and theoretical psychoanalysis.

I have discussed this as an axiomatic principle of anxiety appearing in an early form in Freud's pre-psychoanalytic concept of the *work of the specific action*, as intrinsic to Bion's theory of reverie and the container–contained ($♀♂$; Ps $\rightleftharpoons$ D) relationship, and in Winnicott's concepts of holding and going-on-being. It should be clear from the preceding discussion that the patient in analysis has a primary need, even before being understood, to know realistically that they *can* make contact with the analyst, in the realm of being, in order to sense that a channel, or conduit, exists for their emotions, the contents of their mind. The foremost method with which to achieve this is through effecting changes in the external object by the use of various forms of projective identification, and by being able to monitor closely the effects of having done so. Understanding this means to realise that human *contact*, providing a container and a conduit for communication, is logically and psychologically prior to any meaning and symbolisation achievable through it.

So, to reiterate, from the earliest work of Freud on anxiety, and in a line of clinically based thinking through Klein and Bion, we derive the clear understanding that for the human being, impactful contact is the earliest form of communication. Once established, once the infant has been able to avail themselves of a projective identification–accepting object, the confidence grown from the realisation that communication is made possible in this way[2] leads to a much more sophisticated version of that function, in which realistic projective identification is used to induce what Joseph, following Klein, has called total transference situations. These are founded upon the inherent tendency for the human mind to form, out of featureless raw forces, the dramaturgical structures known as 'object relations'.

---

2 Relying absolutely on the acceptance of what Bion (1959, p. 312; 1967a, p. 102) terms *normal degrees of projective identification.*

I maintain that it is this advance in the use and complexity of the projective process, dependent on the person having been able to find and to make use of a container, that makes role relating and role-responsiveness possible.[3] To allow these processes to take place in the analytic setting puts the analyst under different kinds of strain, which I will now consider, beginning with the most commonly discussed difficulty, that arising from being subject to the patient's transference.

The difficulty of being at the focal point of transference

The difficulty of being an analyst, often subsumed under two different but related concepts both called countertransference, has been discussed from various perspectives by clinicians over the years, beginning with Freud – who believed that it was the combination of analytic abstinence with the interrelated phenomena of transference and countertransference that presented the greatest challenge to us in the work. In relation to the transference he wrote (1912b, p. 108) of a "struggle between the doctor and the patient, between intellect and instinctual life, between understanding and seeking to act . . . played out almost exclusively in the phenomena of transference". "It cannot be disputed", he stated further, "that controlling the phenomena of transference presents the psycho-analyst with the greatest difficulties".

When analysis of the unconscious transference relationship became of central importance to Freud it is clear that he considered that the part of the patient's personality with which he engaged, the particular dynamic structures whose painful functioning brought the patient into treatment in the first place, were patterns of mental life very much in flux – primed, as it were, like psychological 'tropisms', in seeking to attach themselves to himself as the analyst, and to achieve that in an intense, dramatic and personal manner. He found that they did so by taking account of, and making use of, the patterning of the analyst's own personality, as they perceived this to be, coloured, of course, by their own complexes. The effect, and the unconscious aim of transference, was to weave the analyst as actor into the living pattern of the patient's own pre-existing dynamics in order to maintain the integrity of an underlying structure, felt to be essential in terms, primarily, of anxiety – its binding and its disposition. As we would say now, the equilibrium to be thus protected and maintained by the personality and its internal group-structure is that of its realisation-seeking model of experience and object-relating (Britton 2015, p. 22).

Freud understood that it was an arduous business for the analyst to accept fully the task of taking on such transferences and to work within them while at the same time retaining a capacity to be separate, and to observe that with which they were also to some degree participant. For Freud, taking the transference relationship seriously, as "the illness's new production" to be addressed in the immediate present, involved recognising that the entirety of the patient's painfully conflicted inner and outer relationships became concentrated, as he said,

3 See Bion, 1961a, p. 148; Sandler, 1976; and Sandler & Sandler, 1978.

"upon a single point – his relation to the doctor". The "new edition", formed by the transference, of what originally in life were the patient's early object relations, places the analyst at the centre of their love, hate, anxiety, fear and confusion, and at the heart of their basic needs for protection, understanding and structure. In keeping with this understanding, Freud saw that this places the analyst not only in a simultaneously hazardous and yet highly responsible situation, but that if it can be tolerated without abandoning the analytic position, being treated as an object of the patient's inner world offers an unprecedented opportunity to begin navigating their world. Freud stated the achievement of the therapeutic task in terms of this view of the transference:

> We have followed this new edition of the old disorder from its start, we have observed its origin and growth, and we are especially well able to find our way about in it since, as its object, we are situated at its very centre. All the patient's symptoms have abandoned their original meaning and have taken on a new sense which lies in a relation to the transference.
>
> *(Freud, 1917, p. 444)*

When Freud stated that what happens in an analysis, in the events that we combine under the concept of transference, is that *the whole of his illness's new production is concentrated upon a single point – his relation to the doctor,* and when he implied that the staging of that "new production", the revised edition of its drama, so to speak, becomes such that we are *well able to find our way about in it since, as its object, we are situated at its very centre,* it is clear that he was speaking of a very demanding task for the analyst. It also makes absolutely clear why the German analyst Frieda Fromm-Reichmann (1950) wrote succinctly that, "The patient needs an experience, not an explanation". Freud had explained that we cannot confront and work through our conflicts simply by discussing them in representational terms.[4]

Emotional storms: the need of the patient to impact the analyst emotionally

Because psychoanalysts do not direct how a meeting with a patient unfolds, and provide no agenda for their interchanges, no topic for discussion, they have to withstand an uncommon level of uncertainty as to what is going to happen each time they meet a patient. Freud, as I described earlier, recommended that analysts start to make contact with the unconscious from a position in which they *simply listen* to the patient's productions – their ideas, thoughts, phantasies, reports of the events of the day, their recollections, dreams, opinions, associations to what

---

4 Freud, 1912b, p. 108: "It cannot be disputed that controlling the phenomena of transference presents the psycho-analyst with the greatest difficulties. But it should not be forgotten that it is precisely they that do us the inestimable service of making the patient's hidden and forgotten erotic impulses immediate and manifest. For when all is said and done, it is impossible to destroy anyone *in absentia* or *in effigie*".

the analyst says or does – and that this is done with the same evenly suspended attentiveness, holding in check our expectations, based on past events, of what *will* happen, and taming our tendency to act from an idea of what *should* happen – that is to say, our inclinations. This recommendation found its way, via the particular clinical experience of Bion in his work with severely thought-disordered patients, and supplemented too by his growing interest in his study of 'apophatic' methods[5] in theology and drama,[6] into Bion's psychoanalytical attitude of suspending memory and desire, which holds a stronger affinity with Freud's key recommendations than is usually appreciated.

Such a working attitude not only places on the analyst a burden of strain due to voluntary uncertainty and ignorance, it greatly increases the probability of detecting, in the psyche of the patient and arising in the space between the participants, various varieties of emotional turbulence. Concerning these, Freud, in *The Interpretation of Dreams*, described an "emotional storm" as having occurred in his own mind while he had been sleeping:

> all of this combined to produce the emotional storm which was clearly perceived in my sleep and which raged in this region of the dream-thoughts.
>
> *(Freud, 1900, p. 481)*

Such turbulence, inevitable when two personalities meet, led Bion to emphasise that in an analysis it should be recognised that there are two quite frightened people in the room. The meteorological analogy should not, however, be taken as an impersonal one, because what is tempestuous is of *turbulent human drama*, and not merely 'emotional weather'. The forces of such a storm correspond not to the patterns of natural science, but to unmapped inward events far stranger, far less familiar, than those to which we have become accustomed in the everyday 'outer' world of social and material convention. As Bion[7] said of this "other-worldly" turbulence of *mind*, it "obeys no man-made 'laws of nature'".

A second feature of an emotional storm is that its embodiment, in what meets us in the form of transference and countertransference, shows the boundary between what strikes us as the intrapsychic and the interactional realm to be indeterminate for much of the time, in what Britton has called "the ordinary muddle of clinical practice". It is in the nature of these processes that both parties feel not merely *construed* by one other but also, through complex and subtle action, mysteriously *re-configured* by one another.

This I mean dramaturgically, and in the sense given by the etymology[8] of fashioning and being fashioned by the other according to an existing design, pattern

---

5 The writings of the contemplative theological philosophers, Meister Eckhart (Eckhart von Hochheim) and St John of the Cross (Juan de Yepes y Álvarez).

6 Stimulated by his therapeutic contact in the 1930s with Samuel Beckett.

7 Bion, 1991, p. 240: "For fear of the turmoil – the turbulence that obeys no man-made 'laws of nature'. Far worse than any zoo."

8 OED: ad. L. configūrāre, to fashion after some pattern, f. con- together + figūrāre to shape.

or model, but in the specialised sense that the re-fashioning is not only limited to inanimate dimensions, but reaches a psychological depth afforded by the animated world of dramatic relations. It is human relationships that are figured and reconfigured in the peculiar relationship that evolves between the unique patient and the analyst that is unique to them. Existentially, what I am calling 'reconfiguring' bears a similarity to what Sartre, as I described earlier (Chapter 6) called 'the look of the Other', and something of the sense of this experience, in the sphere of action, is expressed beautifully in the following lines from Shakespeare's *Hamlet*:

> Why, look you now, how unworthy a thing you make of me! You would play upon me. You would seem to know my stops. You would pluck out the heart of my mystery. You would sound me from my lowest note to the top of my compass. And there is much music, excellent voice, in this little organ, yet cannot you make it speak? 'Sblood, do you think I am easier to be played on than a pipe? Call me what instrument you will, though you can fret me, yet you cannot play upon me.
>
> *(Shakespeare, c.1901,* Hamlet, *Act III, Scene ii)*

This resonant passage arises in the part of the play in which Claudius, the King – and also Rosencrantz and Guildenstern – have just been 'played' by the play-within-a-play staged by Hamlet. This is the play of which Hamlet says, "The play's the thing, therein to catch the conscience of the King". In other words, the play is crafted to serve as an investigative tool. It is a drama with the specific capacity to reveal hidden actions and motives through the reactions to it of its target audience, reactions that can be read by the designer of the play, according to which he who allows himself to be played is thereby enabled to gain an unprecedented picture of what has been going on in the mind of the other. Shakespeare uses the metaphor of the musical pipe to demonstrate Hamlet's awareness of how simple and malleable Rosencrantz and Guildenstern imagine him to be. Hamlet shows his mastery concerning when to stay open, when to 'play along' – in the case of his having assumed an antic disposition – and when to allow himself to be 'fretted' in order for resonance with the player to 'affect' him, as a way of revealing their intentions. The affinity with the psychoanalytical situation is clear. We can see how the analyst is required to allow something of a play within a play in herself – to allow herself to be impacted and affected by the patient, through the projective processes of transference and countertransference, in order to be in a position to reveal the predicament of the patient in their world. But, like Hamlet, the analyst while being fretted by the patient, must exercise limitation and judgement moment by moment in order not to be 'played' unwittingly, and to avoid becoming, completely, through enactment, the role ascribed. A deeper understanding of the part played in clinical work by countertransference experience helps the analyst to do what Hamlet says in the passage quoted above – which is to some degree, and up to a point – to allow themselves to be affected and impacted by the patient, and to some extent to be configured by them, in order to be in a position to understand the predicament of the patient in *their* world.

One day, after having spent a long time with a young child patient who had spent the majority of a session drowning me out with shrieks whilst 'surrounding' me with multiple versions of herself in the guise of what she called her 'ghoul-ghosts', I suggested that by doing this to me she had needed to make sure that I understood how silenced, terrified and surrounded by monsters she feels, she stood stock-still, looking straight into my eyes, head on one side, and said gravely, "Welcome to my world mister". In a very direct countertransference experience I had been brought unusually close to a terrifying region of this child's world by being put, for a while, in her place, and it had felt important for a while to endure this and not to speak, and not to turn away from it. Analysts have to be open to being affected emotionally, in their countertransference, to be able to recognise what the patient, in their 'play within a play' – in other words in the transference relationship – is unconsciously trying to bring about, and why. Being willing to be affected thus is to accept the transference and the normal projective identification of the patient, in the service of understanding it through experiencing it. Arguably it is the only means by which we gain a real understanding of the forces that are in action in the analytic hour, and the position in which we achieve some answers, however transitory, to the question[9] of "who, in what state of being, is doing what, to what object, in what state, and with what consequences"?

Without any sign of strain in the other, we remain uncertain as to whether we have affected them; how are we to know that our distress has found a home of any kind, however fleetingly, in them? The existence of a living container is shown by its having to change to allow access to us with our pain, which is why it is so harmful when narcissistic parents, partners or analysts who consciously or unconsciously pride themselves on remaining detached and unaffected, are experienced as immune and obstructive to our need to be contained by them. It is the full recognition of the necessity for the analyst to be receptive to the impact made on them by the patient that led Paula Heimann (1950, p. 82), Bion's clinical supervisor, to supplement Freud's fundamental principle of evenly suspended attentiveness with her own recommendation that the analyst develops and learns to value a "freely roused emotional sensibility" in the work.

All of the foregoing discussion conforms closely with what we could call the standard model of psychoanalysis, focusing as it does on the difficulty for the analyst in being subjected to the inevitable and ubiquitous forces that we understand as transference.

Transference and ontological anxiety

Most discussions of transference and countertransference are taken up with the analyst's *ontical* experience of the forces at play – to use the distinction that I have been exploring throughout this book. That is to say, in the transference situation described by Freud, the analyst does in fact experience herself being at the centre

---

9 A paraphrasing of the question asked by Henri Rey, in relation to object relations.

of the patient's unconscious production, one that is to a large extent a reliving of a pre-existing model of relationships, and she does come to feel herself, as a consequence, present to a "sense of being a particular kind of person in a particular emotional situation" (Bion, 1961b, p. 148), and, we would add, with a particular kind of anxiety. How this happens, in its dynamic and dramaturgical detail, comprises a large part of the task of what we call the analyst's 'working-through' of the experience. I consider it, following Bion's model, to be an aspect of her alpha-function. This working-through on the part of the analyst is necessary and valuable in helping her not to become an obstacle to the necessary unconscious communications of the patient (see Bion, 1959, p. 312). However successful an analyst's management of her conscious and unconscious experience of being impacted by her patient may be – of being played by him, featured by him in his phantasy productions, characterised and sometimes hoodwinked by him, sometimes drawn into playing a pale role, a bland partner, a cruel tormentor even – there still remains the *ontological* experience. This derives from the very fact that the patient, as Other, is free to make of us what they will. That these complex events can happen at all is not solely a function of the ways in which the unconscious works, but that they are a specialised sub-set of human relating in which we are all subject to what Sartre termed 'the look'.

This concept, of an inescapable experience that stems from the human being's awareness of our existence *for* others, is discussed in Chapter 6. In 'taking the transference', a useful phrase central to the work of Mitrani (2001; and 2011, p. 677), the analyst is also having to 'take the ontological anxiety' of being subject to the-look-of-the-Other, namely the patient. From the existential perspective of analysis, the analyst has to be able to bear not only the particular strains induced in them by the patient's specific projections from their world, but they also have to be willing and able to put up with Sartre's *être-pour-autrui*, the inescapable being-for-others, which in the analytic relationship means, amongst other things, *being subject to being characterised*.

As well as the experience of being subject to the existential conditions just described, being subject to the look of the Other, and to being characterised *by* the Other – for which I will give a clinical illustration in a moment, the very nature of language, meaning, and personal identity are questioned and thrown into doubt in any approach in which transference is opened up to scrutiny, and doubly so if the use of apperceptive understanding is reduced to the extent that I am suggesting.

Here is an illustration from clinical practice to describe the predicament, both ontic and ontological, of an analyst who, during his training, made a very unwelcome discovery: He realised that his job included being made to feel invaded by his patients, and sometimes 'taken over' by them.

Illustration: the sense of outrage at being played by the patient

Mr A, a candidate in his third year of psychoanalytic training, brought to his analyst his own "quite special internal difficulty" in being with his patient, Dr S, a thirty-two-year-old senior medical registrar. It emerged that his special difficulty lay less in the giving of interpretations than in finding himself at the receiving end of his patient's transference onto him – or to be more precise, his patient's thrusting *into* him the characters of her own inner drama, in ways that not only impacted him but also, in some strange way, were felt to "configure him".

These were his words, his way of trying to get over to me that he resented viscerally the horrible sensation that somehow he was, invisibly, "being altered" by her, "*and not only in her mind!*". This he referred to as "being characterised" by the other. He had been made to feel a character in her drama.[10] He hated this feeling of being 'characterised' in the relationship, even though he 'knew' – but merely consciously – that this was the very essence of the job of being a psychoanalyst. As *his* analyst, I felt that Mr A was expressing something that went beyond a heightened sensitivity to what I described earlier (Chapter 6) as Sartre's concept of 'the look' – the painful ontological truth that all human beings are subject to objectifying perception by the Other. I felt that Mr A was conveying to me an experience that did not stop at a feeling of being perceived by his patient, but that it had moved into his growing sense, in the countertransference, of being *changed* as a person, away from who he thought he was, to someone familiar to the patient but unfamiliar to himself. In other words, his patient was, in the dramaturgical sense, felt by him to be *making him strange to himself.*

I recognised in Mr A's pained communications to me the presence of the helpless feelings that we are generally helped by our own analysis to *take,* as an ordinary part of countertransference experience, which if contained can yield insights (see Mitrani, 2001) but at the same time I felt more acutely for his sense of being made to feel, *in relation to his own personality*, the ontological awareness I described earlier as the 'not-at-home'. This was especially the case when his perceptive patient noticed or intuited aspects of her analyst that were true, but of which he appeared to be unconscious.

This quality of experience was discussed by Bion in his 1952 addendum to his group papers, where he referred to the analyst being made to feel estranged and constrained by patients in "being a particular kind of person in a particular emotional situation" (Bion, 1961b, p. 141). For Bion, a full recognition of the strangeness of the drama into which he had been recruited, as well as an insight that it is playing from the inner world of the patient, becomes numbed by the patient's specialised use of projective identification.[11] For my patient, however, there was no question of his awareness, of being made strange to himself, being numbed, he was excruciatingly hyper-aware of it. Further exploration of instances in his analysis in which he had felt unable to voice his feeling that my interpretations of his experience had objectified him, in which his predominant feeling had been that I had misunderstood him and had, in the moment, reminded him too much of a mother who had conveyed an

10 See Bion, 1961b, "Experiences in groups", pp. 148–9.
11 In its variant known as 'evocatory' projective identification (Spillius, 1988, p. 83).

oppressive sense of "knowing him better than he could ever know himself", enabled a deeper understanding of his situation with his patient. In needing to use projective measures to pull Mr A into the drama of her own world, in which a powerful narcissistic mother had done much the same to her as Mr A's mother had played out with him, she had ensured a painful experience of estrangement for her analyst that resonated strongly with her own experience, but on this stage, the stage of the analysis, she played the part of her mother and pressed Mr A into serving the role of her childhood self, feeling invaded by her mother's omniscient projections to such an extent that she felt her very being had been usurped. It will be clear from this way of formulating the experience, undergone first by his patient in relation to her mother, and in the 'new production' of events by Mr A as the projected-into child, with Dr S as the mother, the total transference situation, is at least potentially an act of communication, and not merely one of discharge and the turning-of-tables. What had made it difficult for Mr A, my patient, to contain his emotional reactions to his patient's projections into him of the anxiety-situation, and to come to experience the events as a communication through re-enactment, was that one of his most powerful internal objects tended to project forcefully into *his* ego, in times of great uncertainty, its sense of knowing everything about him – just as he often felt that I oriented towards him in just such a way. This left him bereft of a capacity to feel himself to be an adequate analyst, or even an adequate being, which became a predicament shared with his vulnerable patient. Because he had been feeling so heavily persecuted, and was almost at one with the patient's experience of being annihilated as a self, he had temporarily lost the capacity to recognise that the patient had needed to give him an experience of what it was to *be* her.

Once Mr A could understand, through his transference relationship to me, that his sense of visceral outrage came from feeling projected into, physically and totally by an omniscient object who left him with a hollowed-out and detracted sense of being, he found himself able once again to be a help to his patient. In passing, it may be observed that this example illustrates both the original sense in which the conception of countertransference was explored, that is to say the difficulties of the analyst as they obstruct the capacity and willingness to be with the patient – and the modern post-Kleinian application of the concept, in which the total transference situation impacts the analyst and induces in them not only feelings but propensities to action and partial-action, in which the dramaturgical patterns to some extent re-enacted are potentially highly informative of the inner world of the patient.

Having introduced the strain for the analyst in taking the transference, which, as I say, includes not only the anxiety at being recruited into role relationships, and not only having painful feelings evoked, but also the ontological anxiety connected with the calling into question of who and what the analyst *is*, I now consider the difficulty due to an ominous sense in the analysis that an unwelcome discovery is about to happen.

Many therapists will be able to recall moments in which the familiar activities of 'talking about', appraising the importance of history, or creating a coherent narrative, give way suddenly and unexpectedly to a change, *not* in the sphere of knowing but in the more opaque realm of being and becoming. There can be an indefinable sense that 'change is in the air', perhaps even that the analyst may potentially be changed by an experience.

It is the ontological anxiety belonging to such a potentially mutative change in being that produces resistance in a reformulated view of the concept[12] that differs from Freud's two uses of the term. In other words, the kind of resistance that I am considering is evoked when the patient or analyst begins to suffer the early stages of a premonition that an interpretation could precipitate a change from a familiar story to something real but as yet unknown. In my view, moments of threatened impingement into awareness of the real (O → K) produce an additional level of insecurity, stemming from the ontological component (the awareness of mortality, or aloneness, for example), because there is no cure for the ontological, no 'managing it', or 'sorting-it-out', no reducing it through 'knowing about it', only whatever may be mitigated by having someone with us in the experience, one who suffers with us an anxiety of the human condition. This is the difference between the ontic suffering of the patient and the ontological. The modified use of the term 'resistance' to take account of the anxiety felt by the analyst at mutative moments, in relation to the unconscious anticipation of contact with ontological experience, is a development of Bion's 1965 use of the term, and one that brings the conception of the analytic task close to the philosophically informed work of Holzhey-Kunz.

To prepare for discussing methodology suited to making explicit the ontological and the dramaturgical dimensions of psychoanalysis, I will explore a little further the subject of the analyst's unconscious resistance to the ontological.

Resistance to the evolution in the session: O → K

I ended the previous chapter by reminding us of the resistance that arises whenever our relationship to moments of truth and change signal to us the occurrence of turbulence and mental pain. There seem to be moments in the evolution of a child's 'play-thoughts', and in comparable moments in the verbal associations of adult patients, where a particular kind of resistance may be intuited. As I wrote earlier (Chapter 4), Melanie Klein addressed this in terms of what she called the 'point of urgency'. It is hard to define what it is in the practitioner that overcomes the resistance to such moments. I suggest that the concept refers to a sensitivity to the evolution of ontological anxiety in the moment-by-moment flow of the session. It corresponds, I suggest, with Bion's use of the concept of *maternal reverie*. My own clinical experience with children and adults in analytic treatment also suggests the possibility that the 'point of urgency' coincides closely with moments ripe for

---

12 Although Freud sometimes spoke of resistance in the more general sense of the patient's opposition to the efforts of the analyst, his most cogent use of the term referred to a factor opposing relatively free verbal communication in an analysis. Resistance in Freud's original sense can be inferred when the free-associative links of the adult patient, or the mobile 'play-thoughts' of the young child in analysis are interrupted by anxiety.

mutative interpretation. These, it will be recalled, are points at which an analyst may shrink back or swerve away from making a potent intervention that risks real contact and the possibility of change. Klein felt that the common avoidance by analysts of all orientations of taking such opportunities meant that a sense of potential danger stalked such mutative contact. Although, as I have considered earlier, Klein did not manage to go much further with her point of urgency concept, and did not herself link it conceptually with Strachey's ideas about the danger of moments in which mutative interpretations would be requisite, it does seem from her descriptions of child analysis that it is not only the intensity of anxiety, nor its particular content that determines the peculiar potential in such pivotal moments, it appears to reside in a particularly elusive *quality* of anxiety. As I say, I would suggest that Klein found this difficult to define because its chief component is ontological anxiety. Unlike ontic fear, which can be specified in relation to the mental objects in psychic reality into which the anxiety is precipitated, or 'falls', anxiety that remains predominantly ontological partakes of no object, unless, that is, one is 'found' for it for defensive purposes. This eventuality I will describe in a moment when I consider what I believe is the analyst's main psychic defensive manoeuvre against ontological anxiety, which also turns out to be the main defensive construction mobilised by analysts unconsciously when they find themselves veering away from mutative interpretations. These defensive operations I will call, following Bion's initial explorations of them in *Transformations* (1965a, p. 86), 'column 2' defences.

Just as Strachey emphasised that an analyst may react to their own apprehension in moments ripe for a mutative interpretation by breaking off from real contact, the child analyst may retreat unconsciously from picking up the point of urgency in the child's patterns of play. The consequence for continued communication from the child Klein described as follows:

> If the analyst overlooks urgent material of this kind, the child will usually break off its game and exhibit strong resistance or even open anxiety and not infrequently show a desire to run away.
>
> *(Klein, 1932, p. 51)*

Indicating to the child an awareness of their anxiety at these moments of unconscious urgency is an act of the greatest importance. The reason for doing so is not primarily to be soothing to the child, but to offer an understanding of unconscious anxiety in order to keep open a precious portal to the child's unconscious mental life.

Failing to pick up the existence of such crucial moments in the flow of analytic contact, or noticing them but failing to act resolutely in relation to them, are not the only unconsciously influenced defences of the analyst against contact with mental pain in their daily work. Neither is an outright barrier in the analyst to taking in such moments. In fact the most common, and most likely defensive manoeuvres are (a) the 'routine interpretation', usually drawn from an existing stock of theory and based on 'recognition memory', and (b) the unconscious creation of a jointly agreed defensive 'explanation'. Both phenomena can be clarified using Bion's concept of a 'column 2' defence, the effect of which is to bring about a plausible-sounding but collusive agreement. The agreement is to a story to which analyst and patient both prefer to subscribe, as a defence against a truth that is felt to hold excessive disruptive force to both.

'Column 2' statements: a defence of the analyst against the ontological anxiety of being with the patient

The strange title for this concept derives from Bion's study of classes of statement made in analysis according not only to the possibility that language may lead to the patient being understood by the analyst, but that statements can be *put to use* for a variety of other purposes. 'Column 2' formulations have the function of preventing the obtrusion of a hidden alternative statement that are felt to be likely to make unwelcome contact with a truth felt to be disablingly disruptive to both participants.

In terms of Bion's model of the container–contained, the 'column 2' defence would feel necessary in a situation where there is an abrupt and alarming threat of catastrophic anxiety due to growth, or the need for growth, in the self and whatever is felt to be its essential containing structure. If this is a correct view, we would expect that uses of this defence by analysts would be likely to occur when an interpretation or a formulation that is occurring to them is feared as a potentially damaging (or 'parasitic') content, not a 'symbiotic' one if it were to be 'put into' the mind of the patient. I believe it is possible, in such moments that bear the potential for a mutative intervention, that the analyst's own profound ontological anxiety is stirred concerning the dangers of growth, of a sudden transformation of being and becoming.

Money-Kyrle's 'facts of life' as instances of ontological anxiety

In his 1968 paper on cognitive development, and its short elaboration in 1971, Roger Money-Kyrle wrote of anxieties conveyed in analysis that reveal the patient's need to protect themselves against awareness of "the basic structure of the essential facts of life" (1968, p. 693), basic innate preconceptions of the primordial that seem to produce a unique anxiety, and which I would connect firmly with the foregoing descriptions of ontological anxiety, anxiety that is of the human condition. Primary recognitions of experiences that match basic innate human preconceptions, suggests Money-Kyrle, can fail to be made, "because the infant, or some part of the infant, fails to recognize what is intolerable to him". In this he is following Freud's line of thinking in his "Formulations on the two principles of mental functioning" (1911), considering the possibility of a crucial unconscious 'decision' made by the psyche to evade experience rather than to face and to modify it.

Money-Kyrle described how he had moved from thinking of how the patient in analysis was *representing* the internal parental couple, as a prototypic example, to considering the multitude of ways in which they seemed unconsciously driven to *misrepresent* the object relation. "Indeed", he wrote, "every conceivable representation of it seems to proliferate in the unconscious except the right one" (Money-Kyrle, 1968, p. 691). The 'right one' would be that bringing a realisation of *separateness*; the parental couple is a union that in significant respects excludes the child from what is the object of the greatest curiosity, and that the child came from a creative act between them and he was not therefore self-creating – made by his own delusional, megalomanic, "parthenogenetic creativity" (Money-Kyrle, 1971, p. 103). A truthful picture of the couple – first as represented by the conjunction of mouth and nipple, then infant and breast, infant and mother and so on, as foundational for the parental couple itself, is anathema to the omnipotence supporting narcissism. To the extent that a personality is organised omnipotently, the event that Bion indicates by the term 'transformation in O' poses a potential psychological disaster at its foundation (see Chapter 8). The 'stories', told *by* the self *to* the self in order to avert such a catastrophe, the misrecognitions discussed by Money-Kyrle, can be considered instances of what Bion was exploring under his 'column 2' concept, in which every conceivable theory or model is allowed to be considered, *except* the one closest to truth.

Brushes of contact with the real (O) are relatively sporadic in analytic work and do not tend to lead to our becoming informed (K), particularly when the container–contained relationship falters under catastrophic anxiety. In the place of conception and change in the participants following a potential moment of truth, *contra*-ception is achieved by means of 'column 2' substitutions. Instead of what Bion calls the 'language of achievement', 'column 2' activity is marshalled in the service of the 'language of substitution'. The intolerable facts of life – mortality, transience, impermanence, the irreversibility of time – are altered by a process creating alternative stories that are more palatable to the individual and his group.

That no good experience lasts for ever is learned at the breast, as is the recognition that the mother's breast, however disappointing and frustrating in its comings and goings, and fundamentally in its independence from the infant, is primordially good and fundamentally necessary to life. This is Money-Kyrle's first 'fact of life', the second being the perception of the intercourse between his parents as a supremely creative act, and the third recognition is of the immutable inevitability of time and eventual death. This third, not the fear of being destroyed by an object but the recognition that life itself is impermanent, corresponds to Heidegger's specification that human beings are beings-towards-death. As Money-Kyrle writes:

> But to fear death is not the same as to recognize its inevitability, which is a fact forced on us much against our will by the repeated experience that no good (or bad) experience can ever last for ever – a fact perhaps never fully accepted.
> *(Money-Kyrle, 1971, p. 104)*

He ends this paper, the companion paper to the one three years earlier, by stating that he now gives a stronger emphasis in his work to the anxiety of death, both as a main factor in the loss of a record of the earliest good experiences, and with the propensity to seek alternative orientations in life, and to form "spurious substitutes".

The distinction echoes Bion's use of Keats' formulation of a 'language of achievement', with its contrasting form, the 'language of substitution'.

Psychoanalysis as a resistance to the conduct of psychoanalysis

Rather as Britton and Steiner (1994, p. 1070) concluded that there is no definitive way for the analyst, in the heat of the moment, to discriminate without doubt between an overvalued idea and a 'selected fact', it may also be true that shared ontological anxiety in the analytic relationship can render it equally impossible at times to distinguish between an interpretation that would feel likely to precipitate beneficial change, and one that addresses a truth so directly that the consequences for the patient and the analyst could turn out to be harmful.

Bion felt that investigating the analyst's use of 'column 2' statements to the patient in such moments, or agreements with such statements when used by the patient, would prove the most helpful way to study *the most common form of psychoanalytic resistance to the conduct of psychoanalysis itself*. Column 2 statements, then, act as formulations with the function of keeping at bay moments in which something of the real being of the patient, and the analyst, threatens to obtrude into awareness in the session. It is, essentially, in the terms developed across the chapters of this book, a defence against the anxiety of the transition O → K. Here is Bion's own definition of the term, from *Elements of Psycho-Analysis*:

> the statement is known to be false but provides the patient with a theory that will act as a defensive barrier against feelings and ideas that might take its place.
>
> *(Bion, 1963, p. 71)*

In the course of an analysis many statements are asserted, and offered up for agreement, by the patient, and by the analyst too, but the idea of the 'column 2' proposition is that its primary purpose, though unconscious and normally appreciated only in hindsight, is as an *invention* to prevent the evolution into awareness of a potentially disturbing *discovery*. Freud cautioned new analysts against constructions based on their preferred modes of thinking, reminding us that an occupational hazard of the analyst is that of "never finding anything but what he already knows" (Freud 1912a, p. 112).

The dynamics of transference and countertransference often produce the conviction that understanding is not enough, that something practical must be done for the patient. This pressure is especially strong in the analyses where it becomes apparent that the original figures in the patient's life were deficient in their care, they may have been traumatising, unconcerned, pretend, or all four of these. It is natural that the analyst who knows the suffering of the patient as a small child would wish to *be* a better object for them, and to offer a better provision, and in some highly specific areas, such as being a better and possibly more containing listener, this may be possible at times within the bounds of an analytic relationship without distorting the setting and depriving the patient of an opportunity for a real analysis.

As well as the risk of being false, through becoming over-attentive and 'waiterly' in the sense discussed earlier, there is also the likelihood that an over-determined analyst will split off or repress their true feelings in order to appear perpetually kind, only for the feelings to return with emotional violence at some later point. Ultimately, as Paula Heimann[13] taught, there is no substitute for the analyst being real. Moreover, as O'Shaughnessy has pointed out, it is often not recognised that too great a determination on the part of the analyst to be the 'new good object' in the patient's life is very likely to result in them being perceived instead as an 'archaic good object', a highly threatening early object that is felt to demand worship and obeisance, resembling closely the kind of parent who makes mute but compelling claims to be regarded as perfect.

To the extent that analysts take on both Freud's recommendations concerning the specificity of the psychoanalytic method, and Bion's extensions of these (discussed throughout the book), there is the arduous nature of conducting a psychoanalysis directed towards the unknown, towards the unconcealment of psychical reality[14] – as contrasted with what often substitutes for it, the examination of more conscious conflicts in the external world and past history of the patient. Related to the above, but not identical, is the difficulty experienced by the analyst in becoming something of a 'stranger in a strange land'. Holzhey-Kunz has made the point that analytic exploration does not only place us in an estranged and unfamiliar landscape, it even leads to uncertainty concerning the concept of strange. What I mean by this is that the notion and existence of meaning itself becomes subject to doubt in the practice of analysis, and no discussion of the difficulty for the analyst in being with his patient should ignore this fact. We therefore need to consider the need for maintaining and furthering our capacity to tolerate being thrown by analytic listening, and by the forces of transference and countertransference, into estrangement from our everyday conceptions of our inner and outer worlds, including our current conceptions of psychoanalysis itself, since this too is not fixed.

As I discussed earlier, Melanie Klein found that even in her therapeutic work with small children – perhaps especially so – there was an inner resistance felt at the prospect of giving interpretations that were to the point. In 1934 James Strachey wrote of a "lurking difficulty in the actual giving of the interpretation", from which he inferred that the analyst in such a pivotal moment felt overwhelming anxiety, dreading a real yet ill-defined kind of contact between themselves and the patient. It is evident that Strachey and Klein realised that this meant that *real contact itself* constituted a situation of danger.

Strachey wrote, "Such a moment must *above all others* put to the test his relations with his own unconscious impulses" (1934, p. 159, my emphasis). The anxiety to

---

13 "On the necessity for the analyst to be natural with his patient", Heimann, 1989, p. 311.
14 Truth as *alethea* (αλήθεια): unconcealedness, disclosedness.

be faced in such moments may arise from a frightening object or situation coming from the outermost reaches of the patient. It could also be a dawning, on both participants, of the vast area of the unknown, perhaps invoking some dark inner objectification of it resembling Coleridge's "frightful fiend that doth tread close behind".[15] And if it is truly an *ontological* anxiety, with no ready-to-hand object, it is bound to be one that will impact both analyst and patient with hardly any opportunities to be shielded against it.

From all three perspectives considered in this book, the psychoanalytic, the existential and the dramaturgical, the analyst is at the focal point of having their sense of identity, their sense of being a particular person in a particular situation, configured and reconfigured, and, in the process, being 'made-strange' in a manner outside their control. The analytical situation itself is structured to allow the patient to do this, in the interests of eventual change and maturation, and the analyst has to undergo a process that is for the most part under the influence of factors outside their personality. This constitutes an inescapable and unmodifiable reality in the ontological realm, and not only in the domain of knowing and learning, something brought out most clearly in the work of Samuel Beckett in *Texts for Nothing*.

Another anxiety of the analyst stems from their unconscious dread of acting *just like* the frightening objects present in the inner world of the patient, or their own, in which the anxiety is twofold. First there is the anxiety of losing ourselves, who we are and who we consider ourselves to be, though these two aspects may not entirely correspond. This is an ontological anxiety at the heart of being an analyst – for periods of an analysis the transference processes create uncertainty and doubt over the question of who and what we are. Second, and consequent upon the first difficulty, we may feel anxiety at what we will visit upon our patient if, in the turbulent emotional storm created when two personalities meet we were to *become,* and enact upon the patient, one of the destructive objects or parts of the self in our own internal world. Bion put the matter simply:

> When two personalities meet, an emotional storm is created. If they make sufficient contact to be aware of each other, or even sufficient to be unaware of each other, an emotional state is produced by the conjunction of these two individuals, and the resulting disturbance is hardly likely to be regarded as necessarily an improvement on the state of affairs had they never met at all.
>
> *(Bion, 1979; 2014, vol. 10, p. 136)*

All these possibilities can arouse what Bion termed catastrophic anxiety in the analyst, a type of anxiety that lies at the heart of the danger situation of analysis that Strachey and Klein identified in their discussions, and which Strachey reported in his 1934 paper. Here is an illustration of the analyst's anxiety of enacting the part of an object that is detrimental to the patient.

---

15 From *The Rime of the Ancient Mariner*, Samuel Taylor Coleridge.

Clinical illustration

Ms D was an echoistic[16] patient whose mother, a malignant narcissist, had ruled her life until she had managed to move away and get married. This had resulted in the patient having such a powerful internal narcissistic object, she often appeared in sessions as self-blaming and self-loathing. Her repeated subservience to this object's criticisms of her and her procrastination in making any decision, because she had been so used to her mother making all decisions for her, caused both the patient and therapist some frustration. The patient had been in therapy for three years and was aware of the role her object played but at times she became so persecuted by it she was unable to recognize whether she herself or her object were present and at these moments she resorted to statements that sounded like repetitions of something she had been told by her mother and continued to hear from her object.

In one session, after a break, Ms D had spoken of her negligence in remembering to pay her invoice on time, and how she had meant to do it and then thought she had done it and forgotten. The patient gave a long description of how frightened she had been that her mother was going to break into her house and steal her children. The patient at one point had become so fearful when she heard a car in the drive that she had hidden under the bed holding her children to her and holding her hands over their mouths so as not to allow a sound.

Her therapist interpreted that she had been subject to a terrifying mother and had felt herself to be abandoned by the therapist. The patient agreed she had felt alone. When her therapist interpreted that Ms D had felt resentful towards her for leaving her at the mercy of both her internal mother and an actual invasive mother, the patient denied any resentment. The therapist pointed out that the patient had never failed to pay her before and that this was evidence of an unconscious feeling of resentment and wish to punish her therapist for abandoning her. The patient began to cry, and to protest that that had not been her feeling and then after the therapist continued to assert that the patient was too fearful to acknowledge that she had had this wish, she started to question herself and after a while she started to agree. It was in this moment that the therapist was able to be reflexive and recognize that she had not only found herself beginning to bully the patient by trying to make her see what she thought was undeniably true, but that she had taken some sadistic pleasure in doing so. Although horrified at her own sadism, particularly given the vulnerability of such a patient, she was able to remain curious, and had the realisation that something of the early situation was being relived between them, and informing her of her patient's actual experience. From this point the therapist was able to interpret from becoming informed by the experience both had shared.

Strachey thought that the deterrent effect on mutative interpretation came from what he called 'instinctual forces' and 'id-energy'. Today we would be

---

16 Echoism (Savery, 2018) – defined as the silenced response to narcissism – is the clinical counterpart to the first character of Ovid's myth of Echo just as what we meet with in the consulting room and call narcissism relates to the second. Two central clinical features are an absence of self and voice.

more likely to use the concept of the analyst's countertransference anxiety. Dramaturgically speaking, one of the analyst's difficulties in being with his patient is the unconscious or preconscious fear that the objects of their own world will become stimulated to near-action by the transference of the patient's inner drama. This can come about in resonance with the activities of the patient's unconscious pressure to live out in the analytic relationship some of their most intensely felt reactions.

And then there is a further source of the phenomenon noted by Strachey, when the analyst makes contact with something of the *being* of the patient and does not stop at knowing *about* him. Waiting for a moment of contact with the *being* of the patient to evolve allows the analyst to become open to words that arise from this being-with, *and from no other source*. This constitutes part of what Strachey calls a crucial act for the analyst, as well as for the patient, and in this too he is exposing himself to a potential danger – corresponding in the analytic situation to the angst described by Kierkegaard in *Fear and Trembling*, and the nameless dread as discussed by Bion.

Francesca Bion noted in her Montreal address of 1994 that her husband would sometimes emerge from his study, after contemplating his work that day, white-faced and ashen. This is comprehensible to us if we keep in mind that he was above all an explorer whose relinquishment of routine and familiar ways of understanding the phenomena of the consulting room exposed him to being perilously close to the abysmal experiences of nothingness of his most deeply troubled patients. As well as his unequivocal expression of an ontological-philosophical viewpoint in his 1973 discussions in São Paulo, he pursued the approach in talks and discussions throughout the 1970s, for example in two previously unpublished papers,[17] "Negative capability" (1967) and "Break up, break down, break through" (1975).

Beyond these considerations I am suggesting that we supplement Strachey's insights concerning the sense of danger in the analytic contact, and those of Bion, with the realisation that effective interpretations risk not only powerful contact with 'live' menacing objects of the patient and of the analyst, but that they also threaten a brush with the ontological anxieties common to both, and crucially the danger for both parties of *becoming* something as yet unknown. Secondly, ontological anxiety itself, when we meet it, seems to be all the more feared because it is irreducible by the transformation of understanding, except that is for the possibility of having another with us to experience it. This contrasts with ontic anxieties and the phantasies that accompany them, as with these we can obtain a sense of 'ego-syntonic' identity as a demonstrably helpful person, unassailed by the same or even similar anxieties.

A potentially authentic approach to ontological anxiety is to be with the other and to bear witness to the truth of the experience without pretending to be able to have an answer or a 'better' way of understanding. Some solace may be gained by not

17 Published in June 2018 in *Three Papers of W. R. Bion* (ed. C. Mawson), Routledge.

being abandoned or shunned in this condition. This is a kind of anxiety that cannot be removed, and should not be pathologised or reasoned away. Samuel Johnson, in a 1758 letter to Bennet Langton, may well have had something very similar in mind – particularly when we bear in mind that its main subject was sudden death – when he wrote the following lines, quoted by Bion (1970, p. 7) in *Attention and Interpretation*:

> Let us endeavour to see things as they are, and then enquire whether we ought to complain. Whether to see life as it is will give us much consolation, I know not; but the consolation that is drawn from truth, if any there be, is solid and durable; that which may be derived from errour must be, like its original, fallacious and fugitive.
>
> *(Johnson, cited in Boswell, 1934 [1791], vol. 1, p. 339)*

The experience of this kind of crisis, to which Bion gave the term catastrophic change, with its particular kind of anguish, has been described by Bion's colleague, Betty Joseph. She wrote (1998, p. 88) of pivotal moments of change, sometimes detectable within a session, in which the current equilibrium of the whole personality undergoes a shift. She noted especially the *physicality* of the experience, with patients frequently pointing to the region of their lower chest, and yet at the same time not expressing this as an event of their body, nor quite of their mind alone.

Joseph went further, adding something that I believe is crucial concerning the nature of the anxiety as belonging to an ontological realisation, one going beyond what we normally consider anxiety in psychoanalysis:

> I have suggested that the pain is not just anxiety, not just depression. I shall indicate that it is linked with a greater awareness of the self and of the reality of other people, thus that it is linked with a sense of separateness, but it is not just these concepts that I am talking about – I want to explore the experience and the qualities involved. I think that it emerges in patients who, though in many ways living apparently satisfactory lives, have important areas of psychotic anxieties and whose defences have been operating comparatively successfully. They have to some extent achieved peace and freedom from conflict by the use of particular types of relationships with objects, which protect them from realistic emotional experiences.
>
> *(Joseph, 1998, p. 89)*

Clinical illustration

In supervision a colleague described a patient with whom she had been working intensively for some years. The patient, a young woman who had completed a course of training feeling very much alone in the world, without friends, and whose life had until then been solitary, had avoided her feelings of separateness and loneliness through constructing a phantasy world in which she was popular and central. With her analyst's presence she was forced to confront this, and the collapsing, not only of her phantasy world, but also of a self who existed in this world alone, with the terrible consequences of having to face not just her loneliness but her awareness of her own existential nothingness – because beyond the constructed world she did not have a real existence. This painful state encountered by this young woman was made bearable by an analyst who was able to stay with her patient's feelings and interpret from her own 'brush with the ontological' – the most anxiety-provoking truth of the shared experience of the couple in the room. This produced the somewhat counter-intuitive experience in the patient, who felt that now she was no longer alone, and that a more truthful relationship to reality could be borne.

The specific form of anxiety arising from such a shift in psychic equilibrium is connected to a greater awareness of the self and of the *reality* of other people. In other words, their *being*. If the analyst can also, in their own way, make a comparable shift, as in this example, it takes both members of the analytic couple closer to the experience of the real and separate other. The vignette above, therefore, illustrates a new state in a relationship where the analyst can describe to the patient the dreadful feelings evoked by being in touch with the reality of the patient's actual existence, and this can bring about a transformation, first of all in alleviating the experience of isolation, next in finding words for the pain, which opens the way to finding symbols and thoughts. In describing the experience of the patient through staying with her, her analyst had interpreted from O, bringing about a transformation which had enabled thinking and therein some understanding in the realm of K.

This touches on the shift indicated in 1965 by Bion, when he implied that other people may be known as *phenomena*, but that the reality of them cannot itself be *known*, but has to be met first of all through a different sort of relation to them than knowing about them. Bion asked whether the process of interpretive understanding can promote 'a transition from knowing the phenomena of the real self to being the real self' (1965a, p. 148), adding that if such a thing is possible, interpretation must achieve more than increasing knowledge.

Whether psychoanalytic interpretation is adequate to this task, as Bion had hoped, is open to further consideration and study. For now, I would just say that by implication, and in line with the central thesis of this book, *such interpretive activity must first put the patient in touch with elements of his being, disclosed to himself through contacts with the ontological and its unique anxiety*. In the final chapter I will be discussing this as a methodological recommendation to give priority to the making-present of experience over its representation.

I began the chapter asking about the difficulty for the analyst in being with the patient, but in considering the reality of the situation it becomes clear that in fact the difficulty for the analyst resides in being with oneself while with the patient, a truth nicely expressed in the following concise terms by Hiscock:

The difficulty for the analyst in being with the patient is the difficulty to be with oneself enough, in love and in hate, to be free to find and be curious about the patient.

(personal communication, 2018)

I will now, in the final chapter of the book, consider methodological implications of the ideas explored in the preceding chapters.

12

RECOMMENDATIONS ON METHOD

In this chapter I consider elements of methodology suited to effecting the shift that I have been exploring throughout this book – the movement from interpretive activity based primarily on knowing about the phenomena of the patient towards becoming informed through the existential being-with relation, with the conventional faculty of everyday knowledge suspended. To do this I make use of Melanie Klein's term, psychoanalytical attitude, as a unifying concept. What I mean by this is that in the psychoanalytical situation we do not follow a set of delineated textbook procedures, but instead we channel any principles of method learned from experience through our basic disposition towards our patients.

I will discuss methodology in relation firstly to the recommendations at the heart of the standard model of psychoanalytic listening (evenly suspended attentiveness in a relatively abstinent analytic attitude as described by Freud, 1912a, p. 111), secondly as supplemented by the extension to these of Bion's methodology, which I have been considering throughout the book as a basically phenomenological and apophatic psychoanalytical attitude, and thirdly I will be considering elements of our method suited for yet a third expansion of the listening component, to take into account the findings of Holzhey-Kunz in the domain of the patient's fundamental strivings to understand themselves and their world philosophically. Finally I will suggest that these dimensions, the psychoanalytic and the ontological, require the inclusion of a third, that of the dramaturgical, because the principles of drama are inherently part of the structure and dynamic functioning of the mind of the human being, and this is evident in the very nature of object relations. In other words, the concept of inner drama is not restricted to being an analogy to what goes on in the mind, the processes of the mind are dramaturgical in their very nature. Psychological drama is not only of the mind, our object relations take place on a stage within the mind, the inner world, and what we call its 'objects' are in fact its dramatis personae. The claim is that mental objects are not only objects in a conceptual scheme, but correspond to an underlying reality no less real than what we normally take to be the actuality of the outer material conditions of our world. In considering methodology suited to an investigation of the being of the patient, I am taking psychoanalysis, as I have done throughout this book, in its multiple perspectives – the world of the unconscious, the world of the drama of internal relations, and the being-in-the-world of the patient, with its ontological modes of being and anxiety as their fundamental disclosing mood.

The closing section is divided into two parts, first there are aspects of the principal areas of method under consideration, stemming from the body of ideas in the book (mainly theory), to be followed by a treatment of them in relation to their technical handling (mainly practice).[1] As in all communication of psychoanalytic ideas with practical implications, our practice is not only a function of the structure of ideas, and how they are expressed, but of what can be achieved with them by a human being in what Britton calls "the ordinary muddle of clinical practice".

Mainly theory

Evenly suspended attentiveness

As described by Freud (1912a, p. 111) this is the core component of the psychoanalytic method. Although it suspends selection on the basis of expectation and inclination, which partially corresponds to memory and desire, as a primary principle it is subject to one major qualifying factor, that of the primacy of anxiety. Present in the work of Melanie Klein in the form of a technical concept, that of the 'point of urgency', the importance of this over-riding factor was stated by Freud before the psychoanalytic method was established formally. Pain, he wrote in 1895 (p. 307), including mental pain, is "the most imperative of all processes", and that the whole mental apparatus has "the most decided tendency to flee from it". All that we meet in terms of psychological defence and the concealment of the unconscious is founded upon this. In his 1915 paper on repression Freud noted again that pain is imperative, and that if it is not to be dealt with by removal through artificial anaesthesia it requires specific and relevant intervention by being treated appropriately as a *mental* event. He wrote (1915, p. 147) that "It can be allayed by nothing but the action that satisfies it; it keeps up a constant tension". Freud wrote, famously, that in the psychoanalytic situation we should simply listen, and not 'listen for' something. The recommendation was to

> ". . . withhold all conscious influences from his capacity to attend, and give himself over completely to his 'unconscious memory'." Or, to put it

---

1 In making this division I am making use of the structure adopted so effectively by Elisabeth Spillius in her comprehensive book *Melanie Klein Today* (1988). It rests on a distinction marked by the Greek terms *techne* and *episteme* (Shepherd *et al.*, 2006, pp. 90–1).

purely in terms of technique: "He should simply listen, and not bother about whether he is keeping anything in mind".

(Freud, 1912a, 112)

This of course refers mainly to the content of the patient's communications, particularly to its constructed narrative, but it refers also to the expression of affects. Because of the primacy of anxiety in psychoanalysis, however, which is an imperative not only for the patient but also for our listening, on the basis that anxiety is a principal way of access to their minds – a fact known from antiquity and forming the root of psychoanalysis in Freud's "Project" – we orient ourselves to the patient in an attitude of evenly suspended attention yet with great openness to the anxiety both overt and concealed, conscious and unconscious. Bion's contribution to this was with the insight that we do this not predominantly through our senses, but with a different faculty, that of intuition, as I discussed earlier in the book. It is an insight which makes sense of the otherwise obscure recommendations of Bion to suspend the operation of memory, desire and understanding. It is on the basis of exploring those difficult recommendations that the analyst can come to realise just how far their intuitive capacity can be dulled by an excessive preoccupation with supposed external facts and historical narrative that smooth out the contradictions, discontinuities and outright strangeness in the patient's inner and outer life.

A relatively abstinent attitude

This is important in freeing the analytic relationship to become one in which the analyst's personality and mental contents do not over-fill the mental space made available to the patient. This is part of what is meant by the container–contained relationship, which is at the heart of the method of effective analysis. The intrusion of too much of the analyst's own personality is, moreover, normally experienced by the patient as a narcissistic taking over of their own mind, and when it happens it tends to be experienced as a traumatising repetition of an earlier formative relationship.

Memory, desire and apperception

The voluntary restraint of the analyst on the use in the session of the faculty of *memory*, and on their desire for particular developments to happen in the analysis, for the 'betterment' of the patient for example, or to be seen as only a helpful figure in the patient's inner and outer life, becomes an extremely important methodological requirement, unless, that is, the faculty of intuition is regarded consciously or unconsciously as unimportant to the task of being an analyst. Few, if any, practising analysts would say that they wished to do without their intuition, but, as Bion noted, it frequently goes unnoticed that the aptitude for it suffers demonstrably when memory, desire and an excessive drive to explain are indulged, most often due to unacknowledged anxiety in the analyst. Intuition can be dispensed with *unconsciously* by the analyst at times where it is felt to be too dangerous, to the self or the patient, or to both participants, as Strachey (1934) himself intuited. The particular form of understanding posing the greatest obstacle to clinical intuition I described earlier as that of apperception, defined by William James as "to unite a new perception to a mass of ideas already possessed, thereby to comprehend and interpret it". Since the priority of this mode is the generic classification of experience in terms of the already known, it is particularly unsuited to approaching the unknown or largely unknown aspects of an evolving situation between human beings. In addition, it is the mode of knowing that places most emphasis on the subject–object cleavage of the everyday mentality, and therefore it interferes with the sensibility of the analyst not only towards specifically psychical reality, but also their receptivity to being with the patient in the shared ontological realm, in which both analyst and patient share the anxieties of the human condition, about which – as Beckett said, in *Waiting for Godot* – there is nothing to be done.

The dramatic composition of the inner world and its manifestation

Our psychoanalytic method has an inherent dramaturgical dimension. This is revealed in two main areas. Firstly, the processes entrained by both Freud's evenly suspended attention and by Bion's recommendations on memory and desire serve a similar underlying function to a principle known in the study of theatre as the *Verfremsdungseffekt*, which can be translated as 'the making strange of the familiar'. To listen with evenly suspended attention to the verbal content of the patient's communications 'makes strange', for the purposes of discerning unconscious aspects, what otherwise would be received according to the encoding by the patient for a 'preferred reading' of their narrative by their listener in the analytic hour. The patterns of choice, emphasis and weighting of particular words, in place of others in what in structural linguistics is known as the 'vertical' or paradigmatic (sometimes called the metaphoric, or synchronic dimension) of utterances, are revealing of unconscious forces. Those in the 'horizontal' plane of speech, the so-called syntagmatic or diachronic chain, the 'metonymy' in language, as well as being capable of revealing unconscious aspects, can also provide evidence of an underlying pattern or design in the patient's use of communication, whereby the listening habits of the analyst, to which the sensitive patient becomes highly attuned, are recruited unconsciously for defensive enactments in the transference–countertransference relationship. I include these aspects of 'language-in-action' in the dramaturgical realm, suggesting that it is a part of our method to be attuned in the analytic situation to the effects on the countertransference of the analyst of these psycholinguistic processes. This is because of their power to configure role-relationships in the internal world of the analyst in the manner highlighted in Bion's explanation, written in 1952, of the relationship between projective identification and countertransference (1961b, p. 148). The second element of the dramaturgical to be found in the practice of analysis, and to which our attention is turned in our daily work with our patients, is that of the object relations themselves. The dynamic and changing relationships that we discern in our patients, lived out to an extent in the analytic relationship, are in themselves dramaturgical structures. The concept of the theatre of the mind stands not just as an analogy to the processes at work, but as an accurate depiction of their actual nature. In other words, the concept of an inner world of unconscious phantasy rests on there being a dramaturgical dimension of mental life. The psychoanalytic method is a way of accessing its basic structure and functioning.

The ontological dimension in psychoanalysis

The anxiety of human beings has been known from antiquity, as I discussed earlier in the book, as rooted in the ontological. If this is to be reflected properly in our method, together with the awareness that we share, as part of our epistemophilic 'instinct' an inherent philosophical interest in our existence and non-existence, there is a need to understand the practical relevance to our work of ontological-phenomenological philosophy. The recent specifically psychoanalytic version of daseinsanalysis developed by Holzhey-Kunz and her colleagues in Zurich has made a beginning with regard to a Freudian model. The approach pursued across the chapters of this book, by including the dramaturgical dimension of analytic work, allows such an integration to be expanded to embrace theories of object relations, unconscious phantasy and a dynamic inner world. Clinical practice undergoes a particular change of emphasis in this approach in relation to claims to know the patient, which is why I have stressed the importance of the analyst seeing their task as becoming informed by the relationship to being, rather than through an active mode of knowing based on acquisition and relationship to past knowledge. Moving from knowing facts to knowing as a mode of being, by being changed, to some degree, as a result of becoming informed *by the experience of being*, requires the inclusion of ontological-philosophical principles, and this at the practical level. I have attempted to explore this from a number of perspectives to achieve a requisite philosophical grounding for taking further Bion's work of the ontological in post-Kleinian analysis.

Mainly practice

Earlier I introduced an addition made by Giovanna Di Ceglie to Bion's theory of the container–contained, a 'ground condition' that has to exist for the mother to be experienced by her infant as a human and humanising container for anxiety. She calls it *orientation*. I have come to realise that her concept has clinical relevance to what I have been calling our analytic attitude, particularly in the matter of timing – of when to think interpretively in a session and when to suspend that activity in favour of openness to what may strike us from what is present, or which may be made present. In other words, there are times to consider what is *represented* by what confronts us, but for the most part I try to face first what is present, *as* it presents itself, and sometimes this means to explore further in order to reveal what is present but as yet only in a concealed or partially covered form. The purpose is to be-with these experiences and to be impacted by them before considering possible representations,[2] such as those involving, for instance, dream-like transformations such as displacements and condensations of symbolic meaning. This principle is another aspect of allowing priority in the analytic situation to being over knowing, and it emphasises the significance in our method of a basically contemplative attitude.

I have been regarding the analyst's first requirement as being to make herself available for the anxiety of the patient, both ontic (specific fears linked to identifiable psychological objects and situations) and ontological (anxieties of the human condition, with no remedy and no 'object'). The attitude described by Bion as reverie reflects the maternal-receptive element in Freud's core technical recommendation for the practitioner to listen with evenly suspended attentiveness, and each practitioner needs to discover from their own unique experience what this capacity feels like for them. Its way of expressing itself will be different with every individual patient, as will the experience of failure to maintain it. Such discovery is part of becoming an analyst. It is an attitude of openness, unshieldedness and restraint from the ordinary, habitual and familiar 'reading' of events in material reality.

Given the last statement, it is inevitable that all analysts will find themselves closing off, foreclosing exploration or swerving[3] away from listening openly to the patient, usually under the sway of the ontic or ontological anxiety lurking in what is being experienced and conveyed by them. This is expressed by Bion as a dread of the *imminence* of an experience of 'O' as it approaches being formulated in K. This is what I have been considering as becoming informed by being with the patient in anxiety.

I have discussed a particular quality of resistance to that premonitory anxiety, and to explore it further methodologically I made use of a hint of Bion's concerning a potential tool ('column 2') for use at such pivotal moments in a session. I suggested that these probably correspond closely to what Klein called a 'point of urgency'. I will expand a little on this subject now.

Because column 2 defences create comforting and familiar narratives they are often reached for and given the seal of approval by both participants when ontological anxiety threatens to emerge. Many plausible propositions of truth can be made that turn out in hindsight to be 'preferred readings' of the events of the analytic hour, of the patient's 'history', or connections between them. It helps to

2 This was hinted at by Freud (1916) in his letter to Lou Andreas-Salomé of 25 May 1916: "renouncing cohesion, harmony, rhetoric and everything which you call symbolic".

3 Staged in Beckett's production *Quad2* – a short televised piece of choreography, it is a clear depiction of this tendency. Written and first broadcast in simplified form in 1981, it consists of four players, each dressed in a robe known as a *djellaba*, silently pacing the edges of a square, then walking diagonally across it, entering and exiting but without touching and, crucially, without walking on the centre, a position designated as 'O', a centre from which they each swerve.

retain as part of our analytic attitude Freud's (1912a, p. 112) dictum: "it must not be forgotten that the things one hears are for the most part things whose meaning is only recognized later on". What at the time may feel a clear insight may turn out to have been what Britton and Steiner have termed an overvalued idea. Some of these ideas can occasionally be recognised, even at the time of forming them, as unsatisfactory productions, formulations that substitute for something glimpsed in the shadows as holding the potential for a turbulent or explosive realisation. When we really understand from our clinical experience that a true statement can be used as a barrier to a more challenging truth – which is the meaning of Bion's column 2 concept – it becomes possible to grasp how important it is to monitor closely the patient's evolving emotional response after each of out interpretive actions.

I wrote earlier in the chapter about one particular hazard of interpreting from knowing about the patient, which is to do so in a way that makes them feel objectified. We need to be willing and able to remain open to those communications from the patient that can inform us that we have been experienced, through our knowing, as somehow intruding into them, taking over their experience or even their whole personality, in a way that may not have been clear to us at the time. Even if we do not believe that we have done so, it is an important part of our method not to resist or to contradict their feeling or assertion that we have intruded on them. Even where we may have good grounds to consider that a specific transference experience is being felt, we first need to treat the patient's description seriously, as an experience. This is an element of what has been described in the book as being a mental container for the patient's anxiety. John Steiner's (1993) concept of analyst-centred interpretations is useful in this regard, both as a technical principle and as a reminder to practitioners to maintain a constantly refreshed awareness of the significance of the many dimensions of the language that they use in their work. Another methodological aspect arises from the fact that the analyst functioning as a mental container for painful experience, rather than functioning in an intrusive, overpowering 'over-containing' manner, may at times be 'under-containing', through the analyst 'sitting too far back' from the patient and failing to take the projected distress and respond appropriately. The discussion earlier in the book of different forms of silence is helpful in orienting us to the intimate connections between qualities of silence, the container–contained relationship, and the experience of being listened to and understood as a subject in our own right.

Suspending memory, desire and understanding

The methodological implication of Bion's recommendation to practise listening, formulating ideas and interpreting whilst suspending memory, desire and understanding is as relevant to making contact with the patient ontologically as it is to working with their unconscious phantasies, beliefs and impulses. The philosophical 'ear', necessary for modes of being and for the differentiation of ontic fears and their ontological inclusions, requires a comparable suspension of everyday faculties. Practically speaking, this is where the dramaturgical, existential and psychoanalytic perspectives really come together closely in terms of method. Dramaturgically because Brecht's principle in theatre of 'making strange the familiar' has, as I have shown, such a useful affinity with the ontological (*l'habitude*; *das Man*; the 'not-at-home' of angst) and equally with psychoanalysis in its basic method. With the proviso that I take Bion's recommendation for the suspension of understanding to refer not to all understanding, but to (a) its *apperceptive* mode, and (b) its prematurity and foreclosing aspect (Keats' "irritable reaching after fact and reason"), I agree with him that for working with the dynamic unconscious and with the ontological realm, the analyst should be willing to experiment further than using a 'textual' form of evenly suspended attentiveness. What I am recommending is that practitioners undertake a detailed, in-depth study of the part played in their own clinical thinking by their own particular reliance on memory in their work, to interrogate the importance of remembered facts in their individual style of working.

Secondly it is helpful for us to discover in detail how our desires affect our work. If we have a concealed desire that a particular patient, or our patients more generally, should express themselves in ways that suit us, or that they should change in particular ways, or perhaps become more like us, or even that we like them very much and so want them to get over their suffering quickly, it is important that we should be open to realising these things. It is, I think, especially valuable to become aware of our unacknowledged preferences for how we are perceived by our patients. The latter consideration is connected with what I have discussed in the book in terms of Sartre's concepts of *the look*, and the associated mode of being, the *être-pour-autrui* to which the analyst is exposed in the clinical encounter, as well as the patient, and the occupational hazard for analysts of a defensively false imitative posture illustrated by Sartre's description of the self-deceiving waiter.

The earlier chapters of the book deal with some of the disturbing accompaniments of the uncommon state of being that remains *after* the faculties of memory, desire, and apperception have lost their central position in our work. Bion's recommendations remind us that analytic listening is *not* in the ordinary everyday mode, and he goes much further, pointing out that when we prefer and privilege the everyday mode we are unlikely to be able to make use of the full capacity of our method. If the analyst stays too much in the everyday mentality, that which Proust called *l'habitude*, analytic functioning becomes not only blunted and numbed through an excess of concreteness, they are also left with their own ontological anxiety (which is always the case) but in the absence of vitality and human contact in their thinking. It is in this respect that we recall that Heidegger's term for the being of the human being in their world was *Dasein*, literally being-there. The earlier discussion about the analyst's desire to change the patient for the better have a close bearing on this capacity of the helper to be there with the patient, and not simply to 'do-for'. Surrender to the analytic experience, which does not allow us the security of the 'at-home', is a source of great potential anxiety for the analyst.

The anxiety is intensified if the method chosen depends more on intuition[4] than the application of pre-existing knowledge, drawn for example from the patient's apparent history or the analyst's accumulation of theory.

Writers from as early as the thirteenth century have described the sense of dispossession when contemplating the unknown without the support and evidence of the senses and pre-existing doctrine. In my clinical work I have found the mental strain of working with reduced reliance on memory, desire and apperception to be intensified by including openness to the ontological dimension of my patients' experience. I have become convinced, however, that as practitioners we do need to let go of these particular moorings, for openness both to the unconscious as conceived by Freud, and the ontological inclusions that I have been describing in this book. Although mentally demanding, it should not be forgotten that these methodological principles have the potential for expanding our awareness of the depth and richness of the states of being present in our consulting rooms.

The inner world as dramaturgical

I considered two main elements of the dramaturgical dimension of the psychoanalytic method, first as it applies itself to the investigation of the patient's ontical world of mental objects and their transferences, and second as it orients us to the being-in-the-world of the patient ontologically. The first element, the requirement in our listening and in our interpreting to 'make strange the familiar', is – as well as a significant concept stemming from Brecht's innovations in theatre, a distinctive and defining characteristic of the psychoanalytic method. Although analysis has become widely known as the 'talking cure', it is not generally known that its conversations do not follow the conventional pattern of everyday talk. Where psychoanalytic conversations stay mainly with conflicts in external reality, in which attention is directed to helping people to adapt, something crucial to psychoanalysis goes missing. It is important for practising analysts and therapists working in a psychoanalytic way to know that their method is, essentially, in its own way, sharing with the study of theatre and literature the mode known as 'making strange the familiar'. The practice of evenly suspended attention *is* in fact a form of making-strange (*Verfremdungseffekt*), and is inconsistent with ordinary speech patterns of turn-taking or with an interrogative pattern. Instead, listening with evenly suspended attention, and making the occasional exploratory or interpretive intervention, institutes a very 'deconstructive' kind of conversation, one in which both participants find themselves listening to one another, and to themselves, in a new and strange way. The 'languages of production'[5] of the practical arts of theatre, painting, poetry and psychoanalysis, have in common the absence of

4 See Bion, 1970, p. 43.
5 A term used with a specialised meaning by the revolutionary theatre director, dramatist and poet
   Antonin Artaud (1896–1948). See Artaud, 2010, p. 49.

a one-to-one (isomorphic) correspondence between the elements of their internal and external realities.

The second main dramaturgical element that I discussed also has clinical relevance – that the inner world has dramaturgical structure and dynamics for which Aristotle's principles provide a coherent basis from which to consider the intimate relationship of the concepts defining tragic drama with the structure and dynamics of object relations as we find them in the psychoanalytic study of the mind. The ways in which the philosopher considered the workings in tragic drama of character, crisis, recognition and reversal, fear and pity, are of significance to the psychoanalyst in understanding the drama of the inner world as it strikes them in the consulting room. I have found repeatedly that gaining a deeper understanding of the dramaturgical thinking of theatre directors and dramatists has helped in my understanding of difficult situations arising in analysis, and often in practical ways such understanding has provided unexpected support in bearing with interest the strain of the roles and dramatic positions into which my patients need to draw me. These situations are inevitably going to be at the heart of whatever dramas and tragedies have been left unresolved in the inner and outer lives of the patient.

The analyst who does not evade these dramas by becoming defensively remote undergoes them to some degree, and may not always manage to retain a capacity to observe their part at the time. The resulting feeling can be shame and humiliation, especially when their unwitting part in an enactment is revealed in front of others, in a clinical seminar for example. I think that such feelings result from the awareness that one has been, however temporarily, taken over by another, losing one's sense of being oneself. It is the power of projective identification to be able to effect this, and for a while actually to 'reconfigure' another human being. It is not often realised by the general public that analysts open themselves daily to this truly disturbing process. Bion (1961b, p. 148) has spoken of the need of the analyst to wake up from such powerfully disabling effects in order to occupy a position of separation to be able to interpret what has happened to them. Until this can occur, however, the analyst is in fact altered in something close to their being, and shame is frequently the inevitable consequence of becoming awake. The consequence for the little ego is that it has been helpless, and has been seen to have been helpless, to prevent what seems an 'invasion', a penetration into the self by another, and therefore dramaturgically akin to a colonisation of self. Help at such times takes the form of colleagues who can remind them that such events are a normal part of the experience of analysis, however much this may feel an outrage. The working-through and working-out of dramatic role enactments is a part of psychoanalysis, part of working in the realm of interacting transference and countertransference. To engage with this, practitioners need to be prepared to 'roll up their sleeves', so to speak.

I will now consider a second aspect of recovery from countertransference enactment, the soporific effect of the sense of familiarity, engendered mostly through a particular form of action-inducing projective identification known as 'evocatory'. It will be recalled that Bion in his group papers had linked this phenomenon, observable in groups and couples, with the 'numbing feeling of reality' that sees to it that countertransference reactions are likely to remain hidden by being made to feel unremarkable. If this is understood in practice it gives us another reason to value the capacity of the analyst to make strange the familiar.

I shall now alter the perspective and consider the experience from the position of the patient, rather than that of the analyst. What does it mean at depth to the patient to see that their helper struggles? Earlier I considered the relationships between anxiety, my central concept in the book, and its containment – by the mind of the mother with her infant in the early situation and by the analyst in the clinical setting. The mother's management of the anxiety of her baby, it will be recalled, depends upon her being willing and available to function as a *container* for that anxiety, the possibility of imminent extinction being its first and prototypic manifestation. Young infants cannot by themselves withstand such a powerful ontological anxiety erupting from within, but mothers who care for them have to, dating from before their babies are born.

Fail again, fail better:⁶ the importance of learning from the failure to contain

In his paper "On arrogance" (1958),⁷ delivered in 1957, Bion wrote in practical terms of the consequences for the patient when he as the analyst found himself unable to be that container for his patient. He described how he realised only belatedly that to be a real container for his patient's projected distress he needed to face that his insistence on ordinary meaningful verbal communication from his patient was being experienced by that patient as a refusal, an attack even, on the only mode of communication that he was capable of. To the extent that Bion had failed to contain what was actually coming his way, he *was* in fact the obstructive object about which his patient complained, and at the same time he was able to be informed, through being it, of an already existing internalised object of the patient. Bion's eventual comprehension of this is a good example of what, in this book, I have been putting forward as *becoming informed by being*, as distinct from knowing *about* the patient.

This account by Bion, revealing as it does (a) the difficulty of the analyst in bearing with the patient's necessary use of the only means of communication at his disposal, and (b) his recovery of his analytic function consequent on understanding where he had been failing to contain what actually was real in the patient – who in reality was unable to be with another person in the conventionally communicative way for which Bion had been unconsciously hoping and requiring of him, prepares us for what I believe is the most essential feature of the container–contained theory in its practical use: that it is difficult work, it involves struggle, and that we

6 Samuel Beckett "Ever tried. Ever failed. No matter. Try again. Fail again. Fail better". *Worstward Ho* (1983).

7 In Bion 1967a. See pp. 90–1. Also see 1967a, pp. 103–4.

often fail and are experienced accurately by our patients as failing in that work. Denis Carpy (1989) discussed the findings that convinced him that being witnessed by the patients in the midst of this struggle to be an adequate container for them was *in itself* therapeutic, however much it emerged later that interpretation played an important role. I find his paper convincing as a valuable contribution in the company of those practitioners who seek to show analysis as a real job of work involving strain, and I will draw several strands from it in this section because the line of thinking he pursues is so informative about containment in clinical practice.

The patient Carpy presented had, in subtle ways, encroached on him, inducing small degrees of enactment of irritation manifesting in critically toned interpretations back to the patient in moments of strain. He noticed a definite look of triumph as she left the room at the end of the session, a look that Carpy said, "came from her having been able to observe that she had got to me and affected me in this way". This analyst felt that this patient, however victorious she may have felt at seeing him thus affected by her, did at some level appreciate that she was a human being who had made an impact, and that her analyst was a human being who had been impacted, had struggled with the difficulty, and yet had still retained his capacity to function. The importance of this aspect of containment was foreshadowed, it will be recalled, by Freud's 1895 use of the term *Nebenmensch*, which his translator had rendered as 'fellow human being'. In this respect, Carpy had understood that it was more important to consider that his patient had been able to observe him attempting to deal with the brunt of her feelings than to worry too much about having been triumphed over. It is particularly in such moments that our patients observe closely and intuit finely all the activities of the strange being with whom they share the room, to see how and where we swerve aside, and shrink back from them and from what they require us to bear of them. In his paper, Carpy referred to Brenman Pick's (1985) descriptions of this process, of the patient's attunement to when we evade and when we are able to face problematic areas in the session. In addition, Carpy articulated, as the main substantial point of the paper, what I think is the central fact about what we call containing.

> I am suggesting that the normal infant needs to be able to sense that his mother is struggling to tolerate his projected distress without major disruption of her maternal function. She will be unable to avoid giving the infant slight indications of the way she is affected by him, and it is these indications which allow the infant to see that the projected aspects of himself can indeed by tolerated. The infant is able then to reintroject these aspects of himself, along with the capacity to tolerate them which he has seen in his mother. . . . In my opinion, what is 'containing' about this is that the baby will have an experience of being fed by a mother in whom he can sense panic, but who is nevertheless able to give him milk. This is what makes the panic tolerable.
>
> *(Carpy, 1989, p. 293)*

The thesis is that something of the difficulty experienced by the analyst in being a container for anxiety is perceptible to the patient, and awareness of the strain is awareness of the function. In other words that it is *work*. Just as a lake may be virtually invisible unless a wind ruffles the surface, the perception of a containing object probably does depend on perceiving it at work, which means of course that it is perceived under strain. I understand this to be an aspect of authenticity in working as a container for anxiety. It implies that if the mother, or the analyst, affects, through narcissism, an attitude of effortlessness, believing perhaps that a 'naturally gifted' helper feels and shows no strain, the child or patient is not only likely to fail to feel a container–contained relationship at all, they will probably be left feeling inadequate and inferior, faced with an object who appears with perfect equanimity when faced with feelings that are unbearable to themselves.

Carpy's insight is compelling and accords with my clinical experience. It corresponds closely with Bion's description of the roots of the container–contained relationship, where the mother is not required to be a perfect container for her infant's anxiety but one that demonstrably *goes-on-being* a mother, caring for her infant in distress, whilst being rocked internally by an intensity of anxiety, a fusion of her own fear of her infant's extinction and her infant's dread of it, which, if left outside her, would remain unbounded, unnameable and impersonal.

Might there be a principle of praxis to cultivate a sensibility in the analyst for the ontological anxiety of their patients, corresponding in its own way to Bion's recommendations to suppress systematically the functioning of memory, desire and apperception, in the service of psychoanalytic intuition? Some clinicians incorporate an implicit and natural philosophical sensibility in their analytic work, perhaps without feeling it to have equal weight to the more tangibly psychoanalytic. They may feel it to be a useful adjunct to their practice, much as some existential therapists accept specific analytic concepts into their work and clinical thinking. Holzhey-Kunz, in developing and refining daseinsanalysis has brought a philosophical and a Freudian psychoanalytic vertex very close together indeed, and it is valuable to explore the methodology that belongs to her approach, because the line of thinking pursued across the chapters of this book, of moving from knowing facts to knowing as a mode of being, by being transformed, to some degree, as a result of becoming informed by the experience of being, requires the inclusion of ontological–philosophical principles, and this at the practical level. In my opinion it is the use of the core existential concepts of early Heidegger, and of Sartre on modes of being, that supply the requisite philosophical grounding for taking further Bion's work of the ontological. Holzhey-Kunz has provided a model for this integration in terms of Freudian analysis, and it is worth considering its expansion into a psychoanalysis that involves itself with object relations.

The aspect of method I am investigating began with Bion's initiative in suggesting that psychoanalysis has the potential to go beyond furthering the insightful use of knowledge, into promoting the capacity of the patient to be real. I have argued that pursuing this in practice necessitates the development of a particular sensibility in the analyst towards anxiety that is specifically ontological. This means becoming capable of appreciating the centrality in one's own mind of ontological anxiety in order to be sensitive to the implicit strivings of the patient in analysis towards a philosophical understanding of their world. Another way to say this is that it means becoming attuned to the presence of the ontological in what otherwise would present as, and be read as, familiar and specific, tangible concrete experience – what in daseinsanalysis is called the 'ontic'. Holzhey-Kunz suggests that if we can allow this distinction to be real for us, we can recognise that our patient speaks in a 'third channel'; that "in his speech not only past and present experiences but also ontical and ontological experiences are intermingled" (2014, p. 218). The methodological requirement in respect of this, therefore, is to cultivate a sensibility to hear the patient's philosophical strivings and the ontological anxiety pertaining to it. It can be thought of as the philosophical counterpart to Bion's recommendations on memory, desire and precocious comprehension, allowing discernment of the ontological inclusions in the patient's apparently ontical concerns. I am in close agreement with Holzhey-Kunz when she suggests that this gives to the core concept of evenly suspended attention an expanded meaning, which she calls listening with a philosophical ear.

I will now summarize the key technical principles outlined by Holzhey-Kunz that highlight the commonalities and contrasts between psychoanalytic and daseinsanalytic interventions, as the background conceptual framework for doing so has been set out. It is important in reading this to appreciate that these are not competing models, nor are they necessarily to be thought of as integrated.

I will focus mainly on those formulations of Holzhey-Kunz that concern interpretation and the mode of listening in the analytic setting. These are based principally (a) on the ontic–ontological distinction of Heidegger, one that does not have a universally accepted counterpart in the current literatures of psychoanalysis, (b) on Holzhey-Kunz's conception of the human being as inherently philosophically inclined, and (c) on her particular emphasis on anxiety as the primary disclosive mood of our being, that leads her to consider that the patient in analysis 'suffers from their being'.

Listening and interpreting in the ontological dimension

I. Listening

In her writing on technique Holzhey-Kunz occasionally characterises Freud's central technical principle of evenly suspended attention as 'intentionless listening', a phrase that is accurate in part but omits the key deconstructive and 'making strange' aspects implied by the following statement of Freud:

> It will be seen that the rule of giving equal notice to everything is the necessary counterpart to the demand made on the patient that he should communicate everything that occurs to him without criticism or selection.
>
> *(Freud 1912a, p. 111)*

Holzhey-Kunz retains the centrality of interpretation in her method, as revealing what is hidden. Her conception of the unconscious as 'unconcealment' gives a pronounced philosophical accent to the conception of the unconscious, drawing as it does on the ideas about self-deception of authenticity and *mauvaise foi* as they appear in the work of Heidegger and Sartre respectively. Nevertheless it is clear that that for her, evenly suspended attention in listening to her patients is a core technical instrument, one that reveals both the unconscious phantasies and other derivatives of the patient and the concealed ontological anxiety included in these. So too is the important role of psychoanalytic abstinence, in which Holzhey-Kunz maintains a clear analyst–patient role asymmetry, though it is not a rigidly hierarchical one.

These defining features of the psychoanalytic method are maintained in the daseinsanalytic method that she has pioneered. Having said that, there are some instructive differences, and these are what enable her technique to function as a container for the ontological and its anxiety, and for the open and explicit recognition of the patient in analysis as an inherently philosophically inclined being.

An important aspect of listening in the realm of being is Holzhey-Kunz's identification of a painful kind of exquisite sensitivity in some patients to the anxieties of the human condition. For this she uses the terms 'special sensitivity' and *Hellhörigkeit*, for which the most apt translation is by analogy to the faculty of *clairaudience*, the special sensitivity (to sound) beyond the normal range. Our patients who show this special sensitivity are not first of all considered by Holzhey-Kunz as suffering from a pathological condition, although they may be regarded thus psychiatrically, or even think this of themselves. Instead it is her approach to consider them as suffering from the sharp and unwelcome awareness of truths of the human condition. She refers to them (2014, pp. 230, 281; and 2016, p. 21) as "reluctant philosophers" because on them weighs the burden of unshieldedness to those painful ontological truths for which most of us have found a thick and effective defence by residing in what earlier I called Proust's *l'habitude*, and Heidegger's 'the everyday'. Such patients cannot achieve the separation, the 'benign splitting', in their lives and in their minds, between ontological truth and a psyche that organises experience in 'the everyday' (*das Man*), in other words those conventional, domiciliating defences that the philosopher David Hume was able to do, simply by leaving his office.[8]

Holzhey-Kunz writes, "In the daseinsanalytic view, listening with free-floating attention is therefore the necessary correlate to the patient's special sensitivity". In other words, the relationship between an evenly suspended attitude in daseinsanalysis and the patient's acute sensitivity to the ontological, corresponds to the relationship in psychoanalysis between evenly suspended attentiveness and the communications of the unconscious. I would suggest that the attitude of evenly suspended attentiveness correspond to reverie in both methods. In the daseinsanalytic method of Holzhey-Kunz, this means listening with a 'philosophical ear'.

8 See Britton, 2015, p. 38.

Like listening with evenly suspended attentiveness, this kind of listening also requires a commitment to learning.

It is clear that between the 1950s and the 1970s, Bion developed a philosophical ear for the ontological. His retrospective ontological interpretation of a patient horrified by the holes in the material of his socks was expressed in a lecture using the analogy of a tennis court at dusk, dimming the illumination until all that could be seen was the net. His new perspective on the anxiety of the patient was neither a description of psychopathology, nor a transference-based or symbolic interpretation, and neither did it involve speculation about the patient's early life. He had found a third perspective, one that corresponds to Holzhey-Kunz's 'third channel', the philosophical ear.

The gap in the subject: the anxiety in furthering listening to include the ontological

As I discussed earlier, many interpretations made in the course of analysis refer to specific anxieties and phantasies belonging to the emotional world of the patient but without finding a comparable experience in the inner or outer worlds of their analyst, and this is part of the difference between them as people. When the analyst listens from the perspective of the ontological, however, this is no longer the case. Holzhey-Kunz reminds us that we are then open to a dimension in which, because the anxieties communicated are those of the human condition, "everything that the patient reports touches on his own anxiety". Though painful, there is a significant consolation to be found in facing such anxiety. It is the experience of discovery.

Bion (1980, p. 30) reminded us that Freud's way of referring to the function of a 'paramnesia' – essentially an invention intended to fill the space where a discovery could occur – applies not only to our patients but also to ourselves. Psychoanalysis itself, both in its microscopic application in the session, and its macroscopic use in society, can function for us as this 'column 2' activity, as a way of filling the gap that needs to be maintained in order to retain absence and space for further discovery. Rather than producing what Bion cautioned against – "a fine structure of theory in the hope that it will block up the hole for ever so that we shall never need to learn anything more about ourselves either as people or organizations" – what is required, especially when admitting into the practice of analysis a consideration of the being of the patient, is something closer to what Jayne Hankinson (unpublished paper, 2018) describes as a 'periodic table in the consulting room'. By her analogy with Dmitri Mendeleev's seminal structure of discovery, Hankinson indicates the need for an open structure of K that is similar to what I have been sketching out here as $K_{(informed)}$ in contrast to $K_{(apperception)}$. She writes:

> If, as practitioners in the therapeutic world, a sense of curiosity or tolerance of the absence is lacking, then the Periodic Table that comes about in the consulting room (i.e. the sense of order that is arrived at) is filled with elements that have not been discovered through being with the patient. Instead

the table has been filled with prior learning (possibly therefore an illusion built upon an illusion), a misplacing of elements and no awareness of anything unknown, no space available for that yet to be discovered.

In my view Hankinson here is using her analogy to recommend that the analyst strives to develop an inner 'table' of their own, a personal practical epistemology that, in common with Mendeleev's table, is itself a structure "born of not-knowing, chaos and work". It *is,* she states further, a structure that "does not just tolerate the unknown, it provides a place for it". Here, and this is an important and often overlooked point, I am reminded of the importance of remembering that a human being working as a mental container can only function properly *as* a container if it is accepted by them that not everything can be contained, and that the practitioner therefore, in this capacity, is herself subject to change through having to grow to encompass the being and becoming of her patient. We are also perhaps reminded of Bion's encouragement to analysts not to become fixated on *his* epistemological structure, including his actual table, *his* 'Grid' (1963), but to develop our own.

II. Interpretation in the domain of the ontological

Holzhey-Kunz makes a crucial point differentiating interpretations revealing ontological anxieties and defences against them from interpretations of the ontic. Experiences of being, she states, "can only be indicated, without any 'meaning' yet discernible in these experiences" (2014, p. 264). This gives a very clear therapeutic referent to the term 'Dasein', since it means *being there*, or, as Heidegger also put it, "Being there where we find ourselves". In the daseinsanalytic perspective, the function of interpretation differs because of this – ultimately because ontological anxiety is distinguished through having no ready-to-hand object into which it can fall. Moving too quickly to interpret in terms of ready categories and tangible objects is, in fact, a common everyday defence against the ontological, for the analyst at times as well as for the patient who has the special sensitivity. A paradox of interpreting from this perspective is that the analyst may feel that her work could stand to improve by *increasing* her sensitivity to the ontological dimension, whilst at the same time feeling a desire to protect the patient by *reducing*, if such a thing were to be possible, the patient's extreme sensitivity, in other words, the *Hellhörigkeit* that exposes them to being traumatised by the conditions of life to which we are all but habituated, and thereby defended against.

Holzhey-Kunz touches upon a further point about interpretation of anxiety in the ontological domain. We normally give priority to the possible latent meaning 'behind' the patient's open declarations and statements of their experience. This is a normal part of our psychoanalytic attitude, but when the anxiety conveyed is already predominantly ontological, however, and is not heavily concealed within defence mechanisms, it may still nevertheless be hidden 'in plain sight', so to speak, not by use of symbolic condensations and displacements, which is similar to dream-disguise, but by an entirely different kind of defence – the 'falling' of the ontological into the ontic, into descriptions that are steeped in, saturated by, and – more importantly – are highly evocative of assumptions that will proceed unexamined because they are normally an inextricable part of the fabric of the 'everyday' (*das Man*) for both participants.

By 'falling' I mean that there is a psychic defence for human beings against angst that is not covered by our existing psychoanalytic models, but for which a fuller understanding requires the inclusion of key principles of ontological philosophy, as found in the writings of Kierkegaard, Heidegger and Sartre, and described earlier in the book. If this supposition is right, there will be moments in an analysis at which the conventional directionality assumed to hold between the latent and the manifest needs to be reversed, as a practical step, in the formulation and the interpretation of anxiety. When faced with a clinical moment of onto-logical anxiety, in other words, the seeking for a hidden symbolic meaning can in itself be the defence against contact with, and recognition of, the ontological – the anxiety that comes from being – a type of anxiety that affects the analyst in the most direct way possible. As well as summoning the analyst's own unconscious defensive system into play, the ontological anxiety, when severe, quite under-standably mobilises the analyst's feeling of responsibility for the patient and for the entire process of the analysis as itself a source of anxiety to the patient. In this regard, Churcher (personal communication, 2018) has suggested that the analyst's awareness of the field occupied by themselves and the patient is limitless and largely unknown, and that as a consequence

> the analyst nevertheless feels responsible for it, and is thus distracted from the task of being the only person in the situation, other than the patient, who can help the patient to be who they are.

Where ontological anxiety is (perilously) close to awareness, and only the non-action of waiting can show us that it is, suitable interpretation may follow the reverse of the usual pattern – forgoing and suspending attention to detailed specific content, and to the symbolic layers that are, undoubtedly, there in the communica-tions, in order to bring out the existence of the ontological anxiety more directly. It will be realised that a degree of anxiety will be experienced by the analyst in making use of this technical recommendation,[9] because its use means reversing the perspective on yet another normal and familiar part of everyday practice.

It will be recalled that James Strachey wrote of the aversion that analysts will experience because of the premonition of danger when they feel on the verge of making a mutative interpretation. The response to such feelings is often to find various ways of *not* making the interpretation at such a point of urgency, to swerve from it or to shrink back from it.

---

9 Namely, the maintenance of the ontic–ontological distinction, as it affects the domain of the anxi-ety most salient for interpretation, and how such decisions affect the technical handling of what is regarded as latent and what is manifest.

Now, there is a special case that may resemble such a 'Strachey moment', one, that is, in which almost any kind of verbal intervention is considered, or given, other than a requisite one, but which is – because the underlying anxiety is ontological – essentially different. When the feared event of the moment is contact with the ontological, as a special instance of a disturbing truth, as contrasted, say, with sharing with the patient an awareness of a particular unconscious fear or phantasy for example, an approach to *symbolic meaning* may present itself as a 'natural' and ready-to-hand psychological defence against staying with a pro-foundly disturbing ontological anxiety, one that by its nature as stemming from the human condition, and not a neurosis, affects the analyst as well as the patient. Furthermore, as a primary anxiety that requires understanding in its own terms, and not as 'something representing a something else', because by its nature it can-not in any way be alleviated or transformed through the synthesis of understanding, to treat it as a 'symptom' would in itself be an evasion. Strange as it sounds, the act of representation may, under certain conditions, such as I am considering in this section, constitute a fundamentally misrepresenting movement. This proposition, that amounts to a principle of 'letting-be' in the face of ontological experience, has been discussed at some length by Holzhey-Kunz (See 2014, p. 264), whose work from the ontological perspective suggests that that identifying an anxiety as coming from the ontological dimension makes it important to consider an *indicative* interpretation rather than moving to an elucidation of its 'meaning'. She bases this principle on the basis that it is often *the making of an interpretation itself* that is the mobilisation of a defence against anxiety.

> The specially daseinsanalytic interpretation is therefore indicative in nature because what it discovers would be obscured again by a meaning-based interpretation.
>
> *(Holzhey-Kunz, 2014, p. 264)*

In other words, there are critical moments in an analysis where the best thing, even when counter-intuitive, that the analyst can do is to heed the words of Wittgenstein's final proposition in his *Tractatus*,[10] *whereof we cannot speak, thereof we must be silent*. The requisite stance in moments such as I have just described is close to that mode of being that I described in the existential section of the book as *being-with (Mitsein)*. The indicative interpretation of Holzhey-Kunz conveys and stems from this mode of being, and gives priority to *making-present* an experience in the room over *representing* it.

What I am recommending in terms of method is for us to become more capable, and to cultivate this capacity, in shifting (and sometimes reversing) our perspective in a session towards a philosophical understanding of the anxiety of our patients,

---

10 *Wovon man nicht sprechen kann, darüber muss man schweigen*, translated by Pears and McGuinness (1961) as "What we cannot speak about we must pass over in silence".

particularly when the patient is communicating a suffering from their being, an ontological anxiety with its particular quality of angst. I am suggesting that we become sensitive to the differences that do exist between this state of being and what we more commonly attribute to fear of specific objects. Bion's later interpretive approach can be distinguished from his earlier attitude by the much firmer emphasis he came to give to emotional *contact* – particularly contact with what is real. When this is appropriate in a session, I am suggesting that if a true 'philosophical angle' can be found, it may often provide what I think is an indispensable first port of call in making real contact with the being of the patient.

What I mean by this, and this is a major conclusion of the work in this book, is that orienting to the anxiety of the patient concerning his own being is more important than locating a meaningful context outside that experience, *in the first instance*, and probably for a considerable length of time. In relation to the fundamental ontological anxiety lurking[11] in the (ontic) fear of holes, the patient is driven to flee all awareness of *hiatus*, the lack of taken-for-granted continuity and solidity in the world, the lacunary nature of their being in the world. What then, in such a situation, constitutes an indicative interpretation?

It would need to be an intervention capable of doing justice to what Bion called the *extreme capacity for observation which is natural to some patients*, a faculty possessed by the patient, however disturbed he may be by the consequences to him of the intensity of this capacity, and to which Holzhey-Kunz gives the name *Hellhörigkeit*. In short, it would need to be an intervention crediting the patient with the capacity to suffer the anxiety of a truth.

It is clear that Bion believed that the analyst had to be able to experience socks as socks, a tennis net as a tennis net, and one might add that a cigar can be a cigar, whilst at the same time abandoning the security of what I have been calling, following Proust, and Heidegger, *l'habitude* and *the everyday*. Abandoning *l'habitude* together with Bion's triumvirate of memory, desire and apperception, we could interpret indicatively to the patient, perhaps along the lines of saying to him: "You see that it is so, you cannot get away from it, and it terrifies you, doesn't it?"

The aspects of clinical technique and attitude of listening described in this book, and the interpretive ways of responding to them, can be considered by analysts and psychotherapists of many differing modalities and schools of thought, and if they accept that it may be a worthwhile use of time for them to orient themselves to the being of the patient, and to the ideas put forward in this book concerning anxieties that come from their condition of being, and not only from specific fears and objects in their world, it is hoped that they may find themselves gradually developing a widened and deepened openness to what Wilfred Bion (1967b, p.18) called an "increased number and variety of moods, ideas and attitudes".

Expanding my analytic attitude to include the dramaturgical and existential dimensions of the experience of being an analyst has broadened and brought

---

11 See Chapter 10; and Holzhey-Kunz, 2014, p. 264.

greater depth to my contact with many of my own patients, and with previously unknown areas of myself. Through the chapters of this book I have pursued a line of thinking that has moved fairly freely between three main perspectives, each with a conceptual framework that has been developed largely independently of one another in their respective knowledge-bases, but amongst which I can, as an analyst, notice and intuit certain useful affinities. Developing a faith in these affinities has enabled me to write what I have been discovering as I went along, in conjunction with my clinical experiences in daily work with my patients, rather than plotting a course to explain what I already know. In this respect and in one or two others, there has been a reflexivity in that what I have undergone in writing the book has led me into experiencing many of the phenomena written about in the chapters of the book. Alice Holzhey-Kunz wrote of the complexity and richness of potential to be found in the analytic relationship, and that psychoanalysts and daseinsanalysts should be careful not to squander that potential by restricting the perspectives available to them.

My experience of navigating with the help of three perspectives, the psycho-analytic, the dramaturgical and the ontological, has been a discovery in itself. It has led to surprises, and further learning in my work and in my self.

POSTSCRIPT

Following a discussion of particular ontological anxieties – the peril of being alive; the inevitability of dying, not as an idea but as a reality; the impossibility of ensuring the complete protection and the continued well-being and even the existence of our loved ones – the patient mused: "I don't know where that gets me".

This intrigued me. I realised that this visuo-spatial 'travel metaphor', much used by this particular man, and one with which we are so very familiar in our everyday conversations as well as much of our thinking in therapy, is so precisely *inaccurate* when applied to existential truths. There is no advantage to ontological awareness, except (at least potentially) for one that I will mention in a moment. Truths of our common human existence can be experienced by us as harmful, they may actually be harmful, but they do not 'get us anywhere'. This is because, in a manner of speaking, we are 'already there'. This is our *Dasein*: being there, there where we are; here, in fact.

Seen like this, the ontological is where we were, all along, we just didn't realise it.

So, in employing the model of 'where does it get me?' for the experience of the ontological, when it is where we are already, are we unconsciously communicating our wish to 'be elsewhere' – anywhere else will do?

What might be the one advantage to which I alluded earlier? It is in our orientation to time. It is finite. Therefore of inestimable value.

REFERENCES

Aristotle. (1944). *Nicomachean Ethics* (tr. H. Rackham). Cambridge MA: Harvard University Press.

Aristotle. (1996). *Poetics*. Harmondsworth: Penguin Classics.

Aristotle. (1954). *The Rhetoric and the Poetics of Aristotle* (tr. W. R. Roberts). New York: Random House.

Artaud, A. (2010). *The Theatre and its Double* (tr. V. Corti; rev. ed.). Richmond, UK: Alma Classics.

Bateson, G. (1972). *Steps to an Ecology of Mind* (foreword by M. C. Bateson). London: University of Chicago Press.

Beckett, S. (1965). *Waiting for Godot: A Tragicomedy in Two Acts*, 2nd ed. London: Faber and Faber.

Bion, W. R. (1954). Notes on the theory of schizophrenia. *International Journal of Psycho-Analysis*, 35: 113–18.

Bion, W.R. (1958). On arrogance. *International Journal of Psycho-Analysis*, 39: 144–6. And in *Second Thoughts*. London: Karnac Books, 1967.

Bion, W. R. (1959). "Attacks on linking". *International Journal of Psycho-Analysis*, 40: 308–15. And in *Second Thoughts*. London: Karnac Books, 1967. And in *The Complete Works of W. R. Bion* (ed: Mawson, C. [2014]), vol. 6. London: Karnac Books, 2014.

Bion, W. R. (1961a). The conception of man. In *The Complete Works of W. R. Bion* (ed: Mawson, C. [2014]), vol. 15. London: Karnac Books, 2014.

Bion, W. R. (1961b). *Experiences in Groups and Other Papers*. London: Karnac Books. And in *The Complete Works of W. R. Bion* (ed: Mawson, C. [2014]), vol. 4. London: Karnac Books, 2014.

Bion, W.R. (1962a). The psycho-analytic study of thinking. *International Journal of Psycho-Analysis*, 43: 306–10.

Bion, W. R. (1962b). *Learning from Experience*. London: Karnac Books. And in *The Complete Works of W. R. Bion* (ed: Mawson, C. [2014]), vol. 4. London: Karnac Books, 2014.

Bion, W. R. (1963). *Elements of Psycho-Analysis*. London: Karnac Books. And in *The Complete Works of W. R. Bion* (ed: Mawson, C. [2014]), vol. 6. London: Karnac Books, 2014.

Bion, W. R. (1965a). *Transformations: Change from Learning to Growth*. London: Karnac Books. And in *The Complete Works of W. R. Bion* (ed: Mawson, C. [2014]), vol. 5. London: Karnac Books, 2014.

Bion, W. R. (1965b). *Memory and Desire*. In *The Complete Works of W. R. Bion* (ed: Mawson, C. [2014]), vol. 6. London: Karnac Books, 2014. And in *Three Papers of Bion* (ed. C. Mawson, foreword by R. Britton). Routledge, 2018.

Bion, W. R. (1966). Catastrophic change. In *The Complete Works of W. R. Bion* (ed: Mawson, C. [2014]), vol. 6. London: Karnac Books, 2014.

Bion, W. R. (1967a). *Second Thoughts: Selected Papers on Psycho-Analysis*. London: William Heinemann. Repr. London: Karnac Books, 1984. And in *The Complete Works of W. R. Bion* (ed: Mawson, C. [2014]), vol. 6. London: Karnac Books, 2014.

Bion, W. R. (1967b). Notes on memory and desire. *Psychoanalytic Forum*, 2: 272–3, 279–80. And in *Cogitations* (ed. F. Bion). London, Karnak Books, 1992. New extended ed., 1994. And in *The Complete Works of W. R. Bion* (ed: Mawson, C. [2014]), vol. 6. London: Karnac Books, 2014.

Bion, W. R. (1970). *Attention and Interpretation: A Scientific Approach to Insight in Psychoanalysis and Groups*. London: Karnac Books. And in *The Complete Works of W. R. Bion* (ed: Mawson, C. [2014]), vol. 6. London: Karnac Books, 2014.

Bion, W. R. (1976). Facts: Can we awake from them? Unpublished paper for Study Centre for Organizational Leadership and Authority, Los Angeles.

Bion, W. R. (1977). New and improved. In *The Complete Works of W. R. Bion* (ed: Mawson, C. [2014]), vol. 15. London: Karnac Books, 2014.

Bion, W. R. (1978). *Four Discussions with W. R. Bion*. Strath Tay: Clunie Press. And in *Clinical Seminars and Other Works* (ed. F. Bion). London: Karnac Books, 2000. And in *The Complete Works of W. R. Bion* (ed: Mawson, C. [2014]), vol. 10. London: Karnac Books, 2014.

Bion, W. R. (1979). Making the best of a bad job. In *The Complete Works of W. R. Bion* (ed: Mawson, C. [2014]), vol. 10. London: Karnac Books, 2014. Originally published in the *Bulletin of the British Psychoanalytical Society*.

Bion, W. R. (1980). *Bion in New York and São Paulo*. Roland Harris Trust Library. Strath Tay: Clunie Press.

Bion, W. R. (1985). *All My Sins Remembered: Another Part of a Life and the Other Side of Genius: Family Letters*. London: Karnac Books.

Bion, W. R. (1990). *Brazilian Lectures*. London: Karnac Books.

Bion, W. R. (1991). *A Memoir of the Future*. London: Karnac Books.

Bion, W. R. (1992). *Cogitations* (ed. F. Bion). London: Karnac Books. New extended ed., 1994. And in C. Mawson, *The Complete Works of W. R. Bion* (ed: Mawson, C. [2014]), vol. 11. London: Karnac Books, 2014.

Bion, W. R. (2014). *The Complete Works of W. R. Bion* (ed: Mawson, C. [2014]; consulting ed. F. Bion). London: Karnac Books.

Bion, W. R. (2018). *Three Papers of W. R. Bion* (ed. C. Mawson, foreword by R. Britton). London: Routledge.

Birksted-Breen, D. (2016). Bi-ocularity, the functioning mind of the psychoanalyst. *International Journal of Psychoanalysis*, 97(1): 25–40.

Boehlich, W. (ed.) (1992). *The Letters of Sigmund Freud to Eduard Silberstein 1871–1881* (tr. A. Pomerans). Cambridge, MA: Belknap Press.

Bollas, C. (2009). Architecture and the unconscious. *International Forum of Psychoanalysis*, 9(1–2): 28–42. And in *The Evocative Object World*. Abingdon: Routledge, 2009.

Boswell, J. (1934 [1791]). *Boswell's Life of Johnson* (6 vols). Oxford: Clarendon Press.

Brecht, B. (1935). Theatre for pleasure or theatre for instruction, in *Brecht on Theatre: The Development of an Aesthetic* (ed. and tr. J. Willett). New York: Hill & Wang, 1964.

Brecht, B. (1948). A short organum for the theatre, in *Brecht on Theatre: The Development of an Aesthetic* (ed. and tr. J. Willett). New York: Hill & Wang, 1964.

Brecht, B. (1997). *The Caucasian Chalk Circle* (tr. J. & T. Stern, with W. H. Auden). *Collected Plays* (ed. J. Willett & R. Manheim). London: Methuen Drama.

Brecht, B. (1997). *Mother Courage and her Children* (ed. P. Thomson). Cambridge: Cambridge University Press.

Brenman Pick, I. (1985). Working through in the countertransference. *International Journal of Psycho-Analysis*, 66: 157–66.

Breuer, J., & Freud, S. (1893). On the psychical mechanism of hysterical phenomena. *The Standard Edition of the Complete Psychological Works of Sigmund Freud*, vol. 2 (1893–5): *Studies on Hysteria*, pp. 1–17.

Britton, R. (1998). *Belief and Imagination*. New Library of Psychoanalysis Series. Abingdon: Routledge.

Britton, R. (2010). Developmental uncertainty versus paranoid regression. *Psychoanalytic Review*, 97(2): 195–206.

Britton, R. (2015). *Between Mind and Brain: Models of the Mind and Models in the Mind*. London: Karnac Books.

Britton, R., Chused, J., Ellman, S., & Likierman, M. (2006). Panel I: Contemporary views on stages versus positions. *Journal of Infant, Child & Adolescent Psychotherapy*, 5(3): 268–81.

Britton, R., & Steiner, J. (1994). Interpretation: Selected fact or overvalued idea? *International Journal of Psycho-Analysis*, 75: 1069–78.

Caldwell, L. (2018). A psychoanalysis of being: An approach to Donald Winnicott. *British Journal of Psychotherapy*, 34(2): 221–39.

Carpy, D. V. (1989). Tolerating the countertransference: A mutative process. *International Journal of Psycho-Analysis*, 70: 287–94.

Cohn, H. (2002). *Heidegger and the Roots of Existential Therapy*. London: Continuum.

Culbert-Koehn, J. (2011). An analysis with Bion: An interview with James Gooch. *Journal of Analytical Psychology*, 56: 76–91.

Danto, A. C. (1975). *Jean-Paul Sartre*. New York: Viking Press.

Deutsch, H. (1926). Occult processes occurring during psychoanalysis. In G. Devereux (ed.) (1953), *Psychoanalysis and the Occult*. New York: International Universities Press.

Deutsch, H. (1929). The genesis of agoraphobia. *International Journal of Psycho-Analysis*, 10: 51–69.

Deutsch, H. (1942). Some forms of emotional disturbance and their relationship to schizophrenia. *Psychoanalytic Quarterly*, 11: 301–21.

Di Ceglie, G. R. (2013). Orientation, containment and the emergence of symbolic thinking. *International Journal of Psychoanalysis*, 94(6): 1077–91.

Draper, R. P. (2015 [1980]). *Tragedy: Developments in Criticism*. London: Macmillan.

Elliott, D. J., Silverman, M., & Bowman, W. D. (2016). *Artistic Citizenship: Artistry, Social Responsibility, and Ethical Praxis*. Oxford: Oxford University Press.

Eriksson, S. A. (2011). Distancing. In S. Schonmann (ed.), *Key Concepts in Theatre/Drama Education*. Rotterdam: Sense.

Feldman, M. (2009). *Doubt, Conviction and the Analytic Process: Selected Papers of Michael Feldman* (ed. B. Joseph). New Library of Psychoanalysis Series. Abingdon: Routledge.

Ferry, L. (2014). *The Wisdom of the Myths*. New York: HarperCollins.

Freud, S. (1894). Draft E: How anxiety originates. *The Standard Edition of the Complete Psychological Works of Sigmund Freud*, vol. 1 (1886–99): *Pre-Psycho-Analytic Publications and Unpublished Drafts*, pp. 189–95.

Freud, S. (1895 [1950]). Project for a scientific psychology. *The Standard Edition of the Complete Psychological Works of Sigmund Freud*, vol. 1 (1886–99): *Pre-Psycho-Analytic Publications and Unpublished Drafts*, pp. 281–391.

Freud, S. (1897). Letter from Freud to Fliess, 29 December 1897. *The Complete Letters of Sigmund Freud to Wilhelm Fliess, 1887–1904*, pp. 290–1.

Freud, S. (1900). *The Interpretation of Dreams. The Standard Edition of the Complete Psychological Works of Sigmund Freud*, vols 4–5.

Freud, S. (1909). Two case histories: "Little Hans" and "The Rat Man". *The Standard Edition of the Complete Psychological Works of Sigmund Freud*, vol. 10 (1909).

Freud, S. (1911). Formulations on the two principles of mental functioning. *The Standard Edition of the Complete Psychological Works of Sigmund Freud*, vol. 12 (1911–13).

Freud, S. (1912a). Recommendations to physicians practising psycho-analysis. *The Standard Edition of the Complete Psychological Works of Sigmund Freud*, vol. 12 (1911–13).

Freud, S. (1912b). The dynamics of transference. *The Standard Edition of the Complete Psychological Works of Sigmund Freud*, vol. 12 (1911–13).

Freud, S. (1913). *Totem and Taboo. The Standard Edition of the Complete Psychological Works of Sigmund Freud*, vol. 13 (1913–14).

Freud, S. (1915). The unconscious. *The Standard Edition of the Complete Psychological Works of Sigmund Freud*, vol. 14 (1914–16).

Freud, S. (1916). Letter from Freud to Lou Andreas-Salomé, May 25, 1916. *The International Psycho-Analytical Library*, 89: 45.

Freud, S. (1917). *Introductory Lectures on Psycho-Analysis. The Standard Edition of the Complete Psychological Works of Sigmund Freud*, vol. 16 (1916–17).

Freud, S. (1930). *Civilization and its Discontents. The Standard Edition of the Complete Psychological Works of Sigmund Freud*, vol. 21.

Fromm-Reichmann, F. (1950). *Principles of Intensive Psychotherapy*. Chicago: University of Chicago Press.

Gadamer, H.-G. (1989 [1960]). *Truth and Method* (tr. J. Weinsheimer & D. G. Marshall; 2nd rev. ed.). London: Sheed & Ward.

Green, A. (2010). Sources and vicissitudes of *being* in D. W. Winnicott's work. *Psychoanalytic Quarterly*, 79(1): 11–35. (Paper presented at Milan conference on Winnicott, November 1995.)

Greenblatt, S. (2012). *The Swerve: How the Renaissance Began*. London: Vintage Books.

Heidegger, M. (1969). *Discourse on Thinking*. New York: Harper & Row.

Heidegger, M. (2001 [1927]). *Being and Time* (tr. J. Macquarrie & E. Robinson). Oxford: Blackwell.

Heidegger, M. (2010 [1927]). *Being and Time* (tr. J. Stambaugh; rev. D. J. Schmidt). Albany, NY: State University of New York Press.

Heimann, P. (1950). On counter-transference. *International Journal of Psycho-Analysis*, 31: 81–4.

Heimann, P. (1989). *About Children and Children-No-Longer: Collected Papers 1942–80*. (ed. M. Tonnesmann). New Library of Psychoanalysis Series. Abingdon: Routledge.

Heisenberg, W. (1930). *The Physical Principles of the Quantum Theory* (tr. C. Eckhart & F. C. Hoyt). New York: Dover.

Heisenberg, W. (1958). *Physics and Philosophy: The Revolution in Modern Science*. Lectures delivered at University of St Andrews, Scotland, Winter 1955–6. New York: Harper.

Hernandez-Halton, I. (2015). Klein, Ferenczi and the clinical diary. *American Journal of Psychoanalysis*, 75: 76–85.

Hippocrates. (1994). *Epidemics*, Books 2, 4–7 (tr. W. D. Smith). Loeb Classical Library. Cambridge, MA: Harvard University Press.

Holzhey-Kunz, A. (2014). *Daseinsanalysis*. London: Free Association Books.

Holzhey-Kunz, A. (2016). Why the distinction between ontic and ontological trauma matters for existential therapists. *Existential Analysis*, 27(1): 16–27.

Illich, I. (1956). The eloquence of silence. In I. Illich (1970), *Celebration of Awareness*. Berkeley, CA: Heyday Books.

Isaacs, S. (1948). The nature and function of phantasy. *International Journal of Psycho-Analysis*, 29: 73–97.

Jones, E. (1958). *Free Associations: Memories of a Psychoanalyst*. London: Transaction.

Joseph, B. (1989). *Psychic Equilibrium and Psychic Change: Selected Papers of Betty Joseph* (ed. M. Feldman). New Library of Psychoanalysis Series. Abingdon: Routledge.

Josipovici, G. (1994) Proust, a voice in search of itself, in *The World and the Book: A Study of Modern Fiction*. Basingstoke: Palgrave Macmillan.

Jung, C. G. (1925). Marriage as a psychological relationship. In *The Collected Works of C. G. Jung*, vol. 17 (tr. R. F. C. Hull). Princeton, NJ: Princeton University Press, pp. 187–201.

Kavanaugh, K., & Rodriguez, O. (tr.) (1964). *The Collected Works of St. John of the Cross*. New York: Doubleday.

Keats, J. (1817). Letter to George and Thomas Keats, 21 December 1817. In *The Letters of John Keats*, vol. 1 (ed. H. E. Rollins). Boston, MA: Harvard University Press, 1958.

Kierkegaard, S. (1843). *Fear and Trembling* [*Frygt og Bæven*] (ed. D. Nikolic; tr. W. Lowrie). Self-published by editor. Morrisville, NC: Lulu.

Kierkegaard, S. (1844). *The Concept of Anxiety* [*Begrebet Angest*] (ed. and tr. A. Hannay). New York: Liveright, 2014.

King, R. (2018). Openness in psychotherapy: Late Heidegger and the clearing, *Existential Analysis*, 29(1): 77–93.

Klein, M. (1932). *The Psycho-Analysis of Children*. The International Psycho-Analytical Library, vol. 22. London: Hogarth Press.

Klein, M. (1940). Mourning and its relation to manic-depressive states. *International Journal of Psycho-Analysis*, 21: 125–53.

Klein, M. (1946). Notes on some schizoid mechanisms. *International Journal of Psycho-Analysis*, 27: 99–110. 1952 version in *Envy and Gratitude and Other Works* (ed. M. Khan). The International Psycho-Analytical Library, vol. 104, pp. 1–24. London: Hogarth Press, 1975.

Klein, M. (1948). On the theory of anxiety and guilt. In *Envy and Gratitude and Other Works* (ed. M. Khan). The International Psycho-Analytical Library, vol. 104. pp. 25–42. London: Hogarth Press, 1975.

Klein, M. (1952). The origins of transference. *International Journal of Psycho-Analysis*, 33: 433–8.

Klein, M. (1957). *Envy and Gratitude*. In *Envy and Gratitude and Other Works* (ed. M. Khan). The International Psycho-Analytical Library, vol. 104, pp. 176–235. London: Hogarth Press, 1975.

Klein, M. (1958). On the development of mental functioning. In *Envy and Gratitude and Other Works* (ed. M. Khan). The International Psycho-Analytical Library, vol. 104, pp. 236–46. London: Hogarth Press, 1975.

Klein, M. (1975). *Envy and Gratitude and Other Works 1946–1963* (ed. M. Khan). The International Psycho-Analytical Library, vol. 104. London: Hogarth Press.

Lessing, G. E. (1767). Extracts from *Hamburgische Dramaturgie*, nos. 14, 75, 78 and 79 (1767–8); in R. P. Draper (ed.) (1980). *Tragedy: Developments in Criticism*. Basingstoke: Palgrave Macmillan. And in E. Bell (ed.) (1913), *Selected Prose Works of G. E. Lessing* (tr. E. C. Beasley & H. Zimmern). London: George Bell.

Lucretius (Titus Lucretius Carus). (50 BCE). *De rerum natura* (On the nature of things) (tr. W. E. Leonard). London: Forgotten Books, 2007.

Meister Eckhart. (2009). *The Complete Mystical Works of Meister Eckhart* (tr. M. O'C. Walshe). New York: Crossroad.

Milton, J. (1674). *Paradise Lost* (2nd ed.). London: S. Simmons. (1st ed., 1667). Mineola, NY: Dover, 2005.

Mitrani, J. L. (2001). "Taking the transference": Some technical implications in three papers by Bion. *International Journal of Psychoanalysis*, 82: 1085–104.

Mitrani, J. (2011). Excogitating Bion's cogitations: Further implications for technique. *Psychoanalytic Quarterly*, 80(3): 671–98.

Money-Kyrle, R. E. (1968). Cognitive development. *International Journal of Psycho-Analysis*, 49: 691–8.

Money-Kyrle, R. (1971). The aim of psychoanalysis. *International Journal of Psycho-Analysis*, 52: 103–6.

Müri, W. (ed.) (1986). *Der Arzt im Altertum: Greek and Latin Texts in the Original Languages from Hippocrates until Galen.* Munich: Artemis.

Ogden, T.H. (1991). Some theoretical comments on personal isolation. *Psychoanalytic Dialogues*, 1(3): 377–90.

Ogden, T. H. (2016). *Reclaiming Unlived Life: Experiences in Psychoanalysis.* New Library of Psychoanalysis Series. London: Routledge.

Ovid. (2004). *Metamorphoses* (tr. D. Raeburn). Harmondsworth: Penguin Books.

Paget, D. (2004). Case study: Theatre Workshop's *Oh What a Lovely War*, 1963, in B. Kershaw (ed.), *The Cambridge History of British Theatre*, vol. 3, *Since 1895.* Cambridge: Cambridge University Press.

Parsons, M. (2014). *Living Psychoanalysis: From Theory to Experience.* London: Routledge.

Proust, M. (1913–27). *À la recherche du temps perdu* (tr. C. K. Scott Moncrieff as *Remembrance of Things Past*, 1922–31). London: Vintage Books, 1982. (French Pléiade ed., tr. C.K. Scott Moncrieff & T. Kilmartin.)

Racker, H. (1968). *Transference and Countertransference*, The International Psycho-Analytical Library, vol. 73. London: Hogarth Press. And in Psychoanalytic Electronic Publishing (PepWeb).

Rilke, R. M. (1989). *The Selected Poetry of Rainer Maria Rilke* (ed. and tr. S. Mitchell). New York: Vintage International.

Riviere, J. (1936). On the genesis of psychical conflict in earliest infancy. *International Journal of Psycho-Analysis*, 17: 395–422.

Riviere, J. (1952). The unconscious phantasy of an inner world reflected in examples from English literature. *International Journal of Psycho-Analysis*, 33: 160–72.

Sandler, J. (1976). Countertransference and role-responsiveness. *International Review of Psycho-Analysis*, 3: 43–7.

Sandler, J., & Sandler, A. (1978). On the development of object relationships and affects. *International Journal of Psycho-Analysis*, 59: 285–96.

Sartre, J.-P. (2013 [1943]). *Being and Nothingness* (tr. H. E. Barnes. 2013). Abingdon: Routledge.

Savery, D. C. (2015, October). Revealment in theatre and therapy. Hermeneutic circular, Society of Existential Analysis.

Savery, D. C. (2018). *Echoism: The Silenced Response to Narcissism.* London: Routledge.

Segal, H. (1957). Notes on symbol formation. *International Journal of Psycho-Analysis*, 38: 391–7.

Segal, H. (1978). On symbolism. *International Journal of Psycho-Analysis*, 59: 315–19.

Segal, H. (1981). *The Work of Hanna Segal: A Kleinian Approach to Clinical Practice.* London: Jason Aronson.

Shakespeare, W. (*c.*1901). *The Complete Works of William Shakespeare* (ed. R. G. White). New York: Sully and Kleinteich.

Shepherd, G. J., St John, J., & Striphas, T. G. (eds). (2006). *Communication as Techne, Communication as Episteme: Perspectives on Theory*. London: Sage.

Shoaf, R. A. (2014). *Lucretius and Shakespeare on the Nature of Things*. Newcastle upon Tyne: Cambridge Scholars.

Spillius, E. (ed.) (1988). *Melanie Klein Today: Developments in Theory and Practice*, vol. 1: *Mainly Theory*. New Library of Psychoanalysis Series. London: Routledge.

Spinelli, E. (2007). *Practising Existential Psychotherapy*. London: Sage.

Steiner, J. (1993). *Psychic Retreats: Pathological Organisations of the Personality in Psychotic, Neurotic, and Borderline Patients*. London: Routledge.

Steiner, J. (ed.) (2017). *Lectures on Technique by Melanie Klein*. London: Routledge.

Strachey, J. (1934). The nature of the therapeutic action of psycho-analysis. *International Journal of Psycho-Analysis*, 15: 127–59. (Based on a paper read at a meeting of the British Psycho-Analytical Society on 13 June 1933.)

Tate, D. L. (1995). Transcending the aesthetic: Gadamer on tragedy and the tragic. In O. V. Bychkov & J. Fodor (eds) (2008), *Theological Aesthetics after von Balthasar*. London: Routledge.

Tauber, I. (1997). *The Quest for Reality*. New York: New York University Press.

Turri, M. G. (2017). *Acting, Spectating, and the Unconscious: A Psychoanalytic Perspective on the Unconscious Processes of Identification in the Theatre*. London: Routledge.

van Deurzen, E. (2010). *Everyday Mysteries: A Handbook of Existential Psychotherapy*, 2nd ed. Abingdon: Routledge.

Willett, J. (1997). (ed. and tr.). *Brecht on Theatre: The Development of an Aesthetic*. London: Bloomsbury.

Winnicott, D. W. (1941). The observation of infants in a set situation. *International Journal of Psycho-Analysis*, 22: 229–49.

Winnicott, D.W. (1945). Primitive emotional development. *International Journal of Psycho-Analysis*, 26: 137–43.

Winnicott, D.W. (1960). The theory of the parent–infant relationship. *International Journal of Psycho-Analysis*, 41: 585–95.

Winnicott, D.W. (1965). *The Maturational Processes and the Facilitating Environment: Studies in the Theory of Emotional Development*. The International Psycho-Analytical Library, vol. 64. London: Hogarth Press.

Winnicott, D.W. (2017). *The Collected Works of D. W. W. Winnicott*. (ed. L. Caldwell and H. Taylor Robinson). Oxford: Oxford University Press.

Wittgenstein, L. (1961). *Tractatus Logico-Philosophicus* (tr. D. F. Pears & B. F. McGuinness; intro. by B. Russell). London: Routledge & Kegan Paul.

Wright, J. (ed.) (1842), *The Letters of Horace Walpole*, vol. 2, 1749–59. Philadelphia: Lea and Blanchard.

INDEX

Printed in Great Britain
by Amazon